THE BEST
BIKE RIDES
IN THE
MID-ATLANTIC

THE BEST BIKE RIDES IN THE MID-ATLANTIC

Delaware · Maryland · New Jersey · New York
Pennsylvania · Washington, D.C. · West Virginia

by

Trudy E. Bell

A Voyager Book

The Globe Pequot Press

Old Saybrook, Connecticut

Photo credits: Pg. 11: Barbara Lloyd; pg. 43: Carroll County Tourism Office; pg. 137: Mark Scholefield; pg. 215: courtesy of the Washington, D.C., Convention & Visitors Association; pg. 229: Pamela "Sam" Withrow, Camera One. All others by the author.

Library of Congress Cataloging-in-Publication Data

Bell, Trudy E.
  The best bike rides in the Mid-Atlantic: Delaware, Maryland, New Jersey, New York, Pennsylvania, Washington, D.C., West Virginia / by Trudy E. Bell. — 1st ed.
      p.   cm.
  "A Voyager book."
  ISBN 1-56440-380-7
  1. Bicycle touring—Middle Atlantic States—Guidebooks. 2. Bicycle trails—Middle Atlantic States—Guidebooks. 3. Middle Atlantic States—Guidebooks. I. Title.
  GV1045.5.M53B45   1994
  796.6'4'0974—dc20

                                              93-48372
                                              CIP

♻ This book is printed on recycled paper.
Manufactured in the United States of America
First Edition/First Printing

To my parents,
Rev. R. Kenneth Bell and Arabella J. Bell,
for their lifetime of love and friendship

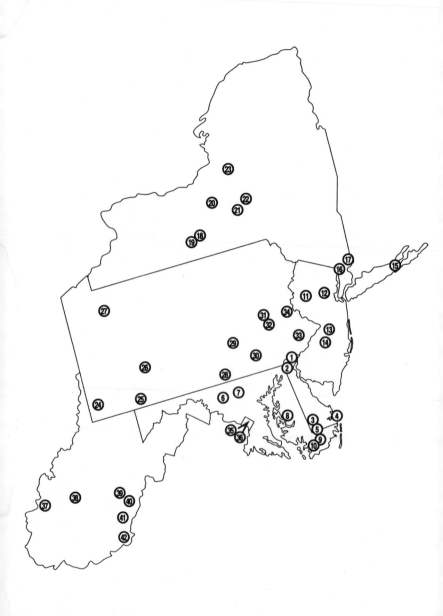

Contents

Introduction

Bike Rides

Appendix

Introduction

A Variety Tour of the Mid-Atlantic

The Mid-Atlantic region of the United States is one of the most beautiful areas of the country in which to bicycle, whether you're a novice wishing to venture beyond your home neighborhood or a strong rider trying for a century (100 miles in a day) every weekend.

Because the Mid-Atlantic states were settled centuries ago, when many byways were still footpaths and dirt wagon tracks join local communities, the region offers a vast network of wandering secondary and tertiary roads bypassed by the more direct interstate and toll highways. Even in today's automobile-oriented society, these small roads are almost undisturbed by cars—and they pass through some of the loveliest countryside a cyclist could hope for.

For scenery you can choose fragrant pine forests, cultivated farm fields, or meandering river valleys. For terrain you have the choice of virtually flat (on New York's Long Island, in southern New Jersey, and in parts of Delaware and Maryland), rolling (in southeastern Pennsylvania), or mountainous (West Virginia). Stop to pet the horses standing next to the rails of a horse farm; pick your own apples in the fall at wayside orchards; open your picnic lunch next to a waterfall; pedal through great Civil War battlefields. And after the day's exercise, camp under the stars in the bracing forest air or luxuriate in a soaking bath at a bed-and-breakfast inn. These and other choices are offered on this book's lovely routes, which were contributed by local bicycle clubs, state tourism organizations, commercial bicycle touring groups, and dedicated individual cyclists.

Some of the rides take you through areas that are the acknowledged favorite of many cyclists—such as the Pennsylvania Dutch farm land, the Finger Lakes region of New York, and the Delmarva peninsula. On a summer weekend in those areas, you are very likely to exchange a wave and a smile with dozens of other riders you pass on the road. Other routes guide you through places as yet largely undiscovered by road-touring cyclists, such as the hills of West Virginia (see "A Special Word about West Virginia" below), where you can pedal for days before meeting another cyclist. Thus, you can even choose a ride based on the society or solitude you seek! In several areas notable for their superb cycling, two or three rides are clustered to give you the option of spending a weekend or longer exploring the region on two wheels.

Something for Everyone

To aid in your selection, the rides in this book are categorized by their difficulty.

Rambles are the easiest, designed to be completed by almost anyone; they are under 35 miles long, and their terrain is flat or gently rolling.

Cruises are intermediate in difficulty, ranging from 25 to 50 miles, with the terrain being rolling or moderately hilly.

Challenges require adequate training and preparation; they range from 40 to 70 miles in total distance and may include long climbs.

Classics, the equivalent of the "black diamond" slopes in skiing, are longer than 60 miles, and their terrain may be hilly or mountainous; they will satisfy the strong, expert rider.

Having noted this, less experienced riders should *not* be discouraged at seeing so many challenges and classics in the list of rides at the beginning of each state chapter. The rides are named after their longest incarnation, and most of the long rides have cutoffs to turn them into shorter cruises or rambles. Alternatively, some of the longer rides can be broken up into shorter rides by staying overnight along the way.

As terrain is as much a factor as distance in determining a ride's difficulty, some long rides that are very flat (such as the 54-mile-long "Strawberries and Wine Cruise" on Long Island) may be easier than some short rides that are very hilly (such as the 25-mile-long challenging "Hillsboro Farm Land Cruise" in West Virginia).

How to Use This Book

Each ride is preceded by a short description to give you a feel for the specific area and what you are likely to see. The description usually mentions roadside attractions, as well as inns or campgrounds for spending the night; where possible, telephone numbers are also provided.

The most crucial section of the description is "The Basics." There you will find information about the ride's mileage, including mileage options for shortened routes; terrain; automobile traffic; and availability of food. Where possible, the routes start near public rest rooms, water, and sources of food, but for a few of the more isolated rides, you will have to bring all your provisions with you.

Last is "Miles & Directions"—a cue sheet, in bicycle touring parlance. As much as possible this book observes several conventions. A "T intersection" is one where the road you are on dead-ends into a perpendicular road where you must turn either left or right. A "Y intersection" is one where the road you are on appears to split into a fork.

A word about maps: Take several. The best is a county map showing all the local streets. (*Note:* Some rides pass through several counties. The names of the counties are given in every ride.) Ideally, if you can find more than one map put out by different publishers, take along two or more. Why weigh yourself down that way? First, maps can help you spontaneously shortcut or add to your ride midway through it, beyond what's shown in this book. Second, road construction begun after this book's publication may block off part of the directed route, in which case a supplemental map can help you find a detour and guide you back to the main route. (If this happens to you, please write to the author so that the rides can be correctly updated in subsequent editions; see "Request and Disclaimer" on page 10). Third, as maps do contain errors in the way roads are drawn and labeled, having two maps by different publishers allows you to compare the versions to ascertain which one best matches your current situation. For more information see "State Bicycling Maps and Guides" in the Appendix.

A Special Word about West Virginia

West Virginia's roads are so different from those elsewhere in the Mid-Atlantic that they require a few notes. The gist is this: The state is gorgeous, but the cycling is only for riders both experienced and strong.

West Virginia is the state of diehard mountain-bikers. Virtually all the bike shops are geared toward mountain-biking as are the tour companies and cycling campgrounds. Trails abound for mountain-bikers, as do packaged tours, books, and informal notes. In contrast, road cyclists are rare: In the five days I spent there in late May—prime weather for cycling—I saw only two cyclists on road bikes on principal roads and *no* road cyclists of any description on the best backroads.

Because of the mountain-bike orientation of West Virginia, one of the West Virginia rides—the "Williams River Trail Cruise"—is an introductory mountain-bike ride that requires a true all-terrain bike with 2-inch knobby tires. For this ride a cross or hybrid bike—one designed for riding on both paved roads and some dirt—is *not* advisable. As mountain-bikers think of rides in terms of maps or landmarks, it was a challenge to transform their knowledge into a cue sheet with mileages; pay greater attention to the physical descriptions, as often gravel roads and trails do not have names on signposts, and odometers are not consistent on rough terrain.

Cue sheets of established road rides in West Virginia are almost impossible to come by; all but the "Sternwheel Regatta Century Classic" and the "Milton Getaway Challenge" were turned into custom cue sheets specifically for this book. In fact, this book may well be the first to publish *road* rides in West Virginia.

Part of the reason so few road tours may exist is that West Virginia has not, until recently, recognized its potential for tourism of any form, according to Greg Cook, West Virginia's bicycle coordinator for tourism and parks. Attracting road cyclists is part of that change in focus. One such effort is the annual international Kmart Classic, a stage race à la the Tour de France. Begun in 1992, the race constitutes a grueling, 500-mile-long course from Morgantown to Elkins to White Sulphur Springs to Charleston; it is run the week preceding Memorial Day and ends with an outdoor music festival in the state's capital. You may want to time your own cycling visit to view the lean professional riders from all countries streaking by.

But West Virginia's roads themselves make the state forbidding to all but experienced road cyclists in peak physical condition. There's a reason West Virginia is called "hill country" or "The Mountain State." Both main and secondary roads commonly grind up miles-long, unremitting climbs and plunge down miles of switchbacks at grades of up to 8 and 9 percent. Believe me, 9 percent is *steep*, as you will see for yourself on the brief 9-percent descent that is unavoidably included in "The Hillsboro Farm Land Cruise." Although grades that steep certainly exist in western Pennsylvania, northern New York, and elsewhere in the Mid-Atlantic, most are mercifully short—under a mile. West Virginia arguably has the *longest* steep grades you're likely to find outside the Rocky Mountains, minus about 10,000 feet in altitude. The hilly terrain is the reason that none of even the shortest West Virginia rides classifies as a ramble.

Many of the main roads are only two lanes and are traveled at 55 miles per hour by cars and logging trucks alike. Scarcely any have paved shoulders. What shoulders do exist are narrow, below pavement level, and inevitably of gravel. There is a *lot* of gravel in West Virginia, and all too much of it ends up on the pavement—so, especially on downhills, ride with *extreme caution.*

That being said, please note that the pavement itself is generally good to excellent, even on the one-lane backroads; you will encounter noticeably fewer potholes than you might find, say, in New York State (undoubtedly due to West Virginia's milder winters producing less frost heave). Moreover, West Virginia's secondary roads have so little traffic that four cars in an hour would be a lot. In fact, it is not an exaggeration to characterize cycling the narrow, paved backroads of West Virginia as almost like riding along your own private paved bike path.

Probably the best road ride in West Virginia is not included as a separate ride in this book: the two-lane Highland Scenic Highway 150 near Marlinton, which describes a 23-mile-long letter *C* through the western part of the Monongahela National Forest, with its northern tip on busy Route 219 and its southern tip on busy Route 39/55. Reminiscent of the gorgeous Blue Ridge Parkway in Virginia, the Highland Scenic Highway commands spectacular views of line after line of the forested ridges that are so beautifully characteristic of West Virginia. Moreover, its pavement is so superb and the summer automobile traffic so light that "we Rollerblade all over it," remarked Gil Willis of the Elk River Touring Center in Slatyfork. The scenic highway has no services outside of primitive campgrounds, however, and there are very long climbs—probably 7,000 to 8,000 feet of altitude gained and lost over the 23 miles, Gil estimates. A short section of this gorgeous road is included in Gil's contributed mountain-bike ride, the "Williams River Trail Cruise."

One appealing aspect of West Virginia is that even on the eve of the twenty-first century, traveling in the state is almost like it used to be driving cross-country in the 1950s: Outside of towns the size of Elkins, Bartow, and Marlinton, major chain hotels, motels, and fast-food restaurants have not yet blighted the countryside with commercialism. Overnight accommodations are often mom-and-pop enterprises that are few and far between and may be open only during the summer.

The flip side is that on some of these routes you may pedal 20 to 40 miles between places to refill your water bottles and stomach—and then your only culinary choices may be what many cyclists consider high-fat "junk": hamburgers, hot dogs, and pizza. Advice: Carry three water bottles, and always take advantage of *any* opportunity to provision up. Better yet, pack more Fig Newtons, sports bars, fruit, and other carbos than you think you could possibly want, for you are likely to need them. Also, as bicycle shops are even fewer and farther between than food and accommodations, carry a more complete set of tools than you might be inclined to take on less isolated rides, and know how to use them.

Safety and Comfort on the Road

Like skiing, boating, and many other sports, bicycling has distinct hazards, some of which have claimed lives. But the chance of injury can be minimized by proper equipment and technique. Moreover, there are ways to increase your comfort, allowing you to enjoy hours in the saddle day after day.

Most important of all: Always wear a helmet. If you bicycle regularly, it is not a matter of *if* you will fall but of *when*. A helmet can make the difference between a serious injury that ends your journey or just some road rash and a story to tell. The old complaints about helmets being hot and heavy no longer pertain; with lightweight, high-impact plastics and styles that provide generous ventilation, you'll scarcely notice you have anything on your head. For maximum protection buy one that has the green or blue sticker inside indicating that it has passed the rigorous safety standards of the Snell Memorial Foundation. A white or yellow helmet will reflect the sun's heat the best and offer maximum visibility at night. Adjust the chin strap so it's loose enough to be comfortable when your neck is extended forward but taut enough so the helmet cannot be pushed off your forehead.

Wear fingerless, padded cycling gloves for two reasons: to buffer road shock to your hands as you ride and to minimize abrasion should you fall. Even roads that look smooth are bumpy enough to make unprotected palms and heels of your hands feel weary at the end of a day's ride. After months of riding this way, you could risk numbness or pain from nerve damage. Encasing your handlebars with protective padding and wearing gloves virtually eliminate both discomfort and the chance of injury. Plus, the open oval on the back above the glove's closure will give the backs of your hands the characteristic "bicyclist's suntan," which can be a nice conversation-starter in social situations!

Use a **rear-view mirror** to monitor automobile traffic approaching from behind. With a mirror you will not be startled if a car quietly materializes to your left and honks. Also, you will not have to take your eyes off the road ahead to know what is going on behind. The most effective rear-view mirrors mount to your helmet; the ones that mount to your eyeglasses tend to have a smaller field of view, and the ones that mount to your bicycle handlebars vibrate too much to stay aligned or to produce a clear image.

Wear light, bright colors so you are visible to motorists, particularly on overcast days or toward sunset. Yellow is the best of both worlds. Some neon colors, such as neon yellow and lime, are even better. For maximum visibility apply reflective tape to your bicycle frame and helmet, especially if there's a chance you'll be riding after dark. Headlights and taillights for the bicycle also alert motorists to your presence. Some cyclists also attach vertical or horizontal international orange flags to their bicycle frames. Remember: You'd rather have a driver think "what a weirdo biker" than miss seeing you, given that many accidents happen only because a driver simply cannot see the cyclist until it is too late.

Last, **ride defensively.** The traffic laws in most states recognize the bicycle as a vehicle, with all the rights and responsibilities thereof. That means stopping at all stop signs and red lights, using left-turn lanes, and using arm signals to indicate your intentions. On roads where you must share the right-hand lane with vehicular traffic, rely on your ears and your rear-view mirror to monitor cars and trucks approaching you from behind. Do not block your ears with earphones; not only are they illegal, but they will deprive you of auditory warnings. Most state laws call for cyclists to ride as far to the right as practicable—but "as far right as practicable" does not necessarily mean blindly clinging to the far right-hand edge in all circumstances. On fast downhills where you feel insecure at the far right because the road's edge is broken or littered with gravel, ride far enough to the left (about where the passenger in a car would sit) so that cars approaching from behind must slow down to pass you—and then immediately move back again to the right when the hazard is passed. When passing parked cars look carefully inside each for the silhouettes of heads of people who might suddenly open a door in your path. Buy a cyclist's bell, and use it to warn cars and pedestrians of your presence; do *not* use a police whistle—not only is it illegal in some places, but it often offends people, and many times they do not think the whistle blast applies to them.

Now that you're equipped for safety, here are a few additional words about simple comfort.

Padded cycling shorts will minimize saddle-soreness. Saddle-soreness is produced by the transmission of road shock from your saddle through soft flesh to your "sit bones" (ischial tuberosity). The most effective padding is made of genuine or artificial chamois; polypropylene is more effective for wicking away moisture than protecting against saddle-soreness. For additional protection you can buy a seat cover of either sheepskin or gel; both are equally effective, although the gel has a longer lifetime. With both a seat cover and cycling shorts, you can ride a cool century without discomfort. A bonus: Cycling shorts, which usually extend down to the knee, also protect the skin of your inner thighs against chafing and blisters that otherwise can be caused by rubbing against either the saddle itself or the seam of ordinary short or long pants.

Bicycling jerseys also serve several practical purposes. Their light colors increase your visibility; their polypropylene or wool fabric increases the wicking of perspiration to keep you dry; their longer cut in the rear shields your lower back from the sun and wind; and their rear pockets allow you to carry a wallet and keys without your legs hitting them at the top of every pedal stroke.

Take at least one water bottle, and always pack a minimum "emergency snack" of raisins or Fig Newtons, even for the shortest rides—your body has a strange way of "hitting bottom" suddenly and unexpectedly. On hot days pack a salty snack as well; ideal are pretzels, which are also low in fat and high in complex carbohydrates.

A word about tools: As many of these routes deliberately take you away from human habitation, you may not find a bike shop nearby. Take bicycle tools—at the very least, tire levers, a patch kit, and a pump for repairing a flat tire—and either know how to use them or travel with a friend who does. In fact, if you anticipate bicycling a lot, one of the best favors you can do yourself is to sign up for a simple "roadside bicycle repair" class, offered by many continuing education schools, bicycle clubs, and youth hostels. If you lack knowledge and tools, a simple flat tire can immobilize you for hours, requiring you to flag down a van or truck to take you back to civilization, whereas if you're equipped, you can fix the problem and be back on the road again in less than twenty minutes.

Delaware

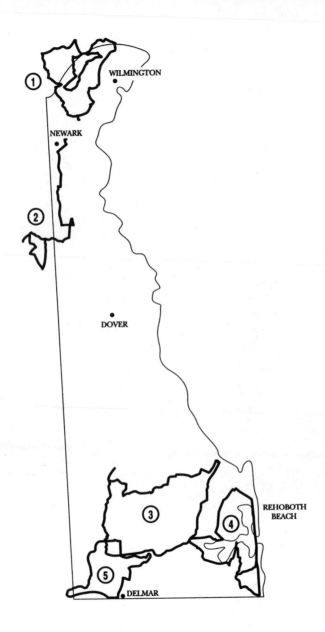

WILMINGTON

①

NEWARK

②

DOVER

③

④ REHOBOTH BEACH

⑤

DELMAR

Delaware

Note: It is an eccentricity of Delaware that most roads—even small farm lanes—are not named, but are instead known by their route number (state or federal) or road number (county). Look for the road numbers on small signs attached to the same pole as stop signs and other road signs. With the advent of 911 emergency service, this custom is now being changed, and you may find that more and more roads are starting to acquire names as well.

1

Delaware-Pennsylvania Hill-Climbing Cruise

Delcastle Recreation Area—Kennett Square
Cossart—Delcastle Recreation Area

This hilly, challenging ride along less traveled roads offers lovely scenery of forest and wooded areas, with many old homes of lots of historical character. You'll wander on backroads that the developers have not yet discovered, as you ride from the outskirts of Wilmington, Delaware (New Castle County), into Pennsylvania toward Philadelphia (Chester County). For the least traffic pedal early on a Saturday or Sunday morning, as some of the main two-lane roads do see heavier automobile traffic during the week, suggests David Shackelford, bicycle-commuter expert of Wilmington's White Clay Bicycle Club, who contributed the ride.

The route is shaped as if you were tracing the outline of the letter *V*. The longer 37.5-mile version dips down into the center of the V to include a stop at the Ashland Nature Center (302–239–2334), where you can stretch your legs on some nature trails. Then the ride continues by taking you through one of Delaware's few remaining covered bridges. The shorter 26.7-mile version eliminates the 10-mile dip down the center of the V-shaped route, turning the route into a simple triangle. Both rides take you near a second covered bridge.

About 9 miles into both the longer and the shorter versions of the ride, you'll pedal along the southern edge of Kennett Square, a small town whose downtown shopping district is quaint but whose outskirts have the typical convenience stores.

Because the ride takes less traveled roads, there are no services on the route itself; neither does the route pass any bike shops or bed-and-breakfast inns, although there are a number in the general area, Shackelford notes. The two covered bridges and the Ashland Nature Center offer scenic places to stop for a packed snack or lunch. Another good lunch stop is a rustic restaurant and bar called Buckley's Tavern in Greenville (5812 Kennett Pike, 302–656–9776), about 30 miles into the longer ride (about 20 miles into the shorter ride); if you plan to stop there, call ahead for the tavern's hours, which are somewhat limited. Another nice lunch stop is the Hoopes Reservoir, where you can sit and enjoy the view of the lake. Near the end of the route, you'll pedal by the Mount Cuba Astronomical Observatory (call 302–654–6407 for information on activities and public observing hours).

The Basics

Start: Mill Creek, Delaware, at the public parking lot of the Delcastle Recreation Area. There are a portable toilet near the tennis courts and permanent toilets near the softball fields; water fountains are scattered throughout the recreation area. To get to the start, take Rte. 41 (Newport Gap Pike) to Mill Creek Rd. Head west on Mill Creek Rd. for 0.3 mile and turn left on McKennans Church Rd. into the Delcastle Recreation Area.

Length: 26.7 or 37.5 miles.

Terrain: Moderately hilly. Traffic is generally light on weekends, although during the week it can be moderate to moderately heavy on some main roads.

Food: There are no convenience stores, restaurants, or water stops directly on the route, although detours of 1–2 miles will bring you plenty in Kennett Square and Chadds Ford. Pack your own snacks and water.

Miles & Directions

- 0.0 From Delcastle Recreation Area, turn right onto McKennans Church Rd. (Rd. 276).
- 0.3 Turn left onto Mill Creek Rd. (Rd. 282).
- 2.3 Turn right at Limestone Hills Park to stay on Mill Creek Rd.
- 4.3 Turn left at the T intersection onto Old Lancaster Pike (Rd. 300), followed by an *immediate right* onto Yorklyn Rd. (Rd. 257).
- 4.9 Turn left onto Old Wilmington Rd. (Rd. 275).
- 5.4 Turn right to continue on Old Wilmington Rd.
- 6.3 Just after crossing into Pennsylvania, turn right onto Chandlers Mill Rd.
- 7.0 Turn left to stay on Chandlers Mill Rd.
- 7.2 Turn right to stay on Chandlers Mill Rd.
- 8.7 Turn right onto Hillendale Rd., which truly takes you over hill and dale. While on Hillendale you may wish to turn left on Kaolin Rd. for about a mile's detour into downtown Kennett Square for grocery stores, restaurants, and shopping.
- 12.2 Turn right onto Rosedale Rd., followed by an *immediate right* onto Norway Rd., so you're headed back almost parallel to the way you just came.
- 13.7 Turn right at the T intersection onto Burnt Mill Rd.

Note: For the 26.7-mile ride, at this T intersection turn left instead onto Burnt Mill Rd. At mile 14.1 turn left onto Center Mill Rd., and then resume following the directions at mile 25.0 below.

- 14.4 Turn right at the T intersection onto Old Kennett Pike.
- 14.5 Make the first left onto Nine Gates Rd. and reenter Delaware.
- 15.6 As you come to a stop sign at Upper Snuff Mill Row, stay on Nine Gates Rd. as it curves to the left.
- 15.7 Turn right at the T intersection onto Snuff Mill Rd. (Rd. 247).
- 15.8 Turn left at the T intersection onto the unmarked Rte. 82

(Creek Rd.). You are now riding alongside Red Clay Creek. Watch for diagonal railroad crossings.

- 16.8 Turn right onto Sharpless Rd. (Rd. 251).
- 17.9 Turn left at the T intersection onto Old Wilmington Rd. (Rd. 275).
- 18.6 Turn left onto the unmarked Brackenville Rd. (Rd. 274).
- 19.8 Turn left onto the unmarked Barley Mill Rd. Now you will be able to see the single-lane covered bridge you will cross. Just before you cross the covered bridge, on your left is the entrance to the Ashland Nature Center.
- 20.1 Immediately after you cross the railroad tracks, turn left at the T intersection onto Rte. 82 (Creek Rd.).
- 20.2 Make the first right onto Ashland Clinton School Rd. (Rd. 287).
- 21.7 Turn left at the T intersection onto Old Kennett Pike (Rd. 243).
- 21.8 Make the first right onto Snuff Mill Rd. (Rd. 244).
- 23.4 Turn left at the T intersection onto Rte. 52 (Kennett Pike).
- 23.9 After crossing back into Pennsylvania, turn left onto Burnt Mill Rd.
- 25.0 Turn right onto Center Mill Rd. *It is at this intersection that the 26.7-mile ride rejoins the longer route.*
- 25.9 Turn right onto Fairville Rd. While riding on Fairville Rd., you will cross Rte. 52 (Kennett Pike). There are several antiques stores (but no food or drink) immediately to your left in the village of Fairville on Rte. 52 (Kennett Pike).
- 26.6 Turn right onto Cossart Rd. Look for the street sign high up on the telephone pole. Enjoy the long downhills here; you'll pay for them later.
- 28.3 Turn right at the T intersection onto the unmarked Rte. 100 (Chadds Ford Rd.). Where the road crosses back into Delaware, it changes its name to Montchanin Rd.
- 29.0 Just after reentering Delaware turn right onto Twaddell Mill Rd. (Rd. 234), where you will begin climbing some steep hills.
- 30.4 Watch for the hidden stop sign at the top of the hill before crossing Rte. 52 (Kennett Pike), and then continue straight

on Owl's Nest Rd. (Rd. 240). At that intersection you're at the center of the historic town of Greenville, containing several offices, boutique and antiques shops, and Buckley's Tavern.

- **32.4** Continue straight where Owl's Nest Rd. joins Rte. 82 (New London Rd.).
- **32.7** Make the first left onto Hillside Mill Rd. (Rd. 269). On this road you'll pass by Hoopes Reservoir and Deer Valley Ln. on your left, which will take you to the Mount Cuba Astronomical Observatory.
- **33.6** Immediately after crossing over the railroad tracks, turn left onto Mt. Cuba Rd. (Rd. 261).
- **34.0** Turn left at the T intersection onto the unmarked Barley Mill Rd. (Rd. 258).
- **35.0** Turn right onto Rolling Mill Rd. (Rd. 263). While on Rolling Mill Rd., as you pass Foxhill Ln., look to the right at another covered bridge.
- **35.6** Turn right at the T intersection onto Rte. 48 (Lancaster Pike).
- **35.8** Make the first left onto Hercules Rd. (Rd. 282), which becomes Mill Creek Rd. after crossing Rte. 41.
- **37.2** Turn left onto McKennans Church Rd. (Rd. 276).
- **37.5** Turn left into the parking lot of Delcastle Recreation Area.

Two-State Breakfast Cruise

Newark—Chesapeake City—Newark

This 48-mile route from Newark, Delaware, to Chesapeake City, Maryland, has long been a popular "breakfast" ride with the White Clay Bicycle Club (WCBC), headquartered in Wilmington, Delaware. The destination: Jack and Helen's Restaurant (410–885–5477), a down-home diner that "serves really good, inexpensive breakfasts, sandwiches, and platters. Very 'bicycle friendly,'" notes Nancy Estilow, the editor of WCBC's newsletter *Tailwind* and the contributor of the cue sheet on which this ride is based.

The ride starts at Casho Mill Barksdale Park near the Newark campus of the University of Delaware in New Castle County. At first you will pedal along some fairly busy roads, but they generally have wide shoulders. Soon you will cross Summit Bridge over the Chesapeake and Delaware Canal and pass through the Canal National Wildlife Area. The canal, which first opened to traffic in 1829, is now one of the busiest canals in the world, averaging more than 22,000 vessels a year; you may be lucky enough to see large international oceangoing freighters plying their way between Baltimore and Philadelphia. You can also hike or mountain-bike along the unpaved service roads paralleling the canal and hunt for fossils in the canal's banks.

As the canal separates the upper and lower Delmarva Peninsula, now you'll feel as though the pace of life has slo-o-owed down. You're cycling through open corn fields and past farmhouses and barns. Once you head west into Maryland, you'll take a scenic loop through some of Cecil County's thoroughbred horse farms.

At this point, 27 miles into the ride, you'll undoubtedly have worked up quite an appetite. Chow down at Jack and Helen's, where the waitresses know everyone, as most of the patrons are locals. "Their pancakes are #1 on our list and are typically what we order," notes Estilow. Crowded on weekends, especially very early in the morning, Jack and Helen's is open before dawn seven days a week.

After remounting your bike, you can pause to let some of the feast digest by stopping less than a mile into the return to gaze at the exhibits in the Chesapeake & Delaware Canal Museum. The 21-mile return leads you back essentially along the outward route minus the scenic loop.

The Basics

Start: Newark, Delaware, at Casho Mill Barksdale Park, at the corner of Barksdale Rd. and Casho Mill Rd. Park cars in one of the three lots. In the summer there are portable toilets set up, but no water. From I-95 take Rte. 896 north along College Ave. South, Christina Pkwy., and Elkton Rd.; turn left onto Casho Mill Rd., right onto Barksdale Rd., and left into Casho Mill Barksdale Park.
Length: 48 miles.
Terrain: Flat to gently rolling. Traffic is generally moderately light to light, except on main roads, where it is much heavier—but the main roads compensate by having wide paved shoulders.
Food: Available near 1 mile and 6 miles into the ride and at Jack and Helen's at mile 27. But carry water and snacks, as there are some long stretches without services.

Miles & Directions

- 0.0 Turn right out of the parking lot of Barksdale Park.
- 0.2 Turn left at the traffic light onto Casho Mill Rd.
- 0.8 Turn right at the T intersection onto Rte. 2/896 (Elkton Rd.). Use caution; this road is busy but has wide paved shoulders. Be very careful in passing the shopping center on your

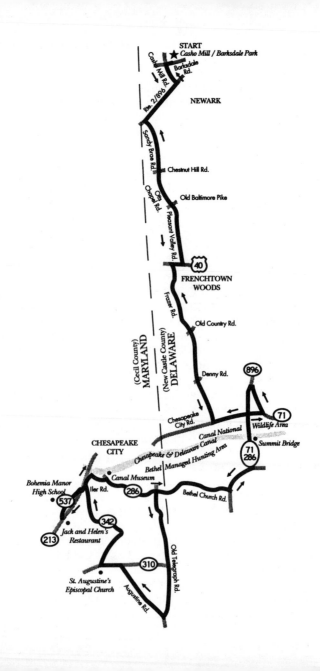

right, watching for cars turning right. (This shopping center includes a grocery store and deli.)

- 2.0 Turn left at the traffic light onto Sandy Brae Rd. This road changes its name several times. After crossing Chestnut Hill Rd., it becomes Otts Chapel Rd. (Rd. 397). At mile 4.3, after crossing the Old Baltimore Pike, keep heading straight on Pleasant Valley Rd. (Rd. 8).

- 5.9 Turn right at the T intersection onto Rte. 40 (Pulaski Hwy.), watching carefully for cars. This road is busy but has a wide paved shoulder. (*Note:* If you were to turn left instead of right onto Rte. 40, you would reach a shopping center with a grocery store, deli, fast-food restaurants, gas stations, and a bicycle shop—Paceline Cycle, 302–834–1156.)

- 6.1 Take the first left onto Frazer Rd. (Rd. 391), a nice rural change of pace after busy Rte. 40. At mile 8.0, cross Old County Rd. (no sign). At mile 9.4 cross Denny Rd. (Rd. 396).

- 10.5 Turn left at the T intersection onto Chesapeake City Rd.

- 11.8 Turn left at the T intersection onto Rte. 71 (Red Lion Rd.).

- 12.6 Turn left at the T intersection onto Rte. 71/896 (Summit Bridge Rd.), which is moderately busy but has wide paved shoulders. Cross Summit Bridge over the Chesapeake and Delaware Canal.

- 14.7 Turn right onto Bethel Church Rd. (Rd. 433).

- 15.6 Turn right to stay on Bethel Church Rd. (Rd. 433), where Choptank Rd. continues straight. At the Maryland border Bethel Church Rd. changes its designation to Rte. 286.

- 17.6 Turn left onto Old Telegraph Rd. At mile 19.5 keep heading straight at the stop sign at the unmarked intersection with Rte. 310 (Cayots Corner Rd.).

- 20.8 Make a sharp right onto Augustine Rd. (the sign says St. Augustine, although the maps say Augustine).

- 22.5 Turn left at the T intersection onto Rte. 310 (Cayots Corner Rd.).

- 23.1 Turn right at St. Augustine's Episcopal Church onto Rte. 342 (St. Augustine Rd. N.).

- 25.9 Turn left onto the unmarked Iler Rd.; watch carefully, for this turn is easy to miss. Immediately cross Rte. 286 and pass under the very high bridge of Rte. 213. At mile 26.7 head straight onto the unmarked Rte. 537 (Basil Ave.).

- 27.0 Bear left at the Bohemia Manor High School to stay on Rte. 537 (Basil Ave.). Cross Rte. 213 to Jack and Helen's Restaurant for a well-deserved breakfast. Leave the restaurant parking lot by turning right to head north on Rte. 213.

- 27.9 Bear right onto Rte. 286.

- 28.4 Turn right at the convenience store to stay on Rte. 286 (here called 2nd St.)

- 28.9 Turn right at the T intersection to stay on Rte. 286. The Chesapeake & Delaware Canal Museum is across the road to your left. At mile 30.3 you'll pass Old Telegraph Rd., and then you'll leave Maryland and reenter Delaware. At the border Rte. 286 becomes Bethel Church Rd. (Rd. 433).

- 32.3 Turn left at the stop sign to stay on Bethel Church Rd. (Rd. 433).

- 33.1 Turn left at the blinking light onto Rte. 71/896 (Summit Bridge Rd.), watching carefully for traffic.

- 35.2 Turn right onto Rte. 71 (Red Lion Rd.).

- 36.0 Bear right onto Chesapeake City Rd.

- 37.3 Make the first right onto the unmarked Frazer Rd. (Rd. 391).

- 41.7 Turn right at the T intersection onto Rte. 40, watching carefully for traffic.

- 42.0 Take the first left at the traffic light onto Pleasant Valley Rd. (Rd. 8), which changes its name first to Otts Chapel Rd. (Rd. 387) and then to Sandy Brae Rd.

- 45.9 Turn right at the T intersection onto Rte. 2/896 (Elkton Rd.), watching carefully for traffic.

- 47.1 Turn left onto Casho Mill Rd. Caution! This intersection is busy. If you happen to miss the turn, you'll know it because the paved shoulder disappears.

- 47.7 Turn right at the traffic light onto Barksdale Rd.

- 47.9 Turn left into the parking lot of Casho Mill Barksdale Park.

3

Inn-to-Inn Triangle Three-Day Ramble

Laurel—Lewes—Greenwood—Laurel

Nestled between Chesapeake Bay tributaries and the Atlantic Ocean lies the gentle, scenic coastal plain of lower Delaware—terrain ideal for cycling at any level of experience. Although strong riders may want to make this flat ride through Delaware's rural Sussex County a one-day near-century challenge, it would be best savored as it was designed: three days meandering leisurely from one luxurious bed-and-breakfast inn to the next.

Designed by the cycling-enthusiast innkeepers Barbara Lloyd of the New Devon Inn in Lewes, Gwen North of the Spring Garden Bed & Breakfast in Laurel, and Sharon Wescott of Eli's Country Inn in Greenwood, this ride takes the route offered as a self-guided package by their outfit Biking Inn to Inn Delaware. (That hassle-free package—which is quite inexpensive—includes three nights in the inns for double occupancy, the transportation of your luggage from one inn to the next, three breakfasts and three dinners, snacks at each inn on arrival, detailed maps and cue sheets of side trips, parking for your car, and secure bicycle storage. For reservations or more information, call the New Devon Inn at 800–824–8754. Tell 'em you read it here.)

This trip begins in Laurel (although beach-lovers may choose to start and end in Lewes). Once a thriving shipping center and port town, Laurel boasts more than 800 structures on the National Register of Historic Places. One of those is your starting point, the Spring Garden Bed & Breakfast (302–875–7015), a restored eighteenth-century country manor furnished with eighteenth- and nineteenth-century antiques and fine art.

After a hearty breakfast you'll head for the beach town of Lewes (pronounced "Lewis")—the "First Town in the First State." The cycling is virtually flat, along agricultural backroads with little traffic. If you choose to relax at the restored twenty-six-room New Devon Inn (800–824–8764), you can walk across the street to King's for homemade ice cream.

After a filling breakfast full of the complex carbohydrates that fuel a cyclist's legs, you'll head cross-country past farm lands and ponds and through historic Milton. One treat will be passing Colvine's Bison Farm—yes, buffalo in Delaware: On Route 16 just before your arrival at Greenwood, you are likely to see the out-of-place-looking creatures pasturing right on the side of the road. Just north of Greenwood is Eli's Country Inn (302–349–4265), a renovated family farm where you can sit and rock forever in the porch swing on the ample front and side porches, listening to the birds trill.

The return ride to Laurel includes passage on Delaware's last free cable ferry across a Chesapeake Bay tributary, the Nanticoke River, and a visit to the quaint shipbuilding village of Bethel, the only village in Delaware listed in its entirety on the National Register of Historic Places. Once again at Spring Garden B&B, you can retrieve your car and wave farewell to Gwen North as you head home.

The first 5 miles of this route coincide with miles 26–31 of Ride 5, and mile 16 overlaps briefly with Ride 4, allowing you to lengthen the ride accordingly. The best times of year to take this ride are spring and fall, as it can "get bleeding hot" in the summer, with high humidity, remarked Barbara Lloyd. You may want to pack some insect repellent as well.

The Basics

Start: Spring Garden Bed and Breakfast in Laurel, 0.2 mile west of Rte. 13 on Delaware Ave. Extended.
Length: 92.3 miles, divided into day-long segments of 32.1, 35.2, and 25.0 miles.

Terrain: Mostly flat. Traffic mostly light, except around the three towns.

Food: Occasional convenience stores en route, but carry some snacks and water. If you do this ride as part of the Biking Inn to Inn Delaware package, your breakfasts and dinners are included, and picnic lunches are available at an extra charge.

Miles & Directions

Note: Follow directions carefully, as not every small street is shown on the map.

First Day (Laurel to Lewes)

- 0.0 From the Spring Garden B&B parking lot, turn left onto Rd. 466 (Delaware Ave.).
- 0.3 After crossing Rte. 13 turn right onto Rd. 465. At mile 1.5 you'll pass Chipman Pond and Old Christ Church on your left.
- 2.2 Turn left onto Rd. 74.
- 3.5 Turn right onto Rd. 447 at Shiloh United Methodist Church.
- 5.6 Bear right onto Rd. 62.
- 6.4 Turn left onto Rd. 472.
- 12.9 Turn left at the T intersection onto Rte. 24. At mile 15.5 cross Rte. 113 and continue straight on Rte. 24 through Millsboro, which has several antiques shops and places to buy lunch. You are now riding on a brief stretch also traveled by Ride 4.
- 17.0 Turn left onto Rd. 305, which becomes Rd. 48 after crossing Rd. 302. At mile 22.8 cross Rte. 5.
- 23.5 Turn left onto Rd. 285. At mile 24.2 you'll pass St. George's Chapel, founded in 1719.
- 29.2 Turn left and then right onto Rte. 9 (business) at Five Points. Immediately cross Rte. 1 and keep heading straight. Rte. 9 becomes Savannah Rd. in Lewes.
- 32.0 Turn left onto 2nd St. At the end of the block, turn left onto Market St., and then turn left into the New Devon Inn parking lot.

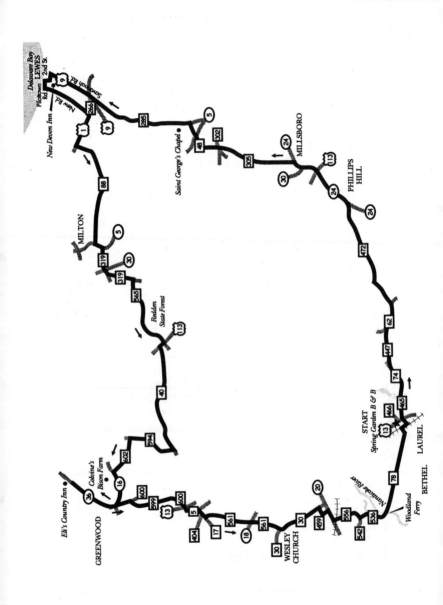

Second Day (Lewes to Greenwood)

- 0.0 Turn right out of the New Devon Inn onto Market St. and make an immediate left onto 2nd St. In 2 blocks turn right at the stop sign onto Shipcarpenter St. In 1 block turn left at the T intersection (tennis courts are across the street) onto the unmarked Pilottown Rd.
- 0.8 Turn left onto the unmarked New Rd. (Rd. 266).
- 3.6 Turn right at the stop sign onto Rd. 266B.
- 3.9 At the yield sign merge onto Rte. 1N.
- 5.5 Turn left onto Rd. 88, following the sign to Milton.
- 11.4 At the stop sign turn left onto Rte. 5 (Federal St.). (Landmarks at this intersection are Tony's TV on your right and the Goshen Methodist Church diagonally across the street on your left.) *Note for a detour:* If you turn right here on Rte. 5 (Federal St.) instead, you can visit the town of Milton, which has a number of lunch spots (the Town Cafe or Norma's), 198 homes on the National Register of Historic Places, a lovely pond, and the mouth of the Broadkill River. King's Homemade Ice Cream is over the bridge and up the hill on Union St. on the left. Pick up snacks at Bodie's or the IGA. After your excursion return here to Tony's to continue the main ride.
- 11.9 Turn right onto Rd. 319 at the produce stand on your left. Cross over the bridge, passing Diamond Pond on your left. At mile 13.3 cross Rte. 30, following the two large arrows pointing left.
- 15.0 Turn right onto Rd. 565 at the sign for Ockels Farm Airport. After a mile or so, you will enter the Redden State Forest, a wonderful area for bird-watching. At mile 18.7 you'll pass a picnic area on your left.
- 19.2 Turn right onto busy Rte. 113. Watch carefully for traffic! (Relax, you'll be on this road only 0.2 mile.)
- 19.4 Make the first left onto Rd. 40, following the signs for Bay Bridge and Bridgeville. At mile 21.5 you'll pass another picnic area on your left
- 25.5 Turn right onto Rd. 594.
- 28.2 Turn left onto Rd. 602 at the sign for the residential development Autumn Acres.

- 30.3 Turn left at the T intersection onto Rte. 16. Soon you should see the buffalo from Colvine's Bison Farm on your right.
- 32.4 Turn right onto Rte. 36.
- 35.2 Turn left into Eli's Country Inn.

Third Day (Greenwood to Laurel)

- 0.0 Turn right out of Eli's Country Inn onto Rte. 36.
- 2.7 Cross Rte. 16 and bear slightly left onto Rd. 600.
- 3.5 Turn right at the Y intersection onto Rd. 599. At mile 3.9 note the horse farm on your right.
- 5.8 Turn right at the T intersection onto Rd. 600. In 1 mile you'll cross Rte. 13.
- 7.0 Turn left onto Rd. 5. In 0.25 mile you can refresh yourself with some fresh produce from Smith & Sons Fruit Market on your left; in the fall the market features fresh-pressed apple cider.
- 7.6 Turn right onto Rte. 404W.
- 8.0 After crossing over the railroad tracks, continue straight through the traffic light onto Rte. 17 (do not follow Rte. 404, as it heads right).
- 8.3 Turn left onto the unmarked Rd. 561; you'll know you've done it right if you pass Delagra Corp. At mile 10.8 cross Rte. 18.
- 12.6 Turn left onto Rd. 30 at the village of Wesley Church.
- 15.0 Turn right onto Rd. 459 (Little League Dr.), on the far side of Nylon Capitol Shopping Center, where you can grab a snack at the pizza parlor or grocery store.
- 15.1 Turn left onto Sussex Ave.
- 15.3 Turn right at the traffic light onto Rte. 20 (Stein Hwy.). You might want to stop in at the unusual shop of Tull Bros.
- 16.0 Turn left onto Rd. 556. Use caution crossing the railroad tracks.
- 16.9 Turn right at Craigs Pond Rd. (Rd. 542A).
- 17.1 Turn left onto Rd. 542.
- 17.7 At the stop sign bear right onto Rd. 536.
- 19.0 Turn left onto Rd. 78.
- 19.2 Turn left to the dock of the Woodland Ferry Crossover.

Take the ferry, which operates seven days a week from 6:00 A.M. to 8:00 P.M. (7:30 A.M. to 6:00 P.M. in the winter) at no charge, whenever its staff see people waiting to cross. Enjoy the two-minute ride across the Nanticoke River. At mile 21.8, to follow the main route continuing on Rd. 78, head straight through the traffic light at Jade Run Sod Farm (for a detour to explore Bethel, turn right instead and ride 0.9 mile). At mile 23.9 use caution in crossing over the railroad tracks. At mile 24.3 cross Rd. 13A (traffic light) onto Rte. 9.

- **24.8** Turn right onto the unmarked Short Dr. at the end of the school field.
- **24.9** Turn left onto Delaware Ave.
- **25.0** Turn left into the Spring Garden Bed and Breakfast. Welcome back!

4

CRABS Challenge

Delaware Seashore State Park—Fenwick Island
Dagsboro—Millsboro—Rehoboth Beach
Delaware Seashore State Park

This tour of the scenic inland estuaries of Delaware is the route featured by the annual Come Ride Around the Bays of Sussex (CRABS) organization in its fund-raising tour early each May, the entrance fee for which benefits the Delaware Inland Bays Estuary education program. The scenery varies from farmland to seashore. Although the land is largely flat, differing from the normal challenge ride by not having long hills, "we regularly have medium to strong prevailing winds that local riders refer to as Delmarva mountains," says CRABS route designer Larry Wonderlin of Rehoboth, Delaware. A steady headwind has often been likened to a hill that never quits.

"I have twice cycled from Portland, Maine to Orlando, Florida with Pedal For Power, and I believe Delaware has the best cycling roads on the East Coast," declares Wonderlin. "Although we have been 'found,' traffic is still lower than in most places." Even the shoulders of Delaware's busy roads are wide enough to be adequate for a single cyclist, if not two abreast. Moreover, motorists are still friendly toward cyclists: "We're over 30 miles into this ride and no one has honked a horn," marveled a cyclist from Sherbourne, New York, who rode in the 1993 CRABS.

Also, wildlife abounds. Delaware is the northernmost point to which pelicans migrate in middle to late June, and you'll also see a profusion of wading birds, such as the egret and the great blue heron. Sussex County is in the north-south flyway for all species of song birds, many of which have flown all the way from South America to arrive at the same time that the horseshoe crabs are mating on Delaware's beaches. By feeding on the crab eggs, the birds double their body weight before crossing the Delaware Bay and continuing north.

The CRABS benefit ride features a metric century (100 kilometers, or in this case 66.4 miles—close enough for government work) and a short ride of 27.5 miles. The shorter version can be ridden by almost anyone. Come hungry for an early lunch, because there are several good opportunities to chow down on the local delicacy of (appropriately enough) crab cakes: Harpoon Hannah's and the Sharks' Cove (at opposite ends of the bridge at mile 11.4) and Tom and Terry's on Route 54 (passed at mile 16.2). Later on in the ride, you can try more crab cakes at The Rusty Rudder (mile 60.0).

There are also nonculinary highlights of the ride. One is Holts Landing State Park on the Indian River (mile 24.5), which has picnic tables, a pavilion, a playground, a boat ramp, and a wading beach. The water is potable, but it sometimes has color, odor, and an obnoxious taste—so do not refill your water bottles unless you are dying of thirst. Another highlight is the museum of the Native American Nanticokes, who live in the Oak Orchard area (miles 41.5–46.5); by timing your visit for the weekend after Labor Day, you'll arrive while they are hosting their large annual powwow. And bring your bathing suit, for there are many opportunities for swimming in either the ocean or the bays. A short stretch of this ride, around mile 37 in Millsboro, overlaps briefly with Ride 3, so the ride may be lengthened accordingly.

If you would like to take this tour in the company of other cyclists at the next CRABS benefit, write to Larry Wonderlin, 28 Marshall Road, Rehoboth, DE 19971, or call him at (302) 227–3697.

For those wishing to stay a night or two in the area, there are many bed-and-breakfast inns and motels in the towns through which you will pass—including Rehoboth Beach, Dewey Beach, Bethany Beach, South Bethany, Fenwick Island, and Millsboro. For specific information call the Delaware Tourism Office at (800) 282–8667 from within Delaware or (800) 441–8846 from out of state.

The Basics

Start: Delaware Seashore State Park Bath House parking lot just south of the Indian River Inlet Bridge on Rte. 1, on the ocean side of the road. The parking lot and beach are accessible year-round, although the bathhouse is open only from May 1 through September 30.

Length: 27.5 or 66.4 miles.

Terrain: Flat, although there can be strong winds requiring low gears in some sections. Traffic is generally moderately light to nonexistent, but in the few populated sections where it is heavy, the roads have wide paved shoulders.

Food: An assortment of fast-food places and restaurants are available from mile 4.0 to 16.0; the next available food is at several cafes in Milford (mile 37.2) and at occasional convenience stores thereafter. Wonderlin's favorite lunch stop is Casapullas at mile 52.7, where the steak sandwiches "rival South Phillie steaks," and Ashby's Oyster House is "better than average" for seafood. Once on Route 1 again, Wonderlin notes, "you're in hog heaven."

Miles & Directions

Note: Follow directions carefully, as not every small street is shown on the map.

- 0.0 Turn right out of the parking lot and make a U-turn under the bridge.
- 0.3 Turn right onto Rte. 1S. At mile 4.8 continue straight at the intersection of Rte. 26. At mile 6.0 do you brake for doughnuts? Here's a Dunkin' Donuts—also a McDonald's for those who want a quick McMuffin.
- 10.8 Turn right onto Rte. 54. At mile 11.4 use caution in crossing the bridge.
- 14.6 Turn right onto Rd. 381. In 1 mile you'll cross over a bridge.
- 16.7 Turn right onto Rd. 384. In 0.5 mile you'll pass Lil Red School House—a nursery school that is indeed painted red. Decision time is approaching.
- 17.6 Bear left at the fork onto Rd. 84.

For the shorter route turn right instead onto Rte. 363. At mile 18.9 bear right to stay on Rd. 363. At mile 21.0 turn right at the stop sign onto Rd. 361 and ride over Little Assawoman Canal Bridge. At mile 22.4 turn right onto Rte. 26. At mile 22.5 turn left onto Rte. 1N. At mile 27.0 do not go over the bridge; instead, turn right into the parking lot alongside the bridge into Delaware Seashore State Park and return to the start.

- 17.9 Turn right to stay on Rd. 84.
- 19.9 Turn left onto Rd. 352.
- 21.0 Turn left onto Rte. 26 in the village of Millville.
- 21.4 Turn right onto Rd. 347.
- 23.5 Turn left at the T intersection onto Rd. 346. (If you were to turn right instead, you would pass the entrance to Holts Landing State Park in about a mile.)
- 27.6 Turn right onto Rte. 26. In a couple of miles, you'll cross over a bridge.
- 32.7 In Dagsboro, turn right to stay on Rte. 26. Keep heading straight onto Rd. 334 where Rte. 26 heads left.
- 33.2 Turn right onto Rd. 331.
- 34.1 Bear left at the Y intersection to stay on Rd. 331. In a couple of miles, cross over a bridge.
- 37.2 You've now entered the town of Millsboro. To avoid waiting at the two traffic lights, turn right onto Morris St. and then turn left at the next corner onto Houston St.
- 37.3 Turn right onto Rte. 24E. Now you are traveling on the brief stretch where this ride overlaps with Ride 3.
- 41.5 Turn right onto Rd. 313A.
- 42.4 Bear left at the Y intersection onto Rd. 312. In 0.5 mile you'll pass the Indian River Yacht Club.
- 44.5 Turn left onto Rte. 5/Rd. 297.
- 46.5 Turn right onto Rte. 24E. At mile 48.0 continue straight through the traffic light. At mile 52.7 Casapullas in Peddler's Village on your left offers good steak sandwiches. At mile 53.2 cross over Love Creek Bridge.
- 54.9 Turn right onto Rd. 275.
- 55.6 Turn left onto Rd. 274.

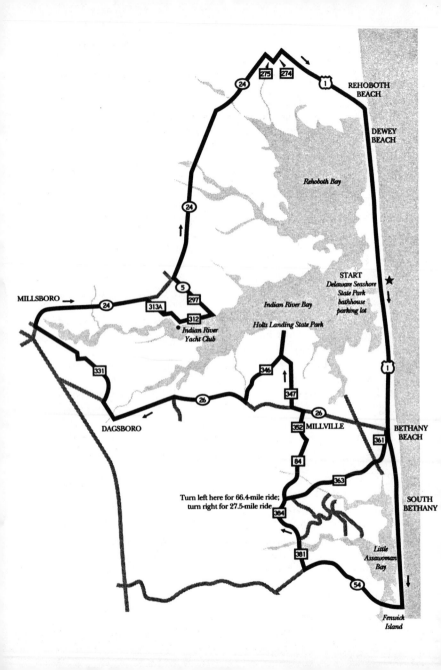

- 55.9 Turn right onto Seaside Dr. into the small housing development of Rehoboth Shores.
- 56.1 Turn right onto Airport Rd.
- 56.4 Turn right onto Rte. 1S to Rehoboth Beach. In 1.5 miles cross over the canal bridge; in another 1.5 miles you'll pass Dewey Beach. A mile later you'll pass the Rehoboth Sailing Club. Five miles later cross over Indian River Bridge.
- 66.0 At the bottom of the bridge, turn right into Delaware Seashore State Park. In 0.4 mile you'll reach the parking lot.

5

Sussex Ponds Cruise

Delmar—Portsville—Bethel—Trap Pond—Delmar

Aside from being ideal for cycling with its almost traffic-free and wooded backroads, Delaware's Sussex County has a fascinating ecology. Two of the ponds this ride passes—Trap Pond and Trussum Pond—represent the northernmost extent of the bald cypress trees growing out of the water in swamps for which the Deep South is famous. At Trussum Pond you may feel as though you're pedaling through a Louisiana bayou instead of in a corner of the Mid-Atlantic. Trap Pond is in a state park, which—in addition to views of the pond—offers picnic tables, rest rooms, drinking water, a camp store, and overnight camping during the summer (for more information call the Delaware Division of Parks in Dover: 302–736–4702).

This ride, devised by Gilbert M. Turner of Salisbury, Maryland, has long been a favorite of the Salisbury Bicycle Club; in fact, all but the last 4 miles were featured as the northern part of a 78-mile ride originating in Salisbury for the League of American Wheelmen's 1989 National Rally.

The outbound route through flat, agricultural land will take you right through the place where the corner of Delaware juts into Maryland—the cornerstone there was the first laid by the surveyors Mason and Dixon in 1768. As the route passes through Portsville, unpack your binoculars for a bird-watching detour into the Nanticoke Wildlife Area. On the eastern side of Laurel beginning at mile 26.2, the route coincides with the first 5 miles of Ride 3, allowing you to consider joining up with a much longer ride by way of an overnight in Laurel.

The Basics

Start: Delmar, a town that straddles the border of Delaware and Maryland (and whose name obviously borrows from both states); at the unpaved parking lot south of Piper's Restaurant. The restaurant is in the Maryland half of Delmar, just south of Rte. 54 and just west of the southbound lane of Rte. 13.
Length: 42 miles.
Terrain: Flat. Traffic is light except on Rte. 54 and crossing Rte. 13.
Food: Many options at the start in Delmar (Piper's Restaurant at the start is a good place for breakfast); a country store just off the route in Bethel about 20 miles into the ride; and seasonal camp stores at Chipman Pond (mile 26) and at Trap Pond (mile 34). No other services in between, so carry snacks, water, and tools.

Miles & Directions

Note: Follow directions carefully, as not every small street is shown on the map

- **0.0** From the unpaved parking lot south of Piper's Restaurant, turn left (west) onto Chestnut St., and then turn right to head north on Woodlawn St. Turn left onto Rte. 54 at the Delaware state line. At mile 7.8 you'll pass the cornerstone monument marking the Mason-Dixon Line and will now be riding briefly in Maryland.
- **8.7** Turn right onto Norris Twilley Rd.
- **9.3** Bear right onto May Twilley Rd. In about 0.75 mile you'll reenter Delaware, where the road you're on becomes Rd. 507.
- **11.2** Immediately after crossing Rd. 76, turn right onto Rd. 508.
- **12.7** Where Rd. 508 jogs right to continue straight, turn left onto Rd. 509.
- **14.8** Turn left onto Rd. 514.
- **15.8** Cross Rte. 24 and continue straight on Rd. 493 into Portsville. (To detour into the Nanticoke Wildlife Area, at Portsville turn left onto Rd. 496 and ride to the end; return the way you

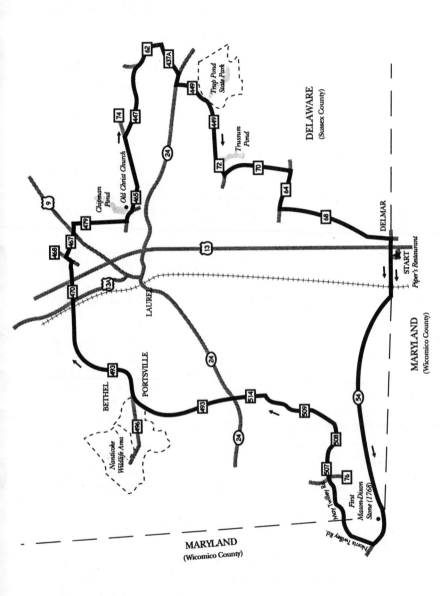

came in.) At Portsville continue on Rd. 493, which bends east past the pond and takes you into Bethel at mile 19.8. Cross the bridge and pass a country store on Main St. Continue on Rd. 493.

- 22.4 Cross Rte. 13A and continue straight on Rd. 470.
- 23.0 Cross Rd. 13 and continue straight on Rd. 470 until the end.
- 23.7 Turn left at the T intersection onto Rd. 468.
- 23.8 Turn right onto Rd. 467. In 0.5 mile you'll cross Rte. 9.
- 24.7 Turn right onto Rd. 479.
- 26.2 Turn left onto Rd. 465. Just after this corner is a camp store, where you can provision up if you're hungry or thirsty. In 500 feet cross over Chipman Pond Dam. Less than 0.25 mile later is Old Christ Church on your left, an early-eighteenth-century "chapel of ease," where the interior—including the pews—is still original, unpainted wood. By the way, for the next 5 miles you'll be riding on the first 5 miles of Ride 3.
- 27.2 Bear left to join Rd. 74.
- 28.5 Turn right onto Rd. 447.
- 30.7 Bear right to join Rd. 62.
- 31.5 Turn right onto Rd. 437A.
- 32.5 Turn right at the T intersection onto Rte. 24.
- 32.7 Turn left onto Rd. 449 at the sign to Trap Pond State Park. At mile 33.9 is the entrance to the park itself. South of the park Rd. 449 bends right (west). At mile 35.5 cross over the dam for Trussum Pond, which lies to your left and is very pretty with its stand of bald cypress trees.
- 35.7 Continue straight on Rd. 72.
- 36.0 Turn sharply left onto Rd. 70 where Rd. 72 curves right. Go slowly here, for this intersection is easy to miss.
- 37.9 Turn right at the T intersection onto Rd. 64.
- 38.9 Turn left onto Rd. 68.
- 42.1 Turn right onto Rte. 54.
- 42.2 Turn left at the traffic light onto Rte. 13.
- 42.4 Turn right into the unpaved parking lot south of Piper's Restaurant.

Maryland

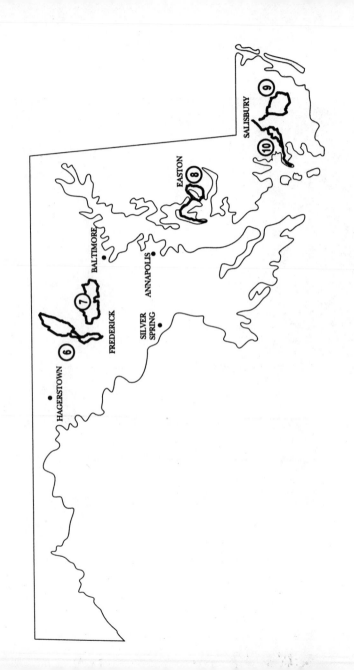

6

Three Covered Bridges Cruise

Frederick—Motters—Thurmont—Catoctin—Frederick

Be sure to pack your camera for this 43-mile jaunt into the northern part of Frederick County. The rolling, lightly traveled roads take you through a valley from which you can gaze at the distant Blue Ridge Mountains. At the northernmost section look for the imposing shrine of Mount Saint Mary's College in the mountains.

Besides the three nineteenth-century covered bridges through which you will ride, you might want to spend some time at the Catoctin Mountain Zoological Park (301–271–7488), one of two privately owned zoos in Maryland. And don't miss the chance to poke around the ruins of an old lime kiln in the historic Catoctin Furnace area; the kiln dates back to the late 1700s. South of Thurmont you'll ride past various fish hatchery ponds.

This ride, one of a series produced by the Tourism Council of Frederick County, Inc., along with the Frederick-based bicycle shop Wheel Base, Inc., is especially nice on a spring day when the orchards are fragrant with flowers, or in the autumn when their boughs are heavy with apples. Leave some space in your panniers to stash a few of each!

For those wishing to break up the 43-mile cruise into an easier two-day jaunt, there are several overnight options in Thurmont, 26 miles into the ride. Campers may set up a tent at the Catoctin Mountain National Park (301–663–9330) or at the Crow's Nest Campground (301–271–7632). Those preferring luxury can rent a secluded cabin at the Ole Mink Farm (301–271–7012) or relax with

---

a free continental breakfast at the quaint Cozy Country Inn (301–271–4301). Staying at Thurmont then makes the second day's return to Frederick a mere 17 miles.

Frederick also has several bed-and-breakfast inns. Particularly notable is the Tyler-Spite House (301–831–4455), an elegantly restored three-story 1814 Federal-style mansion, where your stay includes afternoon tea and an evening carriage ride through the historic district. For information on other choices, contact the Tourism Council of Frederick County at (800) 999–3613.

The Basics

Start: Frederick at the Culler Lake Boat House, at the corner of W. 2nd St. and College Ter. Free parking is available on the street. Rest rooms are open near the tennis courts from May through October. The start on W. 2nd St. is immediately west of Exit 7 off U.S. Rte. 15.

Length: 43.2 miles.

Terrain: Moderately rolling hills. Traffic generally light but heavier around Frederick.

Food: Readily available in Frederick and Thurmont, with convenience stores scattered along the rest of the route. To be on the safe side, carry snacks and water.

Miles & Directions

- 0.0 Turn left out of the Culler Lake Boat House parking lot to head west on W. 2nd St.
- 0.2 Turn right onto Fairview Ave.
- 1.3 Turn left onto Motter Ave.; after crossing Rte. 15 it changes its name to Opossumtown Pike.
- 5.5 Turn right (at Ford Rd.) to stay on Opossumtown Pike.
- 6.1 Bear left at the bottom of the hill to stay on Opossumtown Pike.
- 6.2 Turn right onto Masser Rd.

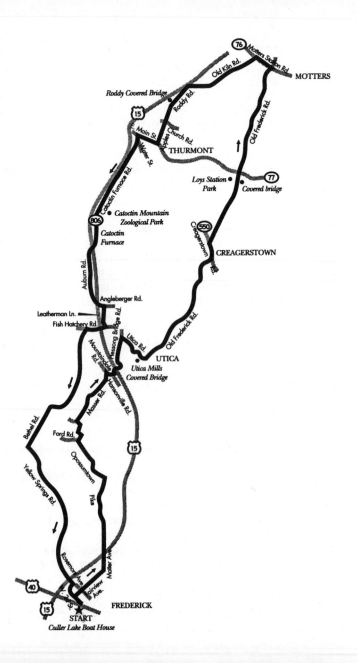

- 8.0 Turn right onto Mountaindale Rd.
- 8.2 Turn left onto Hansonville Rd.
- 8.4 Cross Rte. 15 and turn left onto Rte. 806, here called Hessong Bridge Rd.
- 9.5 Turn right onto Utica Rd. Here you'll pass through the first of the three covered bridges, Utica Mills Covered Bridge, built about 1850.
- 10.7 Turn left onto Old Frederick Rd.
- 14.7 Bear left at the stop sign onto Rte. 550 (Creagerstown Rd.).
- 15.0 Turn right onto the continuation of Old Frederick Rd. At mile 17.1 you'll pass through the second covered bridge at Loys Station, also built around 1850. If you're so inclined, stop to have a snack at the picnic tables at Loys Station Park or to use the rest rooms there.
- 21.0 Turn left onto Rte. 76 (Motters Station Rd.).
- 21.6 Turn left onto Old Kiln Rd. Soon you'll pass the old lime kiln on your right. Watch for gravel on the road.
- 24.1 Turn left onto Roddy Rd. At mile 25.7 you'll pass through the third of the covered bridges, Roddy Covered Bridge, built about 1856. Keep going straight where the road becomes Apples Church Rd., in the village of Thurmont.
- 26.1 Turn right at the T intersection onto Rte. 77 (E. Main St.).
- 26.8 Turn left onto Rte. 806 (Water St.).
- 26.9 Turn right to stay on Rte. 806, which becomes Catoctin Furnace Rd. Several miles ahead the Catoctin Mountain Zoological Park will be on your left. Stay on Rte. 806 as it crosses Rte. 15, changing its name to Auburn Rd. Be careful at that crossing, as traffic is fast and heavy.
- 32.9 Just after Rte. 806 crosses Rte. 15 and becomes Angleberger Rd., turn right onto Leatherman Ln. After Leatherman Ln. bends sharply left, make a right onto Fish Hatchery Rd. and cross Rte. 15 again. Now you will pass fish ponds.
- 33.5 Turn left onto Bethel Rd.
- 38.2 Turn left onto Yellow Springs Rd. at the stop sign. In Frederick this road becomes Rosemont Ave.
- 43.0 Turn right onto W. 2nd St.
- 43.2 Turn right into the Culler Lake Boat House.

7

Sykesville Hill-Climbing Cruise

Eldersburg—Sykesville—Taylorsville—Eldersburg

This hill-climber is made for experienced cyclists wanting a hefty workout on some of the country's most scenic "blue highways." The route winds hill and dale through some of Maryland's loveliest rolling farmland, including that used for horse farms. So get a good night's sleep, fill up the water bottles, and tackle this tour of southern Carroll County.

Among other attractions Piney Run Park and Lake lies just a short jaunt off Route 26. At this day-use park you can take a break to enjoy a picnic lunch or a hike. Two-thirds of the way through the route, reward yourself for your efforts at Little George's, a good stop for ice cream.

This ride is one of ten carefully mapped by the Carroll County Office of Tourism, along with local cyclists. For more routes, plus detailed information about Carroll County (including campgrounds and bed-and-breakfast inns), call the tourism office at the (800) 272–1933.

The Basics

Start: Eldersburg, at the intersection of Ridge Rd. and Gemini Dr. south of the Carrolltowne Shopping Center on Rte. 26. Park cars in the lot of the Carrolltowne Elementary School.
Length: 30 miles.
Terrain: Very hilly. For experienced cyclists.

Food: Convenience stores in Eldersburg, Sykesville, and Taylorsville but scarce elsewhere; carry snacks and water.

Miles & Directions

- 0.0 Turn right onto Ridge Rd.
- 1.2 Turn right onto Brangels Rd.
- 2.4 Turn right onto Arrington Rd. At the T intersection, turn right onto Slacks Rd. and make the first left onto Raincliffe Rd.
- 4.0 Just after crossing Rte. 32 (Sykesville Rd.), turn right onto Village Rd. Make the first left onto Cedar Ave.; then immediately turn right at the stop sign onto Walnut Ave. You're now riding through Sykesville.
- 4.2 Turn right onto Springfield Ave.
- 4.5 Turn left onto Central Ave.
- 4.8 Turn left at the end onto 3rd Ave.; in one block, turn right at the end onto Obrecht Rd.
- 6.8 Turn right onto White Rock Rd. At mile 11.2, if you wish to make a detour into Piney Run Park, turn right onto Martz Rd. to the park entrance.
- 7.9 Turn left onto Streaker Rd.
- 9.0 Turn left onto Rte. 97 (Old Washington Rd.).
- 9.9 Turn right onto Fannie Dorsey Rd.
- 12.2 Turn left at the T intersection onto Woodbine Rd. (Rte. 94); then make an immediate right onto Gillis Rd.
- 13.4 Turn right onto Fleming Rd.
- 14.7 Turn left at the T intersection onto Braddock Rd. You can get snacks at High's Store in Taylorsville.
- 15.8 Turn right onto Rte. 27 (Ridge Rd.). Cross Rte. 26 (Liberty Rd.).
- 17.1 Turn right onto Sams Creek Rd.
- 18.7 Turn left at the triangle onto Salem Bottom Rd.
- 19.4 Bear right onto Arthur Shipley Rd.
- 20.0 Turn left onto Oak Tree Rd.
- 21.1 Turn right onto Bear Branch Rd.

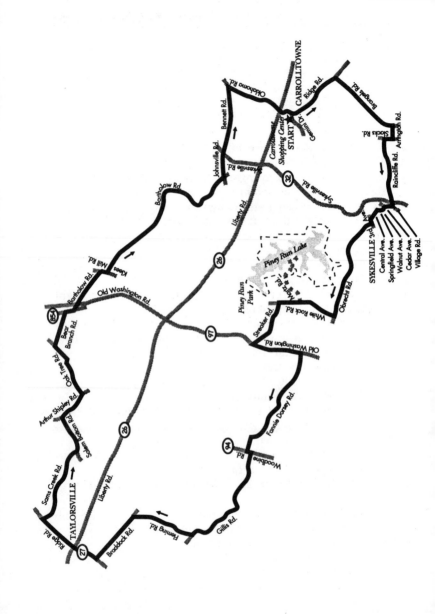

- 21.7 Turn right at the T intersection onto Old Washington Rd. (Rte. 854).
- 21.9 Turn left onto Bartholow Rd., and continue across Rte. 97. Now you're less than 1 mile from the ice cream at Little George's that has been beckoning you for so long!
- 22.8 Turn right at the T intersection onto Klees Mill Rd., just past Little George's.
- 23.0 Turn left to continue on Bartholow Rd.
- 26.6 Turn left onto Johnsville Rd. After you cross Rte. 32 (Sykesville Rd.), continue straight onto Bennett Rd.
- 28.5 Turn right onto Oklahoma Rd. Follow Oklahoma Rd. to Rte. 26 (Liberty Rd.); you'll pass a McDonald's on your right. After you cross Rte. 26, continue straight onto Ridge Rd.
- 30.7 Gemini Dr.—and your starting point.

8

Delmarva Challenge

Easton—Oxford—Saint Michaels
Tilghman—Easton

Delmarva—a long peninsula encompassing *DEL*aware, the eastern shore of *MAR*yland, and a part of *Virgini*A—lies between the Chesapeake Bay and the Atlantic Ocean. Much of it is still commercial farmland for raising chickens, grain, and corn. Most of the land is flat coastal plain and gently rolling farm fields with little-traveled backroads, making for ideal cycling—although at times variable winds, generally from the south, can present stiff opposition on parts of a ride.

Both the shorter and the longer versions of this Talbot County ride have everything for a perfect weekend getaway: lovely views of the water, antiques shops, superb seafood restaurants famous for their Maryland crabs, a nautical museum, a short ride on the oldest continuously operating ferry in the United States. The 27-mile ramble through the Chesapeake Bay, Maryland, towns of Easton, Oxford, and Saint Michaels is an easy, scenic meander that is a favorite of many clubs and commercial bicycle touring companies.

By adding 32 more miles out to Tilghman Island—which most likely will include bucking headwinds on the way out—stronger cyclists can find their match. The full 59-mile challenge to Tilghman Island also includes a view of one of the last remaining fleets of skipjacks: nineteenth-century sailing vessels still used to dredge for oysters. (Another such fleet can be seen on the bicycle ride to Deal Island; see Ride 10). For those antsy to push the pedals even farther, there are also any number of beautiful side jaunts along quiet necks into the water.

There is so much to see and do that, rather than trying to cram all the miles into one day, you would do better to plan your stay to include at least one night. And you can really pamper yourself if you take the whole weekend. This entire area offers a wide assortment of luxurious bed-and-breakfast inns. Among them are the rambling Pasadena Inn in Royal Oak (410–745–5053), the Tidewater Inn in Easton (410–822–1300), the Robert Morris Inn in Oxford (410–226–5111), and Harrison's Chesapeake House on Tilghman Island itself (410–886–2123).

Because this is such a popular resort area, traffic and population density on summer weekends can be higher than someone seeking peace and solitude might desire, particularly in the towns themselves. Try your visit instead in September or October, when the autumn colors can be spectacular. Or play hooky from work to slip away for some midweek R & R and time for yourself and maybe your love. Although a fair amount of the cycling is along main highways (because they are the only access on the narrow necks), the state of Maryland is so civilized that the wide, smoothly paved shoulders are marked as bicycle lanes! Enjoy!

The basic loop ride, contributed by Frank J. Pondolfina of the Freestate Derailleurs Bicycle Club of Baltimore, starts at the Tred Avon shopping center in Easton, where you can park your car. There is also a municipal lot several blocks away. If you plan to stay overnight, park at the inn of your choice and pick up the ride near there instead.

The Basics

Start: Easton, Maryland, at the Tred Avon Square Shopping Center on Rte. 322 and Marlboro Rd. To get to the start from Rte. 50, exit onto Route 322 into Easton and turn west into the Tred Avon Square Shopping Center.
Length: 27 or 59 miles.
Terrain: Mostly flat, although there can be stiff headwinds out to Tilghman Island. Traffic ranges from light to moderate, heavier in the towns and on summer weekends.

Food: Excellent seafood restaurants in the towns, plus convenience stores. You might want to pack a snack, though, for the stretch from Saint Michaels to Tilghman Island.

Miles & Directions

Note: Follow directions carefully, as not every small street is shown on the map.

- 0.0 Turn left out of the Tred Avon Square Shopping Center onto Rte. 322.
- 1.4 Turn right at the second light onto Rte. 333S (Peach Blossom Rd.) toward Oxford, riding in the bicycle lane along the right shoulder. Stay on this road for the next 10 miles until it ends at the ferry dock in Oxford. At mile 3.9 you'll pass Bailey's Neck Rd. on your right—a delightful 8-mile round-trip detour out toward the Tred Avon River if you're feeling energetic. If you're hungry for an early lunch when you reach Oxford, make a sharp left at the tennis courts onto the unmarked S. Morris St. and turn right at the next block onto W. Pier St. for a cyclists' popular lunch stop at the Pier Street Restaurant and Marina. You can also picnic and swim at the beach of the Oxford town park across from the Oxford Mews. Just before the ferry dock, you'll pass the Robert Morris Inn.
- 11.3 Where the road ends at the ferry dock, pay the nominal fare to take the Tred Avon Ferry for a breezy, beautiful, and all-too-short five-minute ride across the Tred Avon River to Bellevue. From the dock continue riding straight.
- 11.6 Turn right at the T intersection onto Bellevue Road, following the signs for Saint Michaels.
- 14.3 Turn left at the stop sign at the T intersection onto Rte. 329 (Royal Oak Rd.), following the signs for Saint Michaels. Royal Oak is a thriving center of antiques stores. In less than 0.25 mile, you'll pass the Pasadena Inn on your right.
- 15.1 Turn left at the stop sign onto Rte. 33W, riding in the bicycle lane on the right shoulder. At mile 18.1 you'll reach Saint

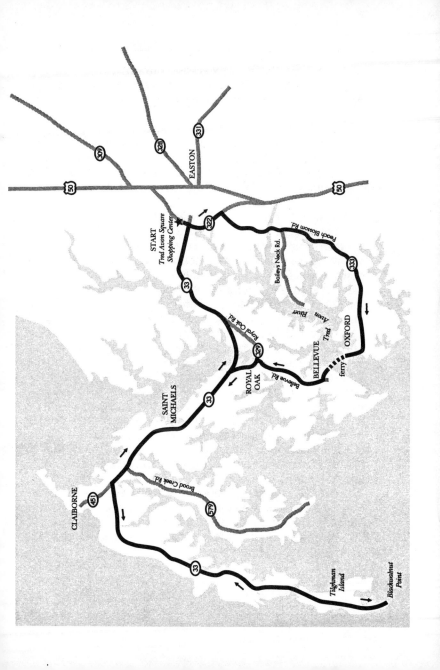

Michaels. Here you may, if you wish, turn right onto Cherry St. to splurge for some calories at Justine's Ice Cream Parlor, or turn right onto Mill St. to explore the Chesapeake Bay Maritime Museum.

If you wish to make this ride only a 27-mile ramble, leave Saint Michaels the way you came in, heading east on the bike lane on the shoulder of Rte. 33E. At mile 27.3 turn left at the first traffic light onto Rte. 322. One block later turn right into the Tred Avon Square shopping center.

■ 18.1 If you wish to visit Tilghman Island, continue heading west out of Saint Michaels on Rte. 33W. At mile 20.6 you'll pass the intersection with Rte. 579 (Broad Creek Rd.) on your left; if you're up for some extra exploring, that spur will lead you down 8 miles along some of the least-traveled roads you are likely ever to pedal, for some views of the sparkling water. At mile 21.2 you'll pass Rte. 451 heading off to your right; that 2-mile optional spur will take you into the charming village of Claiborne and to Rich Neck Manor, the plantation home of Michael Tilghman, a member of the Continental Congress during the American Revolution. At mile 22.8 you'll pass the Wades Point Inn bed-and-breakfast. At mile 30.5 stop at the Tilghman Island drawbridge for a lovely vista of the sailboats. Half a mile beyond that, turn left onto a small wharf where there is one of the last remaining fleets of skipjacks. At mile 31.2 is Harrison's Chesapeake House, an inn popular with duck hunters and sports fishermen. In another 2.5 miles you've reached the end of the line: the Coast Guard station at Blackwalnut Point.

■ 33.7 Turn around and retrace your entire route out Rte. 33W, on which you will remain for the next 25 miles, through Saint Michaels and past the turnoff on Rte. 329 to the Pasadena Inn.

■ 58.6 Turn left onto Rte. 322. In 1 block turn right into the Tred Avon Square shopping center.

9

Iron Furnace Ramble

Salisbury—Furnace—Colbourne—Salisbury

Bicycling doesn't get much better than it does on this ride, one of the favorites of the Salisbury State University Cycling Club. On this ride—an easy 33-mile meander through woodlands preserved by the Nature Conservancy in Wicomico County in southeast Maryland—the scenery is idyllic, the trees shelter you from prevailing winds, the pavement is smooth, the road is flat, and automobile traffic is light. Ah-h-h!

Just to make life even easier, the cycling club has marked the entire route with white arrows numbered *33* (the length of the ride and the number given it when the club first marked it for the 1989 National Rally of the League of American Wheelmen)—markings that have been kept up to date, noted club representative Joseph K. Gilbert, who contributed this ride. All in all, it's a perfect choice for warming up early in the season or for introducing a novice to the joys of two-wheeled touring.

The nominal destination, Furnace Towne, is a restored iron-smelting village. During summer weekends you might see a blacksmith pounding hot iron on an anvil, a candle-maker dipping wicks into tallow, or a broom-maker assembling straw on a wood handle. Stop long enough in Furnace also to stroll along the 0.25-mile-long nature trail, which leads you into a marsh where discreet signs identify exotic cypress trees and other plants.

Although the starting place of this ride is the university campus, you might prefer instead to begin and end from Snow Hill, a couple of miles southeast of the route on Route 12. There you can make a weekend of it at the Snow Hill Inn (410–632–2102), the

Chanceford Hall Bed & Breakfast (410–632–2231), or the River House Inn (410–632–2722); for further information contact Somerset Community Information in Princess Anne, Maryland, at (410) 651–0852. Outside the town is Pocomoke River State Park (410–632–2566), where those preferring to camp can pitch a tent.

In addition to restaurants, canoe rentals, and other services, Snow Hill has *Tilly the Tug:* a tugboat that, for a few dollars, will take you chugging down the Pocomoke River. Keep alert—you might even spot a bald eagle wheeling overhead.

The Basics

Start: Salisbury, at the front of the Maggs Physical Activity Center at Salisbury State University. Parking there is free to the public, although it may be crowded during the school year. To get to the university from Rte. 13, turn west onto Bateman St. and proceed .75 mile.

Length: 32.8 miles.

Terrain: Virtually flat. Mostly on well-paved country roads with very little traffic.

Food: Stock up in Salisbury, because this ride is so rural that there are no places to stop for food or drink unless you make a detour of 4 miles each way to the town of Snow Hill halfway through the ride (adding the detour to Snow Hill lengthens the route to 41 miles).

Miles & Directions

Note: At the start of the ride, follow the big white arrows painted on the pavement until the ride is marked with smaller white arrows numbered *33*. When approaching the university on your return route, follow the green arrows marked with an *H* (for *Home*).

- **0.0** Depart from the exit in front of the gym across from the parking lot.

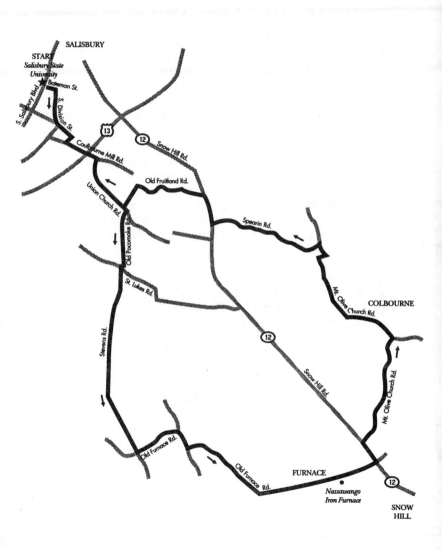

- 0.2 Head straight onto Bateman St., leaving the university. Cross the very busy Rte. 13 (S. Salisbury Blvd.).
- 0.7 Turn right at the T intersection onto S. Division St., which eventually becomes Coulbourne Mill Rd.
- 2.8 Turn right onto Union Church Rd.
- 4.4 Turn right onto Old Pocomoke Rd., which, after crossing St. Lukes Rd., becomes Stevens Rd. (unmarked).
- 10.8 Turn left onto Old Furnace Rd. (the road is unmarked, but follow the sign pointing to Snow Hill). At mile 15.8 you will pass the Nassawango Iron Furnace on your right; the sign to it faces oncoming traffic. This is where you might like to stop and wander around the village restoration and the nature trail. There are also public rest rooms and water.
- 16.9 Turn left onto Rte. 12 (Snow Hill Rd.). *If you wish instead to visit the town of Snow Hill for lunch or other sightseeing, turn right instead and ride 4 miles; although traffic is moderate, there is a lane-wide paved shoulder.*
- 17.6 Turn right onto Mt. Olive Church Rd.
- 23.6 Turn left onto Spearin Rd.
- 26.7 Turn right onto Rte. 12 (Snow Hill Rd.).
- 27.4 Turn left onto Old Fruitland Rd.
- 28.4 Bear right at the yield sign onto the unmarked Coulbourne Mill Rd. After crossing over a bridge, follow the main road as it bears right and joins S. Division St.
- 32.1 Turn left onto Bateman St. Cross Rte. 13 (S. Salisbury Blvd.) Enter the Salisbury State University campus.
- 32.8 Head straight into the Maggs Physical Activities Center parking area.

10

Deal Island Skipjack Challenge

Salisbury—Jason—Deal Island
Princess Anne—Salisbury

Nautical history buffs particularly ought to enjoy this ride, as its destination—Deal Island in the Tangier Sound—is the home of one of the last remaining skipjack fleets. Skipjacks are sailing vessels that by law may not be motorized. In the nineteenth century they were the primary way fishermen tongued for oysters. Today, at the threshold of the twenty-first century, the dozen or so skipjacks at the small Deal Island harbor are one of the last fleets of the waterman's work boats. If you're lucky enough to time your visit for the proper weekend in the spring, you may be able to cheer on the annual skipjack races; for details call Somerset Community Information in Princess Anne at (410) 651–0852.

On the way out, in addition to cycling through miles of pastoral farmland of Wicomico and Somerset counties, you'll pedal through the tidal marshland of the Deal Island Wildlife Management Area. Birders might enjoy packing a small pair of binoculars and looking for great blue heron and other shore birds.

On the return the route takes you through the historic town of Princess Anne. There you will ride by the two-century-old Washington Hotel (410–651–2525), where George Washington's mother once spent the night; if you wish, you can do so today. In the winter the hotel is worth a stop for a steaming bowl of oyster stew; in the spring try the soft-shell crab sandwich. (The weather in this southeastern peninsula of Maryland is so moderated by the surrounding bodies of water that you can comfortably bicycle in all four seasons.)

For the most part the terrain is flat, but don't let that fool you. The land is exposed and there is a significant prevailing wind from the west, and so on the way out "you work," remarked Joseph K. Gilbert, representative of the Salisbury State University Cycling Club who contributed to this ride. But the payoff is that "you have a wonderful tailwind coming home," he added.

The club designed this ride for the 1989 National Rally of the League of American Wheelmen held at the university, marking the pavement with orange arrows and the number 62 (for its mileage). Where roads have not been repaved since, many of those arrows will still guide you.

Because this route is so rural, services are limited. There are two mom-and-pop stores for buying snacks and drinks in Monie and Deal Island, as well as public rest rooms at the gas station on Deal Island. For those wishing to make the ride into a more leisurely weekend trip, Princess Anne has a number of beautiful bed-and-breakfast inns (again, call Somerset Community Information for suggestions). And Salisbury itself has all the major chain hotels, motels, and restaurants.

The Basics

Start: Salisbury, at the front of the University Center at Salisbury State University. Parking there is free to the public, although it may be crowded during the school year. To get to the university from Rte. 13, turn west onto Bateman St. and proceed for .75 mile.
Length: 63.0 miles.
Terrain: Virtually flat, although there can be persistent headwinds on the way out (remember, headwinds have been likened to hills that never quit). Very low traffic, and Rte. 363 has a lane-wide shoulder almost its entire length.
Food: A couple of convenience stores along the way, plus all services in Princess Anne and Salisbury.

Miles & Directions

Note: Follow directions carefully as not every small street is shown on the map. Follow the big orange arrows at the start until the ride is marked with an orange *62* and smaller arrows. When you approach the university on your return, look instead for green arrows marked with an *H* (for *Home*).

- 0.0 Head straight out the exit of the university parking lot. Cross Dogwood Dr. to ride straight ahead onto Wesley Dr.
- 0.2 Turn right onto Pine Bluff Rd.
- 0.3 Turn left onto Camden Ave.
- 2.0 Bear right at the Y intersection onto Allen Rd. After you pass through the village of Allen (which has a small convenience store), the road changes its name to Loretto Allen Rd.
- 8.0 Turn right onto Polks Rd. Stop in at Foggy Bottom, a discount store, for delftware and other items; it has "good prices" and "will ship," noted Joe Gilbert.
- 10.0 Turn left onto New Rd.
- 11.3 Turn right at the T intersection onto Ridge Rd.
- 13.5 Turn left at the T intersection onto Mt. Vernon Rd.
- 14.3 Make the first right onto Black Rd.
- 16.4 Turn left at the T intersection onto Drawbridge Rd.
- 17.1 Make the first right onto Fitzgerald Rd.
- 19.6 Turn right at the T intersection onto Rte. 363 (Deal Island Rd.), and stay on it to Wenona Harbor at the very end. At mile 32.0 you'll reach Deal Island. Stop to explore. To return, turn around and retrace your route, pedaling 18 more miles straight into Princess Anne. At mile 50.2 you'll cross busy Rte. 13.
- 50.3 Turn right onto Mansion St.
- 50.4 Turn left onto Prince William St.
- 50.6 Turn left onto Rte. 675 (Somerset Ave.) and look for the Washington Hotel on your left.
- 52.0 Turn right onto Rte. 529 (Loretto Rd.). At mile 54.6 cross Rte. 13. Watch carefully, as the traffic is heavy and there is no traffic light. After this intersection Loretto Rd. becomes Loretto Allen Rd.

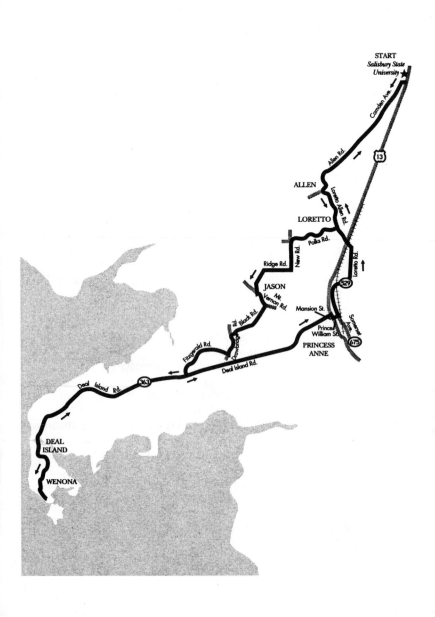

- 56.8 Bear left onto Allen Rd., which eventually becomes Camden Ave.
- 62.7 Turn right onto Pine Bluff Rd.
- 62.8 Turn left onto Wesley Dr.
- 63.0 Head straight into the Salisbury State University parking lot.

New Jersey

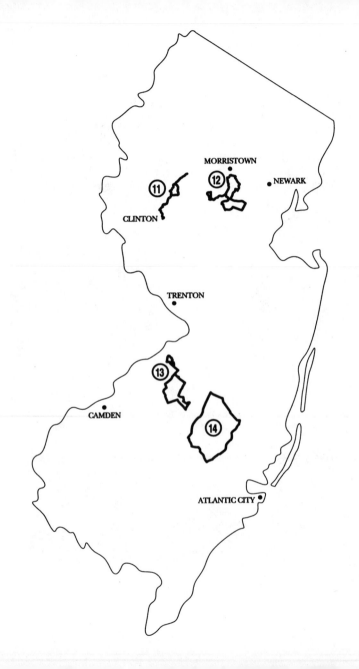

MORRISTOWN

NEWARK

⑪

⑫

CLINTON

TRENTON

⑬

CAMDEN

⑭

ATLANTIC CITY

11

Raritan River Gorge Ramble

Clinton—Califon—Clinton

This peaceful meander in western New Jersey is one of the nicest you're likely to encounter. It is so shaded that it would be cooling even on a hot day; it has almost no automobile traffic; its gently rolling terrain is accessible to nearly everyone; and its scenery—especially the gorge cut out by the Raritan River—is unparalleled. So slow down; bring your fishing rod, binoculars, and picnic lunch; and introduce a friend to the joys of bicycle touring.

This charming ride, based on a route contributed by Leonard C. Friedman and Gail Waimon of Short Hills, New Jersey, starts in the town of Clinton in Hunterdon County. There you can park either along the street or in the public lot in back of the Clinton Bakery, where you can pick up breakfast, snacks, or lunch on any day but Monday. Clinton's small historic downtown district is worth a walking tour, especially the Clinton Historical Museum (908–735–4101) and the Hunterdon Art Center (908–735–8415)—two former gristmills on either side of the cast-iron bridge. The Clinton Falls Country Store and Eatery overlooking the waterfall is a nice place to relax for a drink or bowl of soup after the ride. Clinton is also the home of the Leigh Way Bed and Breakfast at 66 Leigh Street; call (908) 735–4311.

First you'll leave Clinton by Center Street, which is lined by mature trees and gracious old homes. The ride from Clinton to Califon is a net uphill, although generally very gentle; the few significant hills are short enough only to make you glow.

The highlight is the 1.8-mile unpaved section of Raritan River Road (uniformly abbreviated RIVER RD. on the street signs) paralleling the fast-flowing, boulder-strewn south fork of the Raritan River deep in the rocky wooded gorge of Ken Lockwood Gorge Park. Although the rutted dirt road can be navigated even by thin-tire bikes, you'd be happier on a hybrid or true mountain bike, especially if the road is muddy after a rain. In any event take your time—maybe even pause for an hour or two to watch the birders gazing through their spotting scopes or the fly fishermen in waders casting for rainbow and brook trout.

Your destination, Califon, feels like a town that time forgot. The roads are so sleepy that geese sit right in the middle of them, hammocks swing from front porches, and the nineteenth-century buildings of the bank and general store still have false fronts. Sit by the river to enjoy your picnic lunch.

You can return by the path out, if you want to revisit the river gorge. Or you can follow the directions in the cue sheet for a bit of variety, climbing over a ridge just for the challenge (also a good detour for both directions if River Road in the gorge is too muddy). In either case the return to Clinton is a net downhill, and the distance is identical. There are some tricky intersections in both directions, but if you remember not to cross any of the bridges over the Raritan River, you'll do fine.

The Basics

Start: Clinton (exit 15 off I–78), in the public parking lot on Lower Center St. (half a block north of E. Main St.) behind the Clinton Bakery.
Length: 19 miles.
Terrain: Flat to gently rolling, with one steeper hill on the return. After some initial traffic around Clinton, there are almost no automobiles the rest of the ride.
Food: Available in Clinton and Califon but not in between.

Miles & Directions

- 0.0 Turn right out of the public parking lot onto Lower Center St. As soon as you cross the first intersection (Halstead St. heading left over the bridge, Leigh St. heading right), the name changes to Center St.

- 0.8 Turn left at the light, following the signs for Rte. 31N over the overpass.

- 1.0 Turn left at the T intersection, following the signs for Rte. 31N. Now you're pedaling on an onramp.

- 1.1 Turn right onto Grayrock Rd., just before the onramp joins Rte. 31N. Grayrock Rd. immediately becomes a country lane through cornfields.

- 2.2 Turn right onto Old Jerricho Rd. (not crossing the bridge over the Raritan River 0.2 mile ahead). *Watch for the bicycle-tire-eating grates on the curve.* Soon the river will parallel your path on your left.

- 3.0 Turn right at the T intersection onto Arch St. and ride through the right arch of the double-arched stone bridge, paralleling the river flowing through the left.

- 3.4 Turn right at the T intersection onto Washington Ave., which bends left and passes silent factory buildings.

- 3.9 Keep heading straight where Washington Ave. bends right; as soon as you cross over a babbling creek, you're on Raritan River Rd. (Rte. 639). *Note:* The sign will probably say just RIVER RD.

- 5.1 Turn left at the T intersection onto the unmarked Cokesbury Rd., just past the dark green clapboard house on your left. *Immediately* bear right just before the bridge to stay on Rte. 639 (Raritan River Rd.). For the next 4 miles the south fork of the Raritan River will be rushing among the boulders on your left. At mile 5.7 the pavement ends as you enter the Ken Lockwood Gorge and you'll be riding on a flat, rutted gravel road. From time to time wild rabbits may hop alongside your tires. At mile 7.5 the road becomes paved again as you leave the park. At mile 9.5 River Rd. ends at a T intersection with Main St. in Califon.

- 9.5 To return retrace your route back along Raritan River Rd. (Rte. 639).
- 11.2 Turn left onto Hoffmans Crossing Rd. and begin climbing. Near the top stop and look back at the green valley and the distant wooded ridges—now, isn't this solitary beauty worth the effort?
- 12.1 Turn right onto Mt. Grove Rd.
- 13.1 Turn right at the T intersection onto the unmarked Cokesbury Rd., coasting downhill.
- 14.1 Bear left just before the dark green clapboard house onto River Rd. Now you're retracing the route out.
- 15.3 After crossing over a small creek, continue straight onto Washington Ave.
- 15.7 Turn left at the gas station onto Arch St., again just before a bridge over the river. Ride back through the arches.
- 16.2 Turn left onto Old Jerricho Rd. just before a bridge.
- 16.9 Turn left at the T intersection onto the unmarked Grayrock Rd.
- 17.8 Turn left at the T intersection, following the signs to Rte. 31S and to Clinton and Flamingo, and make an *immediate right* onto the overpass over Rte. 31.
- 18.0 Turn right at the traffic light onto Center St.
- 19.0 Head straight across Leigh (or Halstead) St. onto Lower Center St., and turn left into the public parking lot.

12

The Great Swamp and Jockey Hollow Cruise

Convent Station—Green Village—Meyersville
Jockey Hollow—Convent Station

Tours in and around the 6,800-acre Great Swamp National Wildlife Refuge and the Jockey Hollow Encampment Area of the Morristown National Historic Park are ever popular among nature-loving bicyclists. Even in winter you'll get a wave and a smile from one or two lone riders—and on summer weekends you're likely to be overtaken by a whole group from the Bicycle Touring Club of North Jersey or even from the commercial company Brooks Country Cycling and Hiking from New York City. This Morris County ride is one of my personal favorites, and for years a variant of the shorter version has also delighted students in my course "Bicycle Touring: An Introduction" offered by the South Orange–Maplewood Adult School.

The Loantaka Brook Reservation–Great Swamp portion of this ride ranges from flat to gently rolling, with about 1.5 miles of gravel. But the 10-mile extension to Jockey Hollow and the excursion around the park (and any detour to Lewis Morris Park) are very hilly indeed. That is why the full 30-mile ride is designated a cruise. The shorter 20-mile option, bypassing Jockey Hollow, is a nice early-season ramble even for an out-of-shape novice.

When you are first pedaling through the forest and farm land, watching sheep graze in the meadows and turtles swimming in the swamp, you'll hardly believe that the grubby, noisy, crowded steel canyons of New York City are only 25 miles east of you. As in all wildlife areas, you'll see more animals in the spring and fall, especially at dawn or dusk. Pack a small pair of binoculars and tiptoe out on the wooden boardwalks to the bird blinds to watch great blue herons majestically standing in the marsh or swallows swooping for insects. Take along hiking boots and spend an hour or two midway through the ride to explore some of the marked but undeveloped trails. Listen, and in the late afternoon and early evening you will hear a chorus of peepers and frogs. Adjoining the Great Swamp to the east is the 425-acre Lord Stirling Park, home of the Somerset County Environmental Education Center (908–766–2489), offering another 8 miles of trails.

As for Jockey Hollow: You know the old joke about myriad out-of-the-way places trying to attract tourists by advertising "George Washington slept here"? Well, George Washington really did sleep here, along with 10,000 soldiers, who in 1779–80 nearly froze and starved in the sheltered hollows of aptly named Jockey Hollow during one of the snowiest winters of the revolutionary war. There are many sites here preserved from those days, as well as historical restorations and minitours by guides in period costume, so take your time wandering through this park (which is open daily from 8:00 A.M. to 7:00 P.M. (For more information, call 201–543–4030). You'll also get a good aerobic workout on its rollercoaster hills.

Adjoining Jockey Hollow is the 1,154-acre Lewis Morris Park (201–326–7600); a county park at which you can pitch a tent for overnight camping. You might also want to pack a swimsuit for a dip in its Sunrise Lake; the sole disadvantage to refreshing yourself in the lake is that, after you're completely clean and relaxed, the only way back to Jockey Hollow is to grind up the very steep hill that you coasted down to the lake!

Because these are wildlife areas, services are few and far between. There are rest rooms and water for your water bottles at Loantaka Brook Reservation, at the parking lot for the wildlife observation area in the swamp, and at the visitor center at Jockey Hollow. There are only two delis near the swamp. On a Sunday you may want to play it safe and pack a lunch, as the Green Village Deli near the start of the ride is closed and Dom's General Store in Meyersville has limited hours. There are picnic tables and public barbe-cue grills at Loantaka Brook Reservation and at Lewis Morris Park, but eating within either Jockey Hollow or the Great Swamp is dis-couraged. Near the end of the ride, though, you can stuff your mouth with the blackberries growing alongside the road, ripe in late July.

The Basics

Start: Convent Station, in the Loantaka Brook Reservation at the parking area off Kitchell Rd. (Take local Rte. 24 to Convent Station and turn south on Kitchell Rd.; about 1 mile later turn right to enter the reservation.) Here there are rest rooms, water, picnic ta-bles, wooden playground equipment, and a lovely duck pond.

Length: 20.3 or 30.3 miles. Traffic is generally light, with some roads a bit more heavily traveled.

Terrain: Flat to gently rolling in the portion touring the Great Swamp; very hilly in the 10-mile stretch to Jockey Hollow.

Food: Only two places to buy snacks or lunch: Green Village Deli 3.7 miles into the ride (closed Sundays) and Dom's General Store 0.9 mile off the route 9.5 miles into the ride.

Miles & Directions

- 0.0 Start at the northern entrance to the Loantaka Brook Reservation parking lot. Ride straight across the narrow Kitchell Rd. onto the paved bike path—a lovely meander next to the Loantaka Brook through forest glades. At mile 0.7 test your brakes after riding through the shallow brook at the water crossing—or carry your steed across on the concrete stepping-stones.

- 1.0 Turn right onto the intersecting paved bike path, and fol-low it as it bends left. At mile 1.5 cross the moderately busy Loantaka Way and continue straight on the paved bike path.

- 2.9 Turn right at the end of the path onto Green Village Rd. Watch for cars.

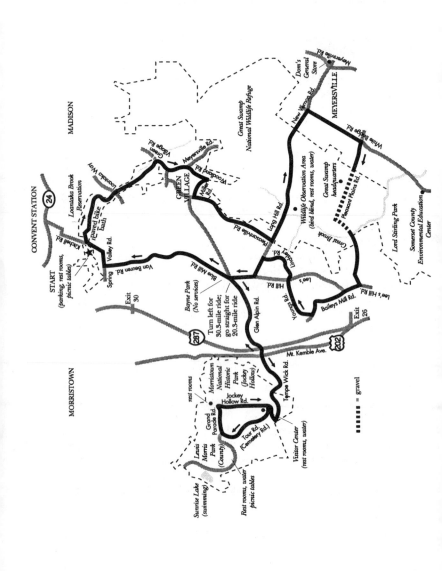

- 3.7 Turn left onto Meyersville Rd. (Just before this turn on your right are a Sunoco gas station and the Green Village Deli, the first of the two chances on this ride to pick up snacks or lunch.) Now you're riding through pastoral farmland.
- 4.0 Take the first right (at the NO OUTLET sign) onto Woodland Rd. (Bird-watchers and hikers take note: If you continue straight here instead, in 1 mile the road will end in a small parking area, which is the trailhead for some of the nature trails into the northern unmanaged section of the Great Swamp.)
- 4.6 Take the first right (at the NO OUTLET sign) onto Miller Rd.
- 5.1 Turn left at the T intersection onto Pleasantville Rd.
- 6.8 Turn left at the T intersection onto Long Hill Rd. At mile 8.3 is the Wildlife Observation Area gravel parking lot on your right, where you can visit the boardwalks and bird blinds (and rest rooms) at the swamp. To resume the ride turn right out of the parking lot to continue on Long Hill Rd. (which eventually changes its name to New Vernon Rd.).
- 9.5 Turn right onto White Bridge Rd. (*Note:* For the second and last chance to buy snacks or lunch, continue straight through this intersection instead. In 0.9 mile, at the T intersection with Meyersville Rd., is Dom's General Store. This crossroads is the town of Meyersville, and the Mexican restaurant Casa Maya is well worth a dinner stop at the end of the day. Then retrace your route 0.9 mile to this intersection and turn left onto White Bridge Rd.)
- 10.7 Turn right onto Pleasant Plains Rd. to ride into the swamp itself. (*Note:* If you want to visit the Somerset County Environmental Education Center, continue straight ahead on White Bridge Rd. for another 1.3 miles and turn right just after the metal bridge. To continue the ride retrace your route and turn left onto Pleasant Plains Rd. into the swamp.) At mile 11.0 on your right is the Great Swamp National Wildlife Refuge headquarters (908–647–1222), which is open Monday through Friday from 8:00 A.M. to 4:30 P.M. and has public rest rooms. Just past the swamp headquarters, the road turns to gravel for the next mile, so ride carefully, following the road as it bends left. A

third of a mile later, a gate blocks a bridge to cars. But the gate is designed in such a way as to admit pedestrians and bicycles— even those with a child seat on the back. After you cross this bridge over Great Brook, the road is paved once again.

- 13.6 Turn right at the T intersection onto Lee's Hill Rd. Watch for cars.
- 13.8 Bear left at the fork onto the quiet Baileys Mill Rd., and begin a gentle climb. Up to now the ride has been generally flat; now it becomes gently rolling.
- 14.8 Bear right onto Youngs Rd.
- 15.7 Turn right at the T intersection onto Lee's Hill Rd., and then make an immediate left onto Lindsley Rd.
- 16.4 Turn left at the T intersection onto Long Hill Rd.
- 16.8 Turn right at the T intersection onto Lee's Hill Rd.
- 17.2 Turn left at the light onto Glen Alpin Rd. toward Jockey Hollow.

For the shorter 20.3-mile ride, do not turn left; instead pedal straight through this light (at this intersection Lee's Hill Rd. changes its name to Blue Mill Rd.), and pick up the directions at mile 27.2.

This is where you'll start doing some serious climbing. At mile 18.9 you'll pass over I–287.

- 19.0 At the light at Rte. 202 (Mt. Kemble Ave.), keep heading straight and uphill onto Tempe Wick Rd.
- 20.4 Turn right at the entrance of Morristown National Historic Park. Keep pedaling uphill.
- 20.8 Bear left at the visitor center to follow the one-way Tour Rd. (Cemetery Rd.) through the park. (The visitor center has literature, a short film about the park's history, and public rest rooms.) This road now becomes almost a rollercoaster, and you may find yourself screaming downhill faster than the posted speed limit of 25 mph.
- 22.1 Bear right at the parking lot for the soldier's huts—which you can see up on the hill ahead of you—onto Grand Parade Rd. (If you wish to picnic or swim at the adjoining Lewis Morris County Park—a detour that will add a hilly mile to your total—

turn left instead and coast down to Sunrise Lake. Then return to this point to continue the main ride.)

- 22.6 Turn right at the yield sign to follow the one-way Jockey Hollow Rd. back to the visitor center. At this intersection is a cylindrical building with public rest rooms and a map of the entire park.

- 23.7 At the visitor center turn left at the T intersection onto the two-way road toward the park exit.

- 24.0 Turn left at the T intersection onto Tempe Wick Rd.

- 25.4 Cross Rte. 202 (Mt. Kemble Ave.) at the traffic light and continue straight onto Glen Alpin Rd.

- 27.2 Turn left at the traffic light onto Blue Mill Rd. At mile 27.3 on your left is Bayne Park, where you can relax on benches and watch geese and ducks in the pond and stream. This manicured park has no facilities or services, not even so much as a garbage can; if you open a snack here, take the remains with you when you leave.

- 28.2 Turn left onto Van Beuren Rd. where Blue Mill Rd. bends right.

- 29.8 Turn right at the T intersection onto Spring Valley Rd. Watch for cars, and ride single-file, as there is no shoulder. In July ripe blackberries dot the bushes on your right.

- 30.1 Turn left onto Kitchell Rd., braking carefully on the descent.

- 30.3 Turn left into the Loantaka Brook Reservation parking lot.

13

Stockton Mills Ramble

Mount Holly—Birmingham—Buddtown
Vincentown—Mount Holly

For an easy ride with little traffic through the bucolic beauty of fields, farms, woods, and small towns of historical note, this exploration of Burlington County in southern New Jersey fills the bill. Devised by Bert Nixdorf of Mount Holly, New Jersey, this lovely route is within the abilities of even the most casual cyclist.

After leaving Mount Holly, you'll pedal through Smithville, once the home of the H. B. Smith Works that made the Star bicycle, famous in the 1890s for its small wheel in the front and large wheel in the rear (just the opposite of the traditional pennyfarthing). Smithville is also where the bicycle railway—a treadle-type railroad—was built to carry commuting riders from Mount Holly to the factory at Smithville. On your ride take a moment to stroll through the Smithville Mansion, former home of H. B. Smith; in the summer the mansion's Victorian courtyard is abloom with the profuse, multicolored plantings of a century past.

As you ride through sleepy Birmingham, you'll find it hard to believe that this town was once the site of a large tourist hotel in the 1890s, catering to the wealthy of northern New Jersey who escaped to the "seclusion in the fresh, aromatic, and healthful air of the pinelands," according to a local history book. Today, however, there are no remnants left. Stockton Mill, the nominal destination of this ride, is the former location of one of the many sawmills in southern New Jersey a century or two ago.

About two-thirds of the way through the route, a perfect lunch stop is Mill Dam Park in Vincentown, where you can gaze out at a pretty dam and pond. According to Bert Nixdorf, there are several nice places on Vincentown's Main Street to buy food: A deli and a well-stocked independent grocery offer choices for a spring or summer picnic lunch. On fall or winter days, the hearty homemade soups at Main Street Deli are satisfying on crisp rides—and the restaurant is open on Sundays.

At the end of the ride, when you return to Mount Holly, there are a number of twists and turns; just follow the directions carefully and you'll do fine.

The Basics

Start: Mount Holly, at the corner of Rte. 541 (High St.) and Ridgley St., near the Trenton Savings & Loan and the Acme Super-Saver market in the Fairground Plaza shopping center. Park behind either Acme or Trenton Savings & Loan. To get to the start, take the New Jersey Turnpike to exit 5, and take Route 541 (Burlington–Mt. Holly Rd.) 2 miles south into Mount Holly. This road becomes High Street.
Length: 25 miles.
Terrain: Mostly flat.
Food: Convenience and grocery stores, some restaurants.

Miles & Directions

Note: Follow directions carefully, as not every small street is shown on the map.

- 0.0 From the front of the Acme Super-Saver market, head south on Rte. 541 (High St.).
- 0.8 Turn right onto Rancocas Rd., at the pharmacy and office buildings. Make an immediate left at Mount Holly State Bank to ride through the bank's parking lot and over the bridge.
- 1.1 Turn left at the T intersection onto Washington St. (Collective Federal Savings & Loan is on your right). In a couple of

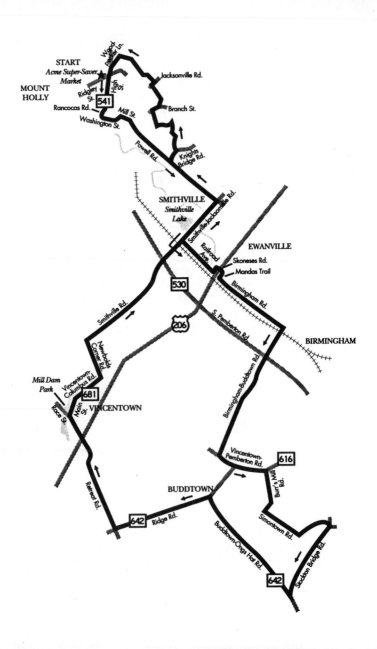

blocks, Washington St. becomes Mill St. and later Powell Rd. If you still want a snack, you have your choice of the Wawa Market or the 7-Eleven.

- 2.1 Turn right onto Smithville-Jacksonville Rd. Shortly you will pass the Smithville Mansion on your right. If the mansion is not hosting a wedding reception or other function, take a moment to stroll through the blooming courtyard, refill your water bottles at the water fountain, or use the public rest rooms off the side entrance.

- 3.0 Turn left onto Railroad Ave., just before the railroad tracks. Now you're riding alongside the tracks, which are to your right. Follow the road as it bends sharply left at the end.

- 4.7 Turn right onto Rte. 206, and then make a quick left to cross the busy highway onto Skoneses Rd. You're now in the tiny burg of Ewanville. In 1 block turn right at the T intersection onto Mandas Trail. In another block turn left at the T intersection onto Birmingham Rd.

- 6.1 At the post office in Birmingham, turn right onto Birmingham-Buddtown Rd. Watch for traffic while crossing busy Rte. 530 (S. Pemberton Rd.), and continue straight.

- 8.3 Turn left at the T intersection onto Rte. 616 (Vincentown-Pemberton Rd.).

- 9.1 Turn right onto Burr's Mill Rd.

- 9.7 Just after the road bends right, turn left onto Simontown Rd. This road will bend sharply left, then gradually right.

- 10.9 Turn right onto Stockton Bridge Rd.

- 12.1 Turn right at the T intersection onto the unmarked Rte. 642 (Buddtown–Ongs Hat Rd.).

- 14.1 Turn left at the T intersection in Buddtown to stay on Rte. 642 (the name changes to Ridge Rd.).

- 15.6 Turn right to stay on Rte. 642 (the name changes to Retreat Rd.). At mile 17.0 cross Rte. 206 and continue straight into Vincentown.

- 17.6 In Vincentown turn left at the library onto Race St. to the town's Mill Dam Park for a snack or lunch al fresco. Leave Vincentown by heading north on Main St., passing Stokes Cannery.

After you leave town, the road becomes Rte. 681 and changes its name to Vincentown-Columbus Rd.

- 18.3 Turn left onto Newbolds Corner Rd.
- 18.9 Turn right onto Smithville Rd. At mile 20.6 use caution in crossing the busy Rte. 530. At mile 21.5 you'll pass the Smithville Mansion again, where once more you can refresh yourself and enjoy the flowers. After crossing the railroad tracks, Smithville Rd. becomes Smithville-Jacksonville Rd., and you'll be retracing a brief section of the outbound route.
- 21.8 Turn left onto Powell Rd.
- 22.7 Turn right onto Knights Bridge Rd. into the Vista's residential development. Now come some quick turns. Take the second left onto Nottingham Way. At the T intersection turn right onto Stonegate Dr., which horseshoes around. Turn right onto Brook Run Rd. At the T intersection turn left onto Dawn Dr. Turn turn right onto Parkview Dr.
- 23.8 At the T intersection, turn right onto Branch St. At the wide intersection bear left to cross Branch St., keeping the Ashurst Mansion on your left. Now for some more quick turns over the next mile: Take the first left onto Ashurst Ln., the first left onto Thornton Rd., and an immediate right onto Stevens Dr. When you reach Jacksonville Rd., jog right to cross it and continue straight on Walton Rd. At the T intersection turn left onto Front St. A block later turn right onto Randolph Dr. Bear left onto Tinker Dr.
- 25.3 Turn left at the T intersection onto Woodpecker Ln. Then turn right into the parking lot of the Acme Super-Saver market or Trenton Savings & Loan at the start.

14

Heart of the Pines Cruise

Atsion—Chatsworth—Green Bank—Batsto—Atsion

The Pine Barrens in the southern part of New Jersey (Burlington County) is a wilderness area covering nearly a quarter of the state. Federal and state regulations protect most of it from development or abuse, thus making it a popular destination of cyclists. Its virtually flat expanse, the backwoods remoteness, sandy soil, and stark scrubby pines and oaks are reminiscent of swamps in the Deep South.

On this ride through Burlington County (and parts of Atlantic and Camden counties), you will see areas of specialized agriculture (blueberry fields and cranberry bogs), pass cedar-lined streams, and cross over three major rivers (the Batsto, the Mullica, and the Wading). Canoeing is popular in this area, and midway through the route at Chatsworth, you can take a break and rent all the equipment you'll need for paddling as well as pedaling.

You'll also ride through some settlements that feel like ghost towns. When you reach Batsto, a former nineteenth-century bog-iron community, take half an hour to walk around the restored gristmill, general store, threshing barn, post office, and the Richards' Mansion, once the home of bog-iron baron Jesse Richards. In the summer and fall Batsto sponsors special events; for more information call the ranger's office at (609) 561–0024.

This ride is thoroughly delightful in any season, according to Bert Nixdorf of Mount Holly, New Jersey, who devised it for the Youth Environmental Society (YES) at Rutgers University. Bert's own favorite season is the autumn, especially the third week of October when the flaming reds and golds of the leaves are at their peak. If your taste runs more to blooming mountain laurel—an ancient relative of the rose—choose to ride the second week in June. Because the ride has precious little shade, it can be blazing hot at the height of summer; on the other hand, the euphoria of sluicing off the sweat and grime by jumping into the refreshing swimming pool at Atsion Lake Camp may make it worth the hot dusty miles. On Tuesday the pool is open free of charge; all other days there is a fee.

For cyclists wishing to sleep out under the stars, there are two campgrounds along the route. One is Atsion Lake Camp on Atsion Rd. at the start; apply for a permit at the Atsion ranger's office (609–269–0444). The other is Godfrey Bridge Camp midway through the ride on Washington Rd. at Jenkins. For that campground you must apply for a permit at the Batsto ranger's office (609–561–0024); if you're interested in that one, you might want to start the ride from the public parking area in Batsto instead of from Atsion.

Because there are so few paved roads in this region, automobiles can be of concern. Traffic can be heavy, especially on weekends. The best time to ride is during the week. Take special care watching for cars along the busy Route 206; Bert notes, however, that the shoulders have been widened and repaved, and many cyclists use this road. (By the way, Route 206 is notable in that it can take you all the way from High Point to Hammonton without going over any major hills, and sections of it are popular with cyclists all along New Jersey's length.)

The Basics

Start: Atsion ranger's station near Atsion Lake Camp in the Wharton State Forest, on Rte. 206, 10.3 miles south of the junction with Rte. 70. Park in the field immediately to the north of the ranger's office.

Length: 52 miles.

Terrain: Mostly flat. Traffic can be heavy on Rte. 206 but is light to moderate elsewhere.

Food: Farm stands, grocery stores, and occasional small restaurants are at the major settlements; there can be 10 or more miles between water stops, so take the opportunity when it comes.

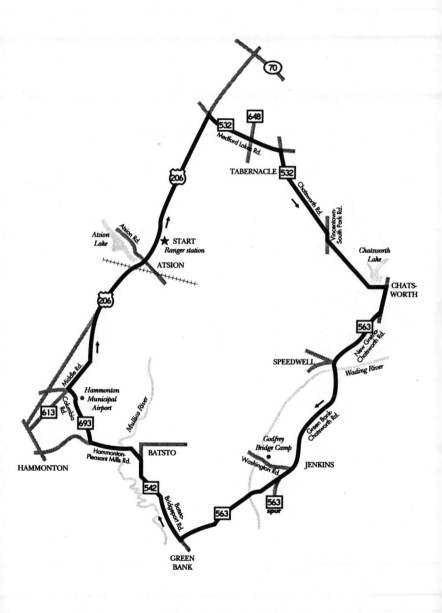

Miles & Directions

- 0.0 Turn right out of the parking lot at the Atsion ranger station to head north on Rte. 206; at mile 7.7 you'll see the sign TO TABERNACLE.

- 9.1 Turn right at the four-way stop onto Rte. 532 (Medford Lakes Rd.). At this intersection there is an open-air farm market on the right where you can buy fresh fruit. After passing Rte. 648 in Tabernacle, Rte. 532 changes its name to Chatsworth Rd. Follow Rte. 532 as it briefly travels south along Vincentown-South Park Rd. before heading southeast again.

- 19.1 Turn right at the firehouse onto Rte. 563. You're now in the heart of Chatsworth.

- 29.1 Just beyond Mick's Canoe Rentals, bear right at the major intersection to stay on Rte. 563 (New Gretna–Chatsworth Rd.). At mile 30.0 you'll cross over the Wading River at Speedwell; this is one terminus of a popular canoeing route. Here Rte. 563 changes name to Green Bank–Chatsworth Rd. You'll cross the Wading River again a few miles later.

- 35.3 In the town of Green Bank, turn right (west) onto Rte. 542 (Batsto-Bridgeport Rd.) at Green Bank General Store. Now you're paralleling the Mullica River on your left

- 39.1 Turn right into the public parking area of Batsto Historic Village, which has a picnic area, water, refreshment stands open in the summer, and public rest rooms. Ask at the park office about the self-guided and conducted tours; there you can also buy topographic maps of the area. When you leave the park entrance, turn right to continue west on Rte. 542, which changes name to Hammonton–Pleasant Mills Rd. when you leave Burlington County and enter Atlantic County.

- 43.7 Turn right onto Rte. 693 (Columbia Rd.).

- 47.2 Just after passing the Hammonton Municipal Airport on your right, bear right at the Y intersection onto Rte. 613 (Middle Rd.).

- 47.9 Turn right at the end of Rte. 613 (Middle Rd.) onto Rte. 206N. *Watch for cars!*

- 51.9 Turn right into the parking lot at the Atsion ranger station.

New York

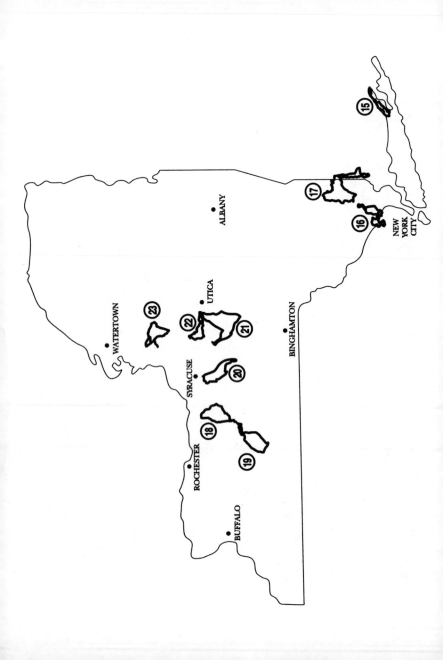

New York

15

Strawberries
and Wine Cruise

Mattituck—Greenport—Orient Point—Mattituck

This flat ride, which is one of my personal favorites, is based in part on the traditional annual "Strawberry Ride" of New York City's American Youth Hostels. It starts at the town of Mattituck on the north fork of Long Island, which each June holds a strawberry festival in the fields of the Mattituck High School. (For the date of the festival each year, call the Greenport-Southold Chamber of Commerce at 516–477–1383.)

If after all those calories you can manage to swing your leg over your bicycle saddle, the route will then take you through some of Suffolk County's best wine country. You'll pedal right past half a dozen vineyards, many of which offer public tours and wine tasting—Peconic Bay Vineyards, Pugliese Vineyards, Bedell Cellars, Pindar Winery, and Lenz Winery—and you can visit more by looking for signs with the symbol of grapes directing you down local side roads. Just use good judgment in sampling the wares: It's even more dangerous to bicycle than to drive under the influence of alcohol, as you are not surrounded by a ton of protective steel.

The midpoint of the ride—perfect for lunch—is a favorite destination for cyclists: Orient Beach State Park, with its refreshment stand, seafood cafe, bathhouse, and pebbly beach overlooking the sparkling Atlantic. This is also the trailhead for a 2-mile hike out to the bird sanctuary at the very tip of Orient Point. The park is friendly to cyclists and is open every day of the year excepting Tuesdays.

Elsewhere on the ride you'll pass some churches and houses dating back to the American Revolution, plus an old lighthouse commissioned by George Washington and now turned into a marine museum. Amateur astronomers might try to time their visit for one of the Saturday observing nights at the Custer Institute Observatory in Southold (516–765–2626), the only astronomical observatory on Long Island to allow the public to look through its telescopes.

Those wishing to make a long weekend of the visit can stay in one of the lovely bed-and-breakfast inns on Shelter Island (for a listing call the Shelter Island Chamber of Commerce at 516–749–0399), a detour that's just a five-minute ferry ride from Greenport. Shelter Island's rolling hills and beaches and lightly traveled roads offer superb cycling—a nice change of pace from the flat terrain of the basic tour on Long Island's north fork.

Although you'll be pedaling on some main roads on this ride (because some places on the north fork are so narrow that there is only one road), Long Island is civilized in offering wide paved shoulders. Just be careful: In some places the shoulder is an inch below the pavement of the main road, and brushing that lip with your tire could cause a spill.

A word about Long Island weather: The eastern tip of Long Island is the last place in the New York City tri-state area for the seasons to linger. Thus, the chill of winter lasts into mid-April, but summer's warmth lingers past the end of September. After Labor Day is perhaps the best time for cycling: You miss the frenetic summer crowds but can swim in the ocean still bathwater-warm from the summer's heating of the Gulf Stream.

The Basics

Start: Mattituck, in the parking lot of the station of the Long Island Rail Road. Take the Long Island Expressway to its very end (Exit 73) and then take Rte. 25 farther east to Mattituck. In town turn left at the traffic light onto Love Ln. and then left into the parking lot of the train station.

Length: 53.6 miles.

Terrain: Virtually flat, although you are likely to run into substantial headwinds while traveling in one direction (usually eastward). Traffic ranges from light on the side roads (mostly on the return) to moderate on the main roads.

Food: Widely available in the various towns and at the concession and restaurants at Orient Beach State Park. But best of all are farm stands: Take advantage of the fresh local produce!

Miles & Directions

- 0.0 Turn left out of the parking lot of the Mattituck station of the Long Island Rail Road, making an immediate right onto Love Ln.
- 0.1 If you're going to the strawberry festival, turn left at the T intersection onto Rte. 25E (Main Rd.) until you reach the Mattituck High School; otherwise turn right onto Rte. 25W.
- 0.2 Turn left at the Handy Pantry convenience store onto New Suffolk Ave.
- 3.2 Turn left at the four-way flashing stop light onto New Suffolk Rd.
- 5.5 Turn right at the light onto Rte. 25E (Main Rd.). You'll now stay on Rte. 25E through all its incarnations for the next 15 miles. In the next 3 miles, you'll pass half a dozen wineries. At mile 9.8 you can turn right onto Corwin Ln. and make an immediate right onto Bayview Rd. to visit the Custer Institute Observatory. At mile 14.8 you'll enter the town of Greenport, where the traffic gets heavier. If you want to visit Shelter Island, at mile 15.1 turn right onto 5th St. and left at the next block (Wiggins St.) to reach the ferry dock. Otherwise continue to follow Rte. 25E (now called Front St.) straight into Greenport. Watch for car traffic!
- 15.3 Turn left at the flashing red signal (T intersection) to follow Rte. 25E out of Greenport.
- 16.3 Turn right at the flashing red signal (T intersection) to stay on Rte. 25E toward Orient Point.

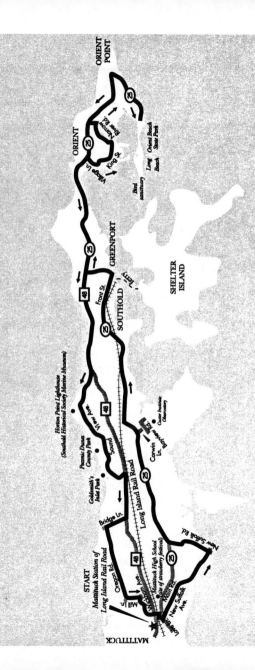

- 20.6 Turn right onto Village Ln., marked with a grassy triangle surmounted by a small obelisk resembling a miniature Washington Monument. You are now entering the village of Orient, with its sparkling bay views and many wonderful centuries-old homes. Stop to read the historical markers to steep yourself in the mood.
- 21.1 Follow the road as it bends left and becomes King St.
- 21.4 Bear right at the Y intersection to stay on King St.
- 21.7 Turn left at the end (yield sign) onto Narrow River Rd. This is a truly lovely stretch past the swaying tall grasses of a salt marsh. Savor it through all its curves.
- 23.5 Turn right at the end (stop sign) onto Rte. 25E, which is now the only road out to Orient Point.
- 25.5 Turn right into Orient Beach State Park.
- 27.7 You've arrived! When you're ready to leave, retrace your route back out the park access road.
- 29.9 Turn left at the T intersection (the only way you can go) onto Rte. 25W, and keep pedaling straight west for the next 11 miles.
- 37.6 Keep heading straight where the yellow flasher marks Rte. 25W's turn back into Greenport; now you're on Rte. 48W.
- 41.0 Turn right onto Sound View Ave., which is bumpy but beautiful, with little traffic.
- 42.3 Bear left at the fork to stay on Sound View Ave. (If you want a little historical detour, bear right instead; the road dead-ends at Horton Point Lighthouse, now the home of the Southold Historical Society Marine Museum. It is open on weekend afternoons in July and August.) Go straight through two four-way stops. At mile 46.6 follow Sound View Ave. as it makes an abrupt left (Goldsmith's Inlet Park will be on your right).
- 46.7 Turn right to rejoin Rte. 48W (here called Middle Rd.).
- 48.2 Turn right onto Bridge Ln.
- 48.9 Turn left at the end onto Oregon Rd., where you'll be cycling past farms and vineyards for the next 3 miles.
- 51.9 Turn left onto Mill Ln., an old concrete road.
- 52.5 Turn right onto Wickham Ave., following it as it curves left through suburbs.

- 53.2 Turn left at the T intersection to stay on Wickham Ave.
- 53.6 After crossing Rte. 48 at the light, turn right onto Pike St. and follow it to Love Ln. and the Mattituck station of the Long Island Rail Road.

16

Two-Reservoir Cruise

Teatown—Lincolndale—Yorktown Heights
Croton Dam—Teatown

The New Croton Reservoir is a favorite of New York City cyclists because this wooded section of lower Westchester County is only 25 miles north. Despite its proximity to what Frank Sinatra immortalized in song as "the city that never sleeps," Westchester County is characterized by wonderfully secluded backroads—in part because the county's affluent citizens would rather have their restful homes passed by dirt tracks than paved thoroughfares. The result is a cyclist's dream.

This ride circles around two Westchester County reservoirs: the New Croton Reservoir, which is part of New York City's water supply, and the smaller Amawalk Reservoir, farther north. The route culminates with a ride across the top of the Croton Dam overlooking the Croton Gorge Park below. Because for the most part the route hugs the shores of the reservoirs, much of it is level to gently rolling, with lovely views of the sparkling water. The sections away from the water give you a chance to get a cardiovascular workout on somewhat steeper roads.

In fact, the inland terrain is so reminiscent of West Virginia or Vermont that Westchester County boasts one of the East Coast's two mountain-bike schools: Croton Mountain Biking Center (10 Sunset Trail, Croton-on-Hudson, NY 10520, 914–271–2640), run by Mike Zuckerman. This route leads you on a few of these peaceful roads, ruts and all, so you may find a fatter-tire bike more comfortable than a thin-tire racing bike.

Should you wish to make a weekend of your visit, you may well enjoy the luxury of a night at the rambling Alexander Hamilton House bed-and-breakfast inn, just a couple of miles from this route at 49 Van Wyck Street in Croton-on-Hudson (914–271–6737). The owner is Barbara Notarius, author of a book on running a bed and breakfast. It was Barbara who suggested the basic route around the New Croton Reservoir and the challenging but beautiful optional loop; the combination of this ride with the circuit of Amawalk Reservoir is an author's original.

Don't be confused by the four versions of this ride. The two longer rides include the trip to Amawalk Reservoir, while the two shorter ones circle only the New Croton Reservoir. The longer ride in each pair also includes a hilly, 4.2-mile-long optional loop simply for the secluded scenery.

The Basics

Start: Teatown Lake Reservation parking lot. To get there from the Taconic State Pkwy., exit at ROUTE 134 OSSINING; drive on Rte. 134W to the second right; turn right onto Spring Valley Rd.; drive 1 mile to Teatown, choosing left at every fork along the way. Turn right into the reservation parking lot.

Length: 17.5., 21.7, 34.6, or 38.8 miles.

Terrain: Gently rolling to moderately hilly. The shortest ride is the most level; the longest one, the most demanding. Traffic ranges from almost nonexistent on the true backroads to moderate on Rte. 129 around the north side of the New Croton Reservoir; very heavy traffic in Yorktown Heights on the return from Amawalk Reservoir.

Food: Bring a full picnic lunch, as there are few services on any of these routes. Teatown Reservation has a soda machine, a couple of hotdog trucks have their regular sites at dusty intersections as noted, and on the two longer rides there is a snack bar at Muscoot Farm 1.1 miles off the main route. Only in busy Yorktown Heights on the two longer rides is there a wide variety of food choices.

Miles & Directions

- 0.0 Turn left out of Teatown Lake Reservation Environmental Education Center onto Spring Valley Rd.
- 0.1 Turn left onto the bumpy, narrow Blinn Rd., which becomes Apple Bee Farm Rd.
- 1.6 Turn right at the T intersection onto Quaker Ridge Rd. At mile 1.8 keep heading straight onto Yorktown Rd. where Croton Dam Rd. heads left. In 0.5 mile the road becomes hard-packed dirt; go slowly, for there are many ruts. At miles 3.7 and 4.0, you'll pass under the southbound and northbound lanes of the Taconic State Pkwy.
- 4.3 Bear right at the T intersection onto the unmarked Arcady Rd., which in 0.5 mile begins climbing. Eventually the road becomes Aqueduct St.
- 5.6 Just across from the entrance to IBM's famous Thomas J. Watson Research Center, turn left onto the moderately busy Rte. 134.
- 7.2 Turn left at the T intersection onto the moderately busy Rte. 100. At this intersection on your left, sometimes there is a hot dog truck. At mile 8.6 head straight at the first light to stay on the wide shoulder of Rte. 100 over the bridge across the New Croton Reservoir.
- 8.9 Head straight through a second traffic light to stay on Rte. 100; usually there is another truck here selling snacks. At this point Rte. 100 develops wonderfully smooth, lane-wide painted shoulders perfect for cycling.

For the two shortest rides, do not head straight, but instead turn left onto Rte. 118 and ride 1.8 miles; at the flashing yellow light, where Rte. 118 goes right, head straight onto Rte. 129 and resume following the directions below at mile 25.0.

- 10.8 Turn left onto Moseman Ave., which begins a long, gradual climb. (For a detour to a snack bar and public rest rooms at Muscoot Farm, do not turn left here but instead continue straight on Rte. 100 for another 1.1 miles. Then return to this intersection and turn right onto Moseman Ave.)

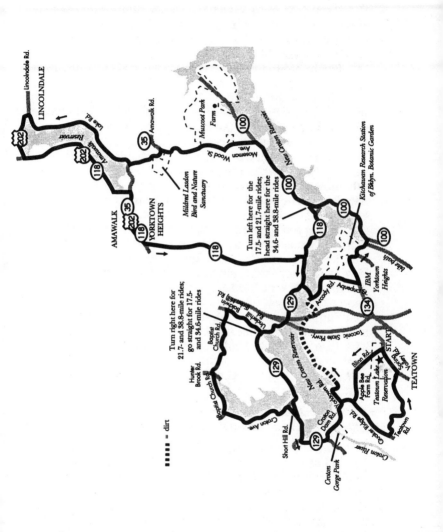

■■■■■ = dirt

LINCOLNDALE

Lincolndale Rd.

Reservoir

Lake Rd.

202

202

118

202

35

Amawalk Rd.

Amawalk Reservoir

AMAWALK

35

202

118

118

YORKTOWN HEIGHTS

Mildred Loslon Bird and Nature Sanctuary

Wood St.

Muscoot Park

Farm

100

Turn left here for the 17.5- and 21.7-mile rides; head straight here for the 34.6 and 38.8-mile rides

118

Moseman Ave.

New Croton Reservoir

100

118

100

100

Kitchawan Research Station of Bklyn. Botanic Garden

IBM Yorktown Heights

bike path

129

134

Arcady Rd.

Aqueducts

Turn right here for 21.7- and 38.8-mile rides; go straight for 17.5- and 34.6-mile rides

Baptist Church Rd.

Underhill Rd.

Baldwin Rd.

Hunter Brook Rd.

Campbell Rd.

129

New Croton Reservoir

Taconic State Pkwy.

Blinn Rd.

START

Apple Bee Farm Rd.

Teatown Lake Reservation

Spring Valley Rd.

TEATOWN

Baptist Church Rd.

Croton Ave.

129

Short Hill Rd.

Croton Dam Rd.

Hickory Kingdom Rd.

Spring Valley Rd.

Grant Ridge Rd.

Teatown Rd.

Croton River

Croton Gorge Park

- 11.5 Turn right onto Wood St., which climbs more steeply through woodlands and trout streams.
- 12.9 Turn left at the T intersection onto the moderately busy Rte. 35 (Amawalk Rd.).
- 13.6 Just before the yellow flashing light, make the first right onto Lake Rd. As you're coming downhill rather fast, make sure you don't miss this turn.
- 16.5 Turn left at the T intersection onto Rte. 202W (Lincolndale Rd.), which is rather busy but has a decent shoulder.
- 17.7 Turn left at the T intersection (traffic light) to stay on Rte. 202W, which is joined by Rte. 118S. The traffic can be moderately heavy and fast, but there are good shoulders. Just 0.1 mile after this turn, you'll pass Geary's Deli.
- 20.5 Turn right at the T intersection onto Rte. 35W/202W/ 118S, which will take you into Yorktown Heights. Traffic can get heavy as you approach town, so pedal with extreme caution.
- 21.9 Head straight through the light at the main intersection onto Rte. 118S; Rte. 35W and Rte. 202W turn right. After you leave town, traffic thins out somewhat; on this downhill coast the shoulder is wide but bumpy and gravelly, so ride with caution.
- 25.0 Turn right at the T intersection (red flashing light) onto Rte. 129. *Here is where the two shorter rides join the two longer ones.*
- 27.3 Turn right onto Underhill Rd. and begin climbing; you have now begun the rather challenging optional loop of rutted road and quiet beauty circling an inlet of the New Croton Reservoir.

For the 17.5- and 34.6-mile rides, do not turn right, but instead continue straight on Rte. 129 and resume following the directions at mile 33.3.

- 27.7 Turn left onto Baldwin Rd. (Echo Hill Rd.). Watch carefully for this intersection, as it is easy to miss. Continue climbing.
- 28.0 Turn left onto Baptist Church Rd. Now you're plunged into a bumpy but gorgeous, forested rollercoaster ride.
- 29.5 At the stop sign make a quick jog left onto Hunter Brook Rd. (unmarked) and then immediately right to continue on Baptist Church Rd.

- 31.7 At the yield sign turn left onto Croton Ave., noting the island in the inlet on your left. This narrow section of road is level and smooth, with very few cars.
- 33.2 Turn right at the T intersection onto Short Hill Rd. True to the road's name, you'll climb up a short, steep hill.
- 33.3 Bear right at the stop sign onto Rte. 129, *rejoining the 17.5- and 34.6-mile routes*.
- 34.3 Turn left onto Croton Dam Rd. Watch carefully for this almost hidden intersection after Rte. 129 starts descending. In a few moments you're pedaling across the top of the New Croton Dam.
- 35.2 Turn right at the T intersection onto Quaker Ridge Rd. (You'll recognize the intersection from the beginning of the ride, as Yorktown Rd. goes to the left.)
- 36.5 Turn left onto the beautiful Teatown Rd. The last section of this one-lane, winding road descends in tight switchbacks almost like San Francisco's famous Lombard St.
- 38.3 Turn left at the T intersection onto the unmarked Spring Valley Rd. Soon you'll pass Teatown Lake on your left.
- 38.8 Turn left into Teatown Lake Reservation parking lot.

17

A Taste of New England Challenge

Bedford—Ridgefield—North Wilton
Pound Ridge—Bedford

This ride, a somewhat abbreviated version of the 60-mile Bedford Silver Spring Sally of the Long Island Bicycle Club, Inc., is a tour of places reminiscent of New England. In fact, some of it is technically in New England, as part of the route dances back and forth across the New York border into Fairfield County, Connecticut. But most of it takes you through some of the hills in the eastern part of New York's Westchester County.

The shorter version of the ride is a brisk cruise for cyclists in moderately good condition; the rollercoaster terrain is challenging enough that the longer version should appeal to strong cyclists. The starting point in Bedford is close enough to New York City that the route can make a good one-day ride for city-dwellers who own or rent cars; but the forest is so quiet that you will be tempted to linger overnight as a momentary respite from city life.

If you want to make a weekend of it, that's easily done. You may luxuriate at a number of noted bed-and-breakfast inns in Ridgefield, Connecticut. Among them are the West Lane Inn (203–438–7323) and The Elms Inn (203–438–2541), Ridgefield's oldest continuously functioning inn, taking in guests since 1799.

For those preferring the wide open spaces, try camping at one of Westchester County's beautiful parks. At the 4,700-acre Ward Pound Ridge Reservation 6 miles north of Bedford, you can rent an open-faced lean-to cabin large enough to shelter eight sleeping bags

(914–763–3493). Farther north try one of the rustic cabins or tent sites at the 1,000-acre Mountain Lakes Campground, where some of the campsites also have showers (914–593–2618 or 669–5793).

This route is perfect for a crisp autumn ride to gaze at the golden and fiery leaves. But please note that on nice weekends the traffic on some stretches can be moderate to moderately heavy. Also, this section of the world seems to have very sandy soil, and a fair amount of sand finds its way onto the road shoulders. Please, ride with caution.

The Basics

Start: Bedford, New York, at the village green (intersection of Rte. 172 and Rte. 22). To get to the start, take Exit 4 off I–684 onto Rte. 172E, and follow Rte. 172E into Bedford's village green.
Length: 34 or 52 miles.
Terrain: Moderately hilly to hilly. Traffic ranges from light to moderately heavy. *Please watch for sand.*
Food: Available in Bedford, New York, and Ridgefield, Connecticut, and at widely spaced convenience stores as noted; if in doubt, stock up.

Miles & Directions

- 0.0 Head north on busy Rte. 22 (you'll have done it right if, after leaving the village green, you immediately pass the Bedford Playhouse on your right).
- 0.3 Bear right at the triangle onto Rte. 121N.
- 2.0 Turn right onto Rte. 137.
- 3.0 Take the first left onto the secluded Honey Hollow Rd., following it as it eventually makes a sharp left.
- 6.0 Turn right at the T intersection onto Rte. 121N. In 0.75 mile you'll pass the entrance to Ward Pound Ridge Reservation. If you ride into the park, there are public rest rooms with water in the building on your right, just before the guard's kiosk.
- 6.9 Turn right at the T intersection where Rte. 121N joins Rte. 35E. Here are a deli and market.

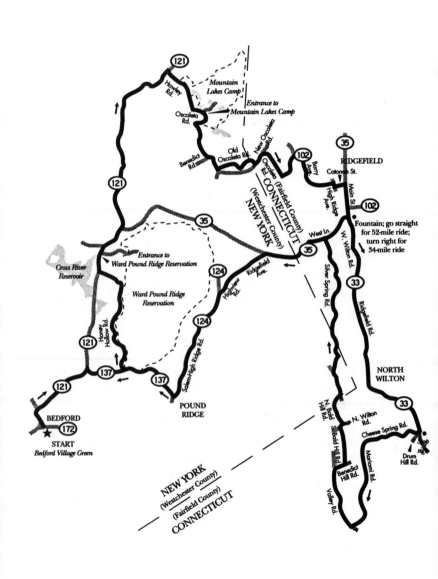

- 7.5 Turn left at the light to stay on Rte. 121N; at this intersection are a gas station and deli—the last opportunity for food or snacks until Ridgefield in another 14 miles.
- 12.0 Turn right onto Hawley Rd. at the blue sign for Mountain Lakes Camp.
- 13.2 Follow the road as it bends sharply left at another blue sign and becomes unmarked Oscaleta Rd. In 0.3 mile on your left is the entrance to Mountain Lakes Camp.
- 14.5 Bear left at the Y to stay on Oscaleta Rd. (Benedict Rd. heads right).
- 15.0 Turn left onto Old Oscaleta Rd., just before the stop sign at Main St. Note the old painted wooden street sign. This is a lovely rollercoaster ride that takes you across the border into Connecticut.
- 15.8 Turn left at the T intersection onto the unmarked New Oscaleta Rd.
- 16.1 Make the first right onto Oscaleta Rd., which plunges down (if you erroneously stay on New Oscaleta Rd., you'll continue to climb).
- 17.6 Turn right at the T intersection onto the unmarked Rte. 102 (Barry Ave.), which leads you into the town of Ridgefield.
- 20.6 Turn right at the T intersection to stay on Rte. 102 (here called High Ridge Ave.).
- 20.7 Turn left at the stop sign to stay on Rte. 102 (here called Catonah St.).
- 21.0 Turn right at the light to stay on Rte. 102 (here called Main St.,) which joins Rte. 35. There are many places to stop to eat along this stretch. Watch carefully for auto traffic. At mile 21.4 keep heading straight on Rte. 35 where Rte. 102 turns left.
- 21.6 Keep heading straight at the fountain onto Rte. 33, where Rte. 35 (here called West Ln.) bears right.

For the 34-mile cruise turn right at this fountain instead to stay on Rte. 35 (West Ln.), passing West Lane Inn on your right. In 0.6 mile, where Silver Spring Rd. comes in from the left, pick up the directions at mile 39.8 below.

Now enjoy the 5-plus-mile downhill coast along Rte. 33. The

road changes its name from W. Wilton Rd. to Ridgefield Rd. at the border of Wilton Township, but remains Rte. 33. The road is narrow but has a good surface and painted shoulder; however, watch for sand. And toward the end of this coast, prepare to stop.

- 26.9 At the stop sign turn right onto Drum Hill Rd. Make an immediate right onto quiet Cheese Spring Rd., which becomes Mariomi Rd. at the border of New Canaan Township.
- 30.1 Turn right at the T intersection onto Valley Rd.
- 31.4 Shortly after crossing a small concrete bridge, turn right onto Benedict Hill Rd.
- 31.6 Turn left onto S. Bald Hill Rd.
- 32.4 Jog right at the T intersection onto the unmarked N. Wilton Rd., and make an immediate left onto the one-lane N. Bald Hill Rd.
- 32.6 Bear left at the Y intersection to continue on N. Bald Hill Rd. This is a beautiful stretch. As you reenter New York State, the road becomes graded dirt.
- 33.7 Turn left at the T intersection onto the unmarked Silver Spring Rd. Although it starts out as graded dirt, it becomes paved again as you reenter Connecticut.
- 36.0 Bear left at the Y intersection to stay on Silver Spring Rd., and ride to the end.
- 39.8 Turn left at the T intersection onto the unmarked but busy Rte. 35 (West Ln.). *This is where the 34-mile ride rejoins the 52-mile route.* If you were to turn right instead, you would pass two antiques stores, a pizza/deli, and the West Lane bed-and-breakfast inn. At mile 41.6, after Rte. 35 changes name several times, you'll reenter New York for the final time. At mile 41.8 keep riding straight through the light to stay on Rte. 35.
- 42.1 Turn left onto Ridgefield Ave. (Watch carefully, for it's easy to miss!) Eventually it changes its name to Highview Rd.
- 43.9 Turn left at the T intersection onto Rte. 124 (Salem–High Ridge Rd.).
- 46.7 Turn right onto Rte. 137N in Pound Ridge.
- 49.5 Turn left at the T intersection onto Rte. 121.
- 51.2 Turn left at the T intersection onto Rte. 22S.
- 51.5 You're back at Bedford's village green.

18

Great Finger Lakes Wineries Challenge

Watkins Glen—Ovid—Interlaken
Reynoldsville—Burdett—Watkins Glen

The Great Finger Lakes are so popular for cycling that at least one publisher has devoted an entire guidebook to them for cyclists (*20 Bicycle Tours in the Finger Lakes,* by Mark Roth and Sally Walters, Backcountry Publications, second edition, 1987). But neither this route nor its companion, the "Wonders of Glass Cruise" (Ride 19) has been published there or, until now, elsewhere.

The Finger Lakes are eleven long and thin bodies of water gouged out by glaciers umpteen thousand years ago during the Ice Age in what is now western New York State. Seneca Lake, whose shore is hugged by the initial part of this ride, is the second largest of the lakes: 40 miles long, 4 miles wide, and so deep that its bottom is 200 feet below sea level. The southern end of Seneca Lake, where this ride guides you, is tucked between forested high hills relieved by valleys that cradle dairy farms, vineyards, and orchards.

This ride begins and ends at Watkins Glen State Park (607–535–4511), which has a splendid gorge featuring rock caverns and nineteen cascading waterfalls—and an Olympic-size swimming pool for sluicing off the road grime. You can make the park your base of operations for both rides by setting up camp at one of its 305 tent/trailer sites just 0.5 mile west of the park's lower entrance on Route 329. Alternatively, if your idea of roughing it is making do with black-and-white television, you might prefer to stay in one of Watkins Glen's bed-and-breakfast inns. For a brochure listing the many lovely inns in the area, contact the Finger Lakes Bed and Breakfast Association (309 Lake Street, Penn Yan, NY 14527; 315–536–1238 or 800–695–5590).

The cycling through Schuyler, Seneca, and Tompkins counties is moderately rolling to undeniably hilly, although the traffic outside of the town of Watkins Glen is generally light. As upstate New York is the largest wine-producing area in the United States outside of California, this route passes a number of vineyards. You'll have the chance to stop in at Rolling Vineyards Farm Winery, Chateau La Fayette Reneau Winery, Poplar Ridge Vineyards, Hazlitt 1852 Winery, Wagner Vineyards, Wickham Vineyards Ltd., and other wineries, all of which allow visitors to sample their fare. (If you choose to do so, be sparing: Remember that cycling under the influence of alcohol is even dumber than driving while intoxicated, since you have no protection of a metal shell.)

The town of Ovid, the northernmost point of the ride not quite halfway through, holds a strawberry festival the second Saturday in June. An attractive village square with surrounding stores and churches makes this town a perfect rest or lunch stop any time of the bicycling season.

This route is from the Great Finger Lakes Bicycle Tour, held annually by Southern Tier Bicycle Club, Inc. (STBC). Each June the two-day tour, which can be joined by any cyclist for a modest fee, features different routes; this route is the day 1 portion of the 1991 tour, devised by Augie Mueller of Vestal, New York. The companion ride in this book, Ride 19 is the day 2 portion. (If you wish to join the group for its annual Great Finger Lakes Bicycle Tour, call Augie Mueller at 607–722–6005.)

The Basics

Start: Watkins Glen, at the lower entrance to Watkins Glen State Park on Rte. 14. To get to the start, take Rte. 17 to Elmira and then Rte. 14N to Watkins Glen.
Length: 56.6 miles.

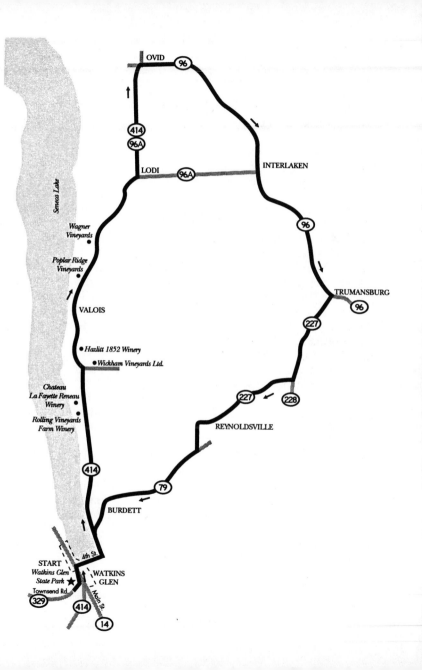

Terrain: Rolling to moderately hilly. Traffic is generally light except in Watkins Glen.
Food: Several stores in Watkins Glen, Burdett, Trumansburg, Interlaken, and Ovid but nowhere else, so plan carefully for this long ride.

Miles & Directions

- 0.0 From the lower entrance to Watkins Glen State Park, head left to ride north on Rte. 14 (Main St.).
- 0.4 Turn right at the light onto 4th St., following Rte. 414N. In 500 feet you'll pass Tobe's Coffee and Danish.
- 2.1 Bear left to stay on Rte. 414N. Now you just cruise along here for the next 21 miles, with Seneca Lake (renowned for its trout fishing) off to your left. Along the way you'll pass a number of vineyards and wineries, and the Ginny Lee Cafe ("Excellent!" exclaims Augie Mueller) at the town of Lodi (mile 18.1). Continue north on Rte. 414/96A.
- 23.6 In the town of Ovid, turn right onto Rte. 96S. Continue through the village of Interlaken (mile 31.0), passing Rte. 96A and bearing left to stay on Rte. 96S.
- 38.2 Just before the village of Trumansburg, turn right onto Rte. 227. Or if you feel like a pleasant rest stop, continue 100 yards and visit the village known locally for its unique architecture, good food, and friendly residents.
- 42.2 Turn right at the intersection of Rte. 228 to stay on Rte. 227, continuing on toward Reynoldsville.
- 48.3 Merge right onto Rte. 79W where Rte. 227 ends. After entering the village of Burdett, veer left to stay on Rte. 79, carefully braking on the steep downhill into Watkins Glen.
- 56.4 Turn left onto Rte. 14S.
- 56.6 You are now back at the lower entrance to Watkins Glen State Park.

19

Wonders of Glass Cruise

Watkins Glen—Corning—Monterey—Watkins Glen

This ride, the companion to the "Great Finger Lakes Wineries Challenge" (Ride 18), takes you south from Watkins Glen along lightly traveled roads through the rolling farmland of upstate New York. Your destination: Corning, home of the Corning Glass Center (607–974–8271). Here in the 1940s a twenty-ton, 17-foot-diameter disk of Pyrex glass was cast to become the mirror of the 200-inch Hale telescope on Palomar Mountain, California—a reflecting telescope that for decades retained the distinction of being the largest in the world. The Corning Museum of Glass has fascinating exhibits, among them the Steuben Glass factory, where hot glass is fashioned into world-famous Steuben crystal before your eyes.

On your return from Corning, you'll once again wend your way over hill and dale through rural scenery. You might even be lucky enough to see beavers hard at work building their dams. Because the ride is so rural, there are long stretches of forest and farmland with no services, so pack plenty of snacks and water. You'll burn up a lot of energy on the hills.

This ride through Schuyler, Steuben, and Chemung counties is one of the Great Finger Lakes Bicycle Tours, held annually by Southern Tier Bicycle Club, Inc. (STBC). Each June the two-day tour, which can be joined by any cyclist for a modest fee, features different routes; this route is the day 2 portion of the 1991 tour, devised by Augie Mueller of Vestal, New York. The companion ride in this book ("Great Finger Lakes Wineries Challenge," Ride 18) is the day 1 portion. (If you wish to join the group for its annual Great Finger Lakes Bicycle Tour, call Augie Mueller at 607–722–6005.) See the write-up for Ride 18 for information on campgrounds or local bed-and-breakfast inns.

The Basics

Start: Watkins Glen, at the main entrance to Watkins Glen State Park on Rte. 14. To get to the start, take Rte. 17 to Elmira, and then take Rte. 14N to Watkins Glen.
Length: 53.2 miles.
Terrain: Moderately rolling to hilly. Traffic is generally light, although Rte. 414 and Rte. 415 can be busy, especially on Watkins Glen race weekends.
Food: Many places in Watkins Glen and Corning, some on Rte. 415 leaving Corning; none on Rte. 414 or Meads Creek Rd.

Miles & Directions

Note: Road numbers designate county roads.

- 0.0 From the park entrance turn right onto Rte. 14.
- 0.1 Turn right onto Rte. 329; just past the south entrance, turn left onto Rte. 17.
- 1.5 Turn right onto Rte. 16. At mile 5.4 you'll pass the Watkins Glen Grand Prix Race Track. At mile 5.8 you'll pass Townsend Grocery Store.
- 6.1 Turn left onto Rd. 19. Pass through the village of Beaver Dams at mile 8.0. Cross over the railroad tracks at mile 11.1.
- 11.2 At the yield sign turn right (south) onto Rte. 414. Watch for rough pavement. Then just stay on this road for the next 11 miles. At mile 21.8 you'll enter the city limits of Corning.
- 22.5 Turn left onto Rte. 415.
- 22.7 Turn right onto Rte. 414S (Centerway). Less than 0.25 mile later on your left is the Corning Glass Center and museum.
- 23.4 Turn right onto Market St., where you'll find many fine restaurants, cafes, and stores.
- 23.9 Turn right onto Bridge St.

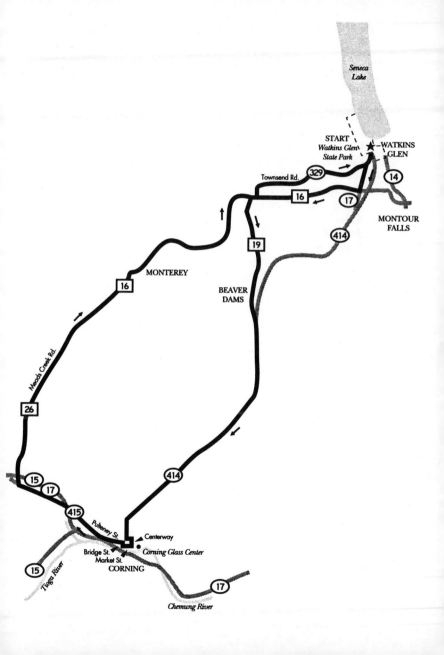

- 24.5 Turn left at a traffic light onto Rte. 415 (W. Pulteney St.). If you haven't eaten, you might want to provision up at the McDonald's or other food options here, for soon you'll be entering a long stretch with no food stops.

- 29.6 Turn right onto Rd. 26 (Meads Creek Rd.); do not follow the signs for Rtes. 17 and 15. Now just stay on Rd. 26 (Meads Creek Rd.) for nearly 18 miles. At mile 36.8, when you cross from Steuben County into Schuyler County, Rd. 26 becomes Rd. 16. Three miles later it curves to the right, and you'll see a sign for the town of Monterey. At mile 47.2 keep going straight at the intersection of Rd. 19.

- 47.4 Turn left onto Townsend Rd. at the Townsend Grocery Store. At mile 47.9 bear right at the fork to stay on Townsend Rd. At mile 50.5 Townsend Rd. becomes Rte. 329, and you'll streak downhill to the town of Watkins Glen.

- 53.2 Turn left into the south entrance of Watkins Glen State Park.

20

Skaneateles Lake Cruise

Skaneateles—Borodino—Scott
New Hope—Skaneateles

Hill-climbers who love rural areas are certain to enjoy this rolling and scenic route circling Skaneateles (pronounced "skinny-atlas") Lake. The second easternmost of the eleven Finger Lakes, Skaneateles Lake offers lovely vistas of sailboats for the first half of this route, as well as fishing and swimming. The lake's water is the purest in the state of New York—so pure, in fact, that it is the source of drinking water for the city of Syracuse. The lightning class of sailboat was developed on its waters, and today the lake hosts many races and regattas. The lake also supports one of the few remaining water-borne mail delivery routes, which leaves every morning at 10:00 A.M.; for a modest fare you can catch it for a three-hour tour (call Mid-Lakes Navigation at 315–685–8500).

This ride, one of four in this book contributed by Peter C. Lemonides, cartographer for the Onondaga Cycling Club, Inc., of Syracuse, New York, begins in the town of Skaneateles and passes through Onondaga, Cortland, and Cayuga counties. The town, which calls itself the Eastern Gateway to the Finger Lakes, has many wonderful nineteenth-century buildings, along with some world-class (and expensive) restaurants. Of local fame is Krebs (founded in 1899), which serves family-style dinners and a Sunday brunch. "Don't miss Doug's Fish Fry!" exclaims Pete Lemonides. The eatery is at the municipal parking lot where you start.

If you wish to stay overnight, you can rest your bones at the Sherwood Inn (315–885–3405), which you pass near the end of the route. Its sixteen guest rooms are decorated in a variety of nineteenth-century styles. A stay at the inn, which traces its origin to a building that fed and housed travelers on Isaac Sherwood's stagecoach line as long ago as 1807, includes a continental breakfast.

The Basics

Start: Skaneateles, at the municipal parking lot on Rte. 321 (State St.) just off Rte. 20 (Genesee St.). To get to the start, take I–81 to Exit 15 just south of Syracuse and then take Rte. 20W into Skaneateles.

Length: 47.8 miles.

Terrain: Hilly. Traffic is light on Rte. 41 and very light on the rest of the roads.

Food: Readily available in Skaneateles; not available elsewhere, so load up on lunch and snacks.

Miles & Directions

- 0.0 Turn right out of the municipal parking lot onto Rte. 321 (State St.).
- 0.1 Turn left (east) onto Rte. 20 (Genesee St.).
- 0.6 Turn right onto Rte. 41S (E. Lake Rd.). Now just enjoy your cruise down the eastern shore of Skaneateles Lake for the next 19 miles. At mile 8.4 you'll pass through the village of Borodino.
- 19.5 In the village of Scott, turn right onto Glen Haven Rd.
- 22.5 Turn left to stay on Glen Haven Rd. and begin climbing a big, long hill. At mile 28.5 in the town of New Hope, continue straight where the road changes its name to New Hope Rd.
- 29.5 Turn left onto Old Salt Rd.
- 30.3 In the village of Kellogsville turn right onto Globe Rd. At mile 31.2, after you cross Rte. 38A, the road changes its name to Twelve Corners Rd.
- 36.5 Bear slightly right onto the unmarked Cemetery Rd., where Twelve Corners Rd. bears left.

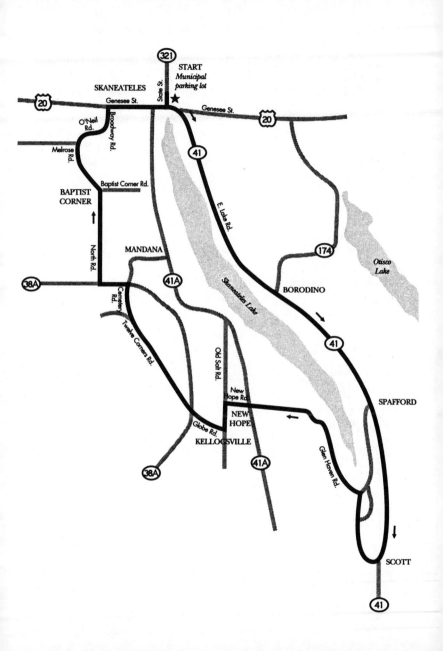

- 37.2 Turn left onto Rte. 38A.
- 38.1 Turn right onto North Rd.
- 41.5 In the village of Baptist Corner turn left onto Melrose Rd.
- 43.3 Turn right onto O'Neil Rd., which is stony and bumpy.
- 44.4 Turn left onto the unmarked Broadway Rd.
- 45.4 Turn right onto Rte. 20E (Genesee St.). Soon you'll pass Krebs and the Sherwood Inn.
- 47.7 Turn left onto Rte. 321 (State St.).
- 47.8 Turn left into the municipal parking lot.

21

Pratts Falls Half-Century-Plus Challenge

Pompey—Truxton—Erieville—Fabius—Pompey

Light traffic, hills, farms, hills, quaint villages, and more hills combine to make the Pratts Falls Half-Century-Plus a pleasant yet challenging day ride. Passing through Onondaga and Madison counties, this ride is a real retreat from automobiles and people: Rolling acres of farms and four-corner towns don't offer much to tourists seeking typical tourist attractions, but they will refresh the spirit of a cyclist seeking solitude and good, scenic, challenging terrain.

The Pratts Falls Challenge is one of four rides in this book contributed by Peter C. Lemonides, cartographer for the Onondaga Cycling Club, Inc., of Syracuse, New York. About 5 miles of this route overlap with the "Cazenovia-Erieville Cruise" (Ride 22). The two can be linked as a 79.3-mile one-day ride, in which case you wouldn't travel the 5.1-mile overlapping section; however, in so doing you would miss a steep climb that rewards riders with one of the best panoramic views of either ride.

This ride begins at Pratts Falls Park, a county-run recreational park offering plenty of parking, covered picnic areas, rest rooms, hiking trails, and a beautiful view of Pratts Falls. (Swimming and overnight camping are not permitted.) The first opportunity to pick up provisions for the road is in the village of Pompey, 3 miles into the ride.

Beginning about 10 miles into the ride, you will be pedaling along Route 91 as it passes through the exceptionally scenic Labrador Hollow and the Labrador Mountain Ski Center. A natural lunch stop is DeRuyter, nearly halfway (26 miles) into the 58-mile loop. DeRuyter is a quaint village dotted with charming bungalows (one of which is an antiques shop). You'll have your choice of grocery stores, several small restaurants, and an ice cream parlor. Three-quarters of the way through the ride is another nice stop: Highland Forest, a county park with picnic areas, hiking trails, bridle paths, and some challenging mountain-bike trails.

The Basics

Start: Three miles north of Pompey, at Pratts Falls Park on Pratts Falls Rd. Take I–81 to Exit 15 just south of Syracuse and follow Rte. 20E into Pompey. Take Henneberry Rd. north to Pratts Falls Rd. and then turn right to the park entrance.

Length: 58 miles. May be increased to 79.3 miles by combining this route with Ride 22.

Terrain: Rolling to very hilly in stretches. Traffic is light in the villages of Pompey and Fabius and extremely light everywhere else.

Food: Occasional convenience stores and neighborhood bar-and-grill restaurants, with some long stretches between.

Miles & Directions

- 0.0 From Pratts Falls Park parking lot, turn right onto Pratts Falls Rd.
- 0.6 Turn right onto Henneberry Rd., and make an immediate left to stay on Pratts Falls Rd.
- 1.3 Turn left onto Sweet Rd.
- 3.5 In the town of Pompey, bear right at the stop sign onto Cherry St. In 1 block cross Rte. 20 and continue straight and slightly left onto Berwyn Rd.
- 5.8 Bear right onto Collins Rd. At mile 9.4 continue straight as the road becomes Berry Rd.
- 9.6 In the village of Apulia, turn left at the T intersection onto Rte. 80.

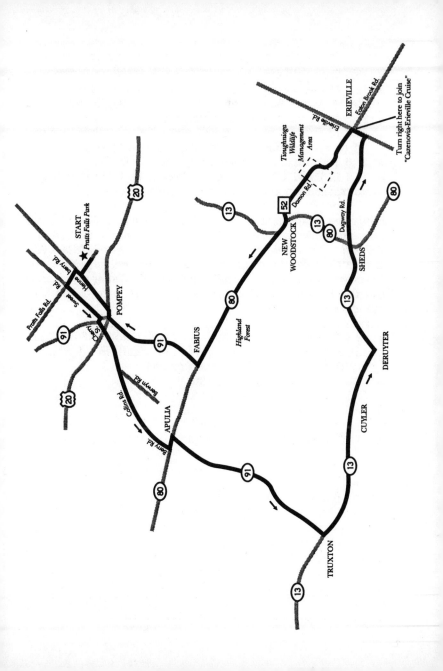

- 9.9 Turn right onto Rte. 91.
- 18.3 In the town of Truxton, turn left at the T intersection onto Rte. 13. At mile 22.7 continue on Rte. 13 through Cuyler.
- 26.6 In the town of DeRuyter, turn left to stay on Rte. 13..
- 31.8 In Sheds continue straight onto the unmarked Dugway Rd. (where Rte. 80E heads right and Rtes. 13W/80W head left).
- 37.0 Turn left at the T intersection onto Erieville Rd.
- 37.4 In Erieville turn left at the Erieville Post Office onto the unmarked Damon Rd. Now you'll begin climbing.

Instructions for turning this 58-mile challenge into a 79.3-mile classic: Instead of turning left onto Damon Rd., turn right onto Eaton Brook Rd. and pick up the directions for the "Cazenovia-Erieville Cruise" (Ride 22) at mile 12.3. Ride to the end of the "Cazenovia-Erieville Cruise" at Cazenovia Lake; then continue riding as if you were starting the cruise at mile 0.0. In New Woodstock at mile 6.7, turn right onto Rte. 80, and pick up the directions below.

- 43.1 In New Woodstock continue straight onto Rte. 80W (Rtes. 13E/80E head left and Rte. 13W heads right). In a few miles you'll pass the Highland Forest on your left.
- 50.2 In Fabius turn right onto Rte. 91.
- 55.3 In Pompey turn right onto Rte. 20.
- 55.5 Turn left onto Henneberry Rd.
- 57.5 Turn right onto Pratts Falls Rd.
- 58.1 Turn left into Pratts Falls Park.

22

Cazenovia-Erieville Cruise

Cazenovia—New Woodstock—Erieville—Cazenovia

Not too far from Syracuse, Cazenovia is in the heart of central New York State, a region steeped in revolutionary war–era history and famed for its lush green valleys and crystal clear lakes. Cazenovia itself overlooks the beautiful Cazenovia Lake, on whose banks you may sit and let your mind wander free, soaking up the spirit of the countryside before mounting your bike. Once you are on the road, the rolling-to-moderately-hilly route to Erieville winds through Madison County's farm country and state wildlife management areas.

This Cazenovia-Erieville Cruise is one of four rides in this book contributed by Peter C. Lemonides, cartographer for the Onondaga Cycling Club, Inc., of Syracuse, New York. Together the four popular day rides are "representative of terrain and gorgeous central New York scenery," Lemonides noted. About 5 miles of the Cazenovia route overlap with the "Pratts Falls Half-Century-Plus Challenge" (Ride 21). Thus, the two could be combined for a 79-mile-long classic (see Ride 21 for a suggested linkage); for the combined route you would not ride the overlapping section and would thus miss pedaling through the Tioughnioga Wildlife Management Area.

The ride begins at the public parking area on the south end of Cazenovia Lake. Grocery stores, minimarts, restaurants, and shops can be found in the village of Cazenovia itself, about 0.5 mile east on Route 20 from the parking area.

If you wish to stay a night or a weekend, rooms are available at the charming Lincklaen House in Cazenovia (315–655–3461); for a more economical and casual setting, try the Cazenovia Motel (315–655–9101), which is at the village's eastern edge and next to the Cazenovia Country Kitchen restaurant. Take a moment to stroll through the formal gardens of the Lorenzo State Historic Site (315–655–3200), which overlooks Cazenovia Lake; time your visit right and you may watch an annual horse-driving competition or other special event. On Thursday evenings during the summer, there is usually a free concert or dancing at the lake-front park.

Four miles north of Cazenovia is Chittenango Falls State Park (315–655–9620), where bike campers might wish to set up a tent or rent a shelter. During the summer you can enjoy hiking on the nature trails or catching fish for dinner; best of all, the campground has hot showers, where you can sluice off the road grime and relax your muscles at the end of the ride.

The Basics

Start: Cazenovia, at the parking lot at the south end of Cazenovia Lake, at the intersection of Rte. 92 and Rte. 20. The start can be reached from I–81 by taking Exit 15 onto Route 20E to Lafayette and following it east to Cazenovia.
Length: 31.4 miles. May be increased to 79.3 miles by combining this route with Ride 21.
Terrain: Rolling to hilly. Traffic is light, but keep an eye out for farm tractors.
Food: Small restaurants and convenience stores in Cazenovia, New Woodstock, and Erieville.

Miles & Directions

Note: To turn this 31.4-mile cruise into a 79.3-mile challenge, see directions in the "Pratts Falls Half-Century-Plus Challenge," Ride 21.

■ 0.0 From Cazenovia Lake parking area, turn left onto Rte. 20. (Albany St.).

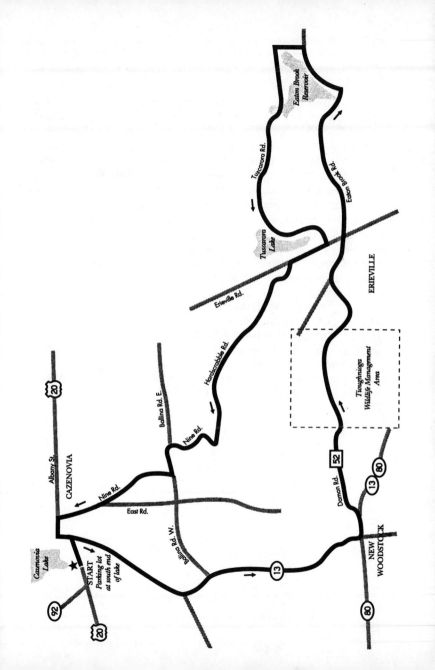

- 0.6 Turn right onto Rte. 13.
- 6.7 In the village of New Woodstock, turn left onto Rte. 80.
- 7.2 Turn left onto Rte. 52 (Damon Rd.) and begin a long, gradual climb. For the next 5.1 miles until you reach the town of Erieville, this route overlaps a section of the "Pratts Falls Half-Century-Plus Challenge" (Ride 21), although heading in the opposite direction. Halfway along the road you'll pass through the Tioughnioga Wildlife Management Area.
- 12.3 In Erieville continue straight where Rte. 52 (Damon Rd.) becomes Eaton Brook Rd. Follow it as it bends left around Eaton Brook Reservoir, where you can stop at the fishing access to dip your feet into the water.
- 16.4 Turn left onto Tuscarora Rd, which eventually bends left taking you around Tuscarora Lake. Unfortunately, here there are no public swimming areas.
- 22.0 Turn right onto Erieville Rd. at the T intersection.
- 22.8 Turn left onto Hardscrabble Rd.
- 26.5 Turn right onto Nine Rd.
- 27.4 Turn left onto Ballina Rd. E.
- 28.0 Turn right to resume pedaling on Nine Rd. At mile 29.3 continue straight where Nine Rd. joins East Rd.
- 30.2 In the village of Cazenovia, turn left onto Rte. 20 (Albany St.) and follow it west back to the start.
- 31.4 Turn right into the Cazenovia Lake parking area.

23

Salmon River Cruise

Altmar—Orwell—Redfield—Ricard—Altmar

The rural countryside of this ride is known primarily for its hunting and fishing. You'll pedal over green rolling hills troubled by few cars, catch isolated glimpses of the reservoir, and pass many spots tempting you to stop and picnic and let your spirit catch up to your body. Although there are no bed-and-breakfast inns or campgrounds in the area, there are fishing lodges for those desiring such accommodations; if you enjoy fishing or swimming as well as cycling, this is definitely the tour for bringing your portable rod and reel or swimsuit. You may also want to pack your own picnic lunch before embarking, as the only food anywhere along the route is the fare offered by convenience stores.

This Oswego County ride, one of four in this book contributed by Peter C. Lemonides, cartographer for the Onondaga Cycling Club, Inc., of Syracuse, New York, begins in Altmar; its main attraction is the large Salmon River Fish Hatchery (315–298–5051), which offers informative tours.

Perhaps the most scenic spot is just off the route about 5 miles into the ride: Turn right onto Falls Road and 1 mile later you will behold a waterfall with a greater vertical drop than Niagara Falls. To see the falls at their best, visit in early spring when the river is swollen from the runoff from winter's snows. But even in the drier summer, the sight of the narrow pencil of water plummeting into the gorge below is dramatic.

The Basics

Start: Altmar, at the public parking lot near the Salmon River at the intersection of Bridge St. and Pulaski St. Altmar has two bars, a gas

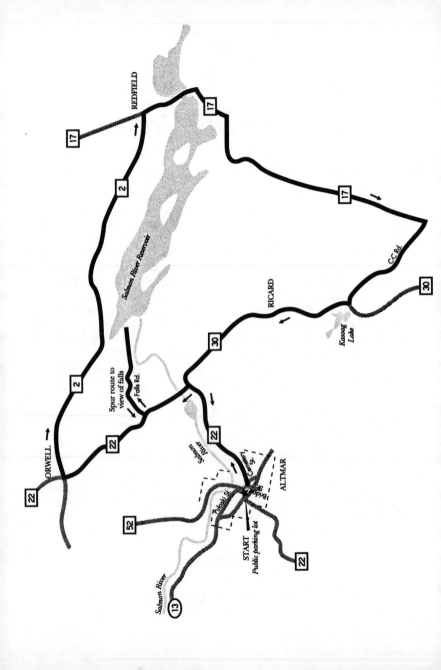

station, and a convenience grocery store. To get to the start, take Exit 36 off I–81 north of Syracuse, and then take Rte. 13 southeast to Altmar.

Length: 37 miles.

Terrain: Rolling (no long hills or steep climbs). Traffic is very light and reasonably polite, if somewhat above the posted speed limits.

Food: Isolated convenience stores.

Miles & Directions

- 0.0 From the public parking lot, ride away from the river up the hill along Bridge St. Three blocks later turn left onto Cemetery St. At mile 1.3 Cemetery St. becomes Rte. 22.
- 3.6 Bear left to stay on Rte. 22. In a short distance you'll cross over the Salmon River, although unfortunately you will not be able to see it. In another couple of miles, Falls Rd. heads right to a view of the high waterfall.
- 7.5 In the rural village of Orwell, turn right onto Rte. 2, and stay on it for the next 9 miles. Eventually you will pass the Salmon River Reservoir, although it will remain unseen behind the trees. You may also want to stop to take a swim.
- 16.6 Turn right at the T intersection in Redfield onto Rte. 17.
- 18.2 Turn right to stay on Rte. 17.
- 19.2 Turn right to stay on Rte. 17.
- 25.4 Turn right onto C-C Rd. (A historical note: C-C Rd. was originally C.C.C. Rd., named after the Civilian Conservation Corps's camp there during the 1930s; somewhere along the line the last C was dropped.)
- 28.3 Turn right at the T intersection onto Rte. 30.
- 33.1 Bear left to stay on Rte. 30.
- 33.4 Bear left onto Rte. 22. As you enter Altmar at mile 36.0, Rte. 22 becomes Cemetery St.
- 36.8 Follow Cemetery St. as it turns right onto Bridge St. Continue straight for another 3 blocks to return to the public parking lot.

Pennsylvania

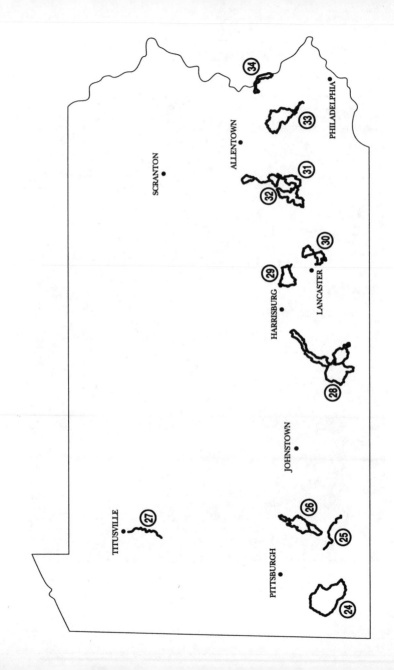

Pennsylvania

Prosperity Covered Bridges Cruise

Prosperity—West Finley—Rogersville—Prosperity

A marvelous old club ride of the 1,000-member Western Pennsylvania Wheelmen (WPW) bicycle club, this route will take you near no fewer than nine covered bridges. Back in the nineteenth century, of course, bridges were covered in part to prevent the accumulation of snow, which could not be plowed, and to minimize wetting of the main structure, thus prolonging a bridge's life by minimizing rot. Time your visit for mid-September and you may be able to take in the crafts, food, live entertainment, and other activities of the Covered Bridge Festival, held every year since 1971 onsite at many of the bridges. For exact dates, events, and bridge locations, call the Washington–Greene County Tourist Promotion Agency at (412) 222–8130.

Although the basic ride route does not take you through these bridges, directions are given for a few short side trips to visit them. You may want to do this ride on a cross (hybrid) or mountain bike, as some of the roads on the main route (and on some of the side trips to covered bridges) are dirt—shown on the map as dashed lines. But the payoff is very light automobile traffic and the back-to-nature romance of recalling an earlier age, notes contributor Noel P. Grimm, board member of the WPW. By the way, these side trips add up: If you visit all nine bridges, you add another 24.0 miles to the route, turning this 51.4-mile cruise into a 75.4-mile classic.

The ride begins about 1 mile south of Prosperity, Pennsylvania, which is about 10 miles south of Washington, Pennsylvania. This tour through Washington and Greene counties heads north through the tiny town of Prosperity, where a stop at the town grocery store provides a glimpse back in history because of its old wood floors, old display cases and shelves, and antique lighting. Then you'll warm up on flat to rolling farm land, paralleling Ten Mile Creek on your left.

About 4 miles into the ride, you'll begin a climb up a 10 percent grade to the top of a ridge—the steepest climb of the entire journey. Once up there you'll pedal along the ridge for the next 12 miles, enjoying expansive views of the farm valleys on your right and left.

After riding through the town of West Finley, you'll coast down into the valley, where there are some good choices for a roadside picnic. The last 20 miles, which parallel railroad tracks, are a slight uphill grade. As this beautiful loop is accessible to most average in-shape cyclists, it is a favorite club ride and no. 63 in the packet of 150 rides in western Pennsylvania available from the Pittsburgh-based WPW.

A few notes about road designations in this part of Pennsylvania: The highways prefixed *PA* have a keystone-shaped sign with a one-, two-, or three-digit number. The PA highways are also marked with State Route (SR) numbers as well as the keystone sign. Four-digit SR roads—which are also county roads—are the less traveled access roads preferred by cyclists; they can be marked either by black letters on white signs or even by small numbers on reflective tape on a 5-foot-high pole about every 0.5 mile. Roads marked with a *T* followed by three digits are township roads that have little traffic and are usually very narrow; when the roads are marked—and often they are not—the *T* designation appears on a green city street sign with white letters. Having noted all this, "the local people will not know the T route numbers and they usually don't know the SR route numbers even though they are signed," remarks Grimm, so pay close attention to the cue-sheet mileages and the map.

The Basics

Start: One mile south of Prosperity, in Washington County, at the intersection of PA221 and PA18. To get there take I–79 south from Pittsburgh and then I–70 west. Drive about 6 miles on I–70, passing exits to Washington, Pennsylvania, and exit onto PA221. Turn left at the end of the off ramp, and make another left onto PA221S. Then drive about 7 miles to Prosperity, a town with a population of about 200. Drive another mile to the south to the starting point at the intersection of PA18. Park on the right (south) side of the road in the gravel parking lot (used for road maintenance).

Length: 51.4 miles (75.4 miles with all the side trips to the covered bridges).

Terrain: Flat to rolling, with a couple of stiff climbs. Traffic is light for most of the ride, although it is moderate on PA21 and PA18.

Food: Sparse. Stock up in Prosperity; other convenience stores are in Graysville (mile 23.3) and Rogersville (off the route at mile 37.5, near Waynesburg restaurant).

Miles & Directions

- **0.0** Turn left (north) out of the parking lot onto PA18/221 toward Prosperity.
- **1.0** Turn left onto PA221N in Prosperity, leaving PA18.
- **3.9** Turn left onto SR3029W toward Pleasant Grove. At mile 5.4 you'll pass through Pleasant Grove.
- **5.9** Bear left at the Y intersection to stay on SR3029.
- **8.3** At the stop sign where the road intersects with PA231, make a quick jog left and then an immediate right to keep heading straight ahead on SR3029.

Side trip to three covered bridges (11.8 miles round-trip): Turn left instead onto PA231. After 2.5 miles turn right onto T414. After another 0.2 mile follow T414 as it turns right to Brownlee Bridge (spanning 31 feet over the Templeton fork of Wheeling Creek). From here the rest of this detour to the next two bridges will take you on dirt roads. Ride

221

3029

PLEASANT
GROVE

Danley
Covered Bridge 379 3029 231

3025

GOOD
INTENT

414 *Brownlee Covered Bridge*

3029

Wyit Sprowls
Covered Bridge

Plants Covered Bridge

408 3035

Sprowls Covered Bridge

Presbyterian Church
(rest rooms)

Crawford
Covered
Bridge 3037

WEST
FINLEY

Longdon Covered Bridge

4016

408

4007

GRAYSVILLE

21

21

****** = dirt

RUTAN

424 *Scott*
Covered
Bridge 21

18

221

PROSPERITY

START ★ 221 18

18

221

339 *Day*
Covered
Bridge

DUNNS
STATION

3039

WEST
UNION

221

DEERLICK

SWARTS

18

4029

SYCAMORE

Albert's Restaurant
(rest rooms) and ice
cream store

18

ROGERSVILLE 18

21

21

WAYNES-
BURG

18

through the Brownlee Bridge and continue on T414 for 2.0 miles. Turn left onto T408 to Plants Bridge (spanning 24.5 feet over the Templeton fork). Ride through that bridge on T408 for 0.9 mile, and turn right onto SR3035. After 0.3 mile turn left onto T450 to Sprowls Bridge (built in 1875, spanning 27.5 feet over the Rocky Run branch of Wheeling Creek). Return to the main ride by retracing this detour route.

- 10.8 Turn left to stay on SR3029.
- 12.6 Continue straight at the junction with SR3025, to stay on SR3029. At mile 12.6 you have your next chance to visit a covered bridge.

Side trip to one covered bridge (4.2 miles round-trip—very steep): Turn right onto SR3025 and ride 0.7 mile to Good Intent. Turn right at the T intersection to stay on SR3025. After another 1.4 miles turn right onto T379 to Danley Bridge, spanning 39 feet across the Robinson fork of Wheeling Creek. Return to the main ride by retracing this detour's route.

- 15.8 Go straight onto SR3035. At this intersection there are public rest rooms behind the Presbyterian church.
- 16.4 Turn left at the T intersection onto SR3037 in West Finley, heading toward Graysville.

Side trip to two covered bridges (4.0 miles round-trip): Turn right instead of left at the T intersection onto SR3037. In 0.2 mile turn right to stay on SR3037. In 0.7 mile turn left onto T307 to Crawford Bridge, spanning 39 feet across the Robinson fork of Wheeling Creek. Return to SR3037 and continue north. In 0.8 mile turn right onto T360. Ride 0.3 mile to Wyit Sprowls Bridge, spanning 43 feet across the Robinson fork. Return to the main ride by retracing this detour route.

- 18.7 The road you are on becomes SR4007 as you enter Greene County.
- 18.9 Bear right at the base of the downhill to stay on SR4007 toward Graysville. At this curve the road heading left is SR4016.

Side trip to one covered bridge (1.8 miles round-trip): Turn left onto SR4016. After 0.6 mile, turn left onto T414, a gravel road. After 0.3 mile you'll see Longdon Bridge—complete with bats—spanning a remarkable 67.5 feet across the Templeton fork of Wheeling Creek. Return to the main ride by retracing this detour route.

Continue straight at the junctions at miles 21.9 and 22.1 to stay on SR4007. At mile 23.4 there is a convenience store on the left.

- 23.5 Head straight onto PA21E, watching carefully for traffic. At mile 27.4 PA21E will take you through the village of Rutan. *At mile 28.5, opposite SR4017, look right: You'll see Scott Bridge, built in 1885; it spans 41 feet across Ten Mile Creek on T424.*
- 31.4 Bear left at the stop sign where PA18N joins PA21E. In 0.5 mile you'll pass through Rogersville. At mile 35.4 keep heading straight at the junction to stay on PA21E/18N.
- 37.5 Turn left onto PA18N (leaving PA21E), following the PA18N signs. (If at this intersection you continue straight on PA21E instead, within 0.5 mile on your left are an ice cream store and Albert's Restaurant, where you can relax with an iced tea and refill your water bottles in the rest rooms. Then resume the main route on PA18N.) At mile 39.6 continue straight at the junction to stay on PA18N.
- 40.7 In the village of Sycamore, turn right onto SR4029, heading north. At mile 42.9 you'll pass through the village of Swarts; keep heading straight at the junction, following the sign to Prosperity.
- 45.3 Bear right at the Y intersection in the village of Deerlick to stay on SR4029. At mile 46.7, after passing through the village of West Union, you reenter Washington County, and SR4029 becomes SR3039.
- 48.5 Head straight at the junction onto PA221N, leaving SR3039.
- 49.3 Turn left at the stop sign to stay on PA221N, heading toward Prosperity.
- 51.4 Bear right where PA18 joins PA221; then make a sharp left into the gravel parking lot at the start.

Side trip to one covered bridge (2.2 miles round-trip): Turn right out of the gravel parking lot and make an immediate right onto PA18S. After 1.1 mile turn left onto T339. There is Day Bridge, built in 1875 and spanning 36.5 feet across Short Creek. Return by this route to your starting point in the parking lot.

25

Youghiogheny River Trail Ramble

Ohiopyle—Ramcat Hollow—Ohiopyle

The Youghiogheny River Trail is a 9-mile-long multipurpose trail for cyclists, hikers, and cross-country skiers. Located entirely within Ohiopyle State Park, straddling the border of Fayette and Somerset counties, the 12-foot-wide, hard-surfaced path of fine gravel runs through the scenic, forested gorge of the Youghiogheny (pronounced "YAHK-ah-gain-ee") River on the old Western Maryland Railway bed. The nearly level 18-mile out-and-back course from Ohiopyle to the Ramcat Hollow Launch area, near Confluence, is highlighted by magnificent river views, cascading feeder streams, and maturing forests. The trail was officially dedicated in 1986, after the Western Pennsylvania Conservancy acquired the abandoned railroad right-of-way from the Chessie System and transferred it to the Bureau of State Parks of the Pennsylvania Department of Environmental Resources.

Although Ohiopyle is nearly due west of Ramcat Hollow, the 900-foot-deep Youghiogheny River gorge carved through Laurel Ridge makes the bike path's trailheads far from a direct route. Cyclists heading upriver from Ohiopyle, for example, will occasionally find themselves pedaling directly north or south as they make their way steadily eastward. Because it was originally designed as a railroad corridor, the bike trail never exceeds a 3 percent grade. The path appears level on the uphill first half toward Confluence, but the grade becomes apparent after you turn around and gradually descend back to Ohiopyle. The gentle slope and smooth trail surface allow easy access to remote sections of the Yough Gorge that were once enjoyed only by white-water rafters, railroad travelers, and determined hikers, hunters, and anglers.

Although cyclists generally prefer loop trails over out-and-back courses because they do not like recrossing the same territory, the scenery on this trail is so varied and breathtaking that you are certain to notice new features from the different perspective of the return ride. Moreover, take the time to venture off the trail for a short distance to visit the riverbank, tributary valleys, waterfalls, and other hidden wonders just off the beaten track. "The trail becomes almost secondary and a simple highway to the wilder and isolated nooks and crannies of the Yough Gorge," remarks Paul g. Wiegman, director of natural science and stewardship of the Western Pennsylvania Conservancy, who contributed this ride (note that the lowercase *g* is not a typo).

Each season has its own appeal. Riding in April and May reveals migrating warblers, blooming woodland wildflowers, and the river swollen with runoff from winter snows. Summer outings are highlighted by field flowers in the meadows, a river temperature that invites swimming, and the pleasant, pervasive fragrance of hay-scented fern. In the autumn the northern and southern hardwoods on the gorge's high, wooded ridges are ablaze with vibrant reds and golds.

Note: As you're heading for the start, on Route 381 just north of Ohiopyle you may want to stop to see Fallingwater, the most famous private house designed by Frank Lloyd Wright (412–329–8501). For information on camping at one of the 223 sites at Ohiopyle State Park, call (412) 329–8591.

The Basics

Start: Ohiopyle, at the bike trailhead parking lot of the single-story frame building that was once Ohiopyle's railroad station. To get to the start, take the Pennsylvania Turnpike (I–76) to exit 9 (Donegal). Turn left onto Route 31E. Drive 2 miles to Route 381 South, and turn right. Stay on Route 381 to Ohiopyle. As you enter Ohiopyle, cross the concrete bridge over the Youghiogheny River and make the first left just before the gas station, following the signs for BIKE/HIKE TRAIL. Make another left into the bike trailhead parking lot. By the way, you can rent bicycles in Ohiopyle, in which case, you might want to park at one of the lots in town and pedal back to the trailhead.

Length: 18 or 22 miles.

Terrain: Flat. No automobile traffic.

Food: In keeping with the gorge's rugged, natural character, there are no drinking fountains, rest rooms, or eating facilities along the trail. Carry all your own water and snacks. There is a deli in Ohiopyle at the western end and in Confluence at the eastern end (open April 1–October 10). There are clean pit toilets at the Ramcat Hollow parking lot.

Miles & Directions

Note: Throughout the trail's length, odd-numbered mileage posts have been placed on the left edge of the path and even-numbered ones on the right. On both the trip to Ramcat Hollow and the return to Ohiopyle, the mileposts are numbered 1 through 9. Because there are no turns off the trail on this trip, the narrative descriptions below are indications of the scenery you will enjoy at different mileposts.

■ **0.0** From the single-story frame building that was once Ohiopyle's railroad station, take the trail down through a 150-yard tunnel of trees. Soon it passes across the top of the wide dirt ramp that serves as a take-out point for canoes descending the river. The path then skirts the edge of a second gravel parking lot and squeezes between four vertical wooden posts designed to keep out motorized vehicles.

Just after this gate you will get your first unobstructed view of the Youghiogheny River. Trees along the left edge soon obscure the river, and your attention will be directed back to the path as you enter a mile-long straightaway. This wide, open stretch al-

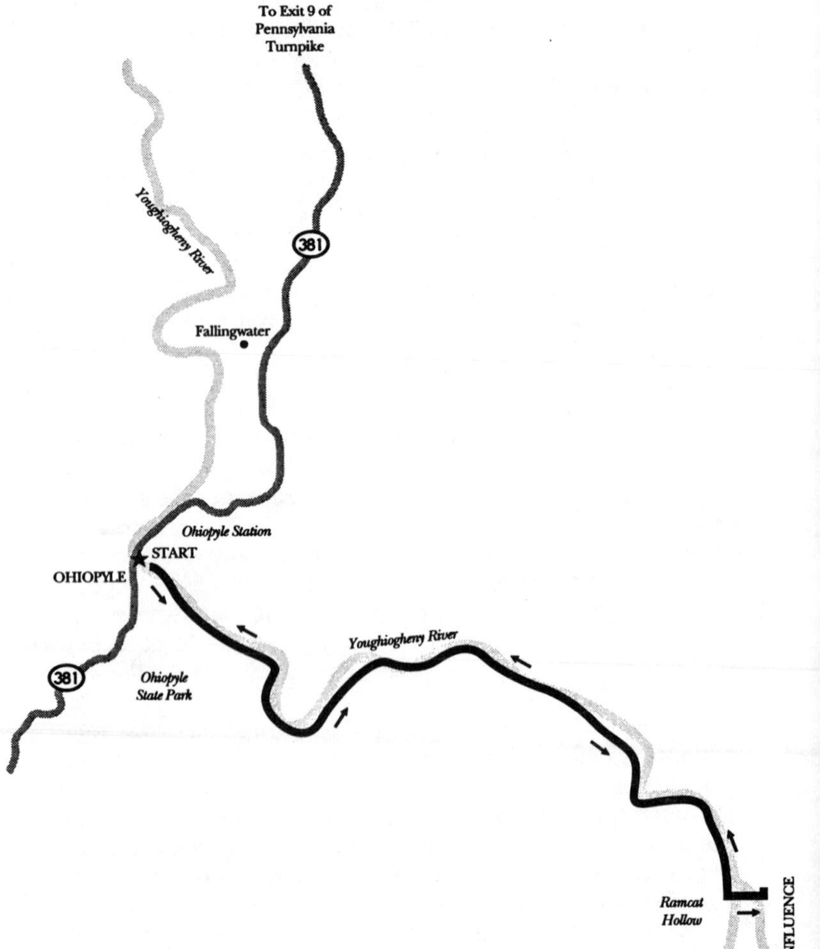

To Exit 9 of
Pennsylvania
Turnpike

381

Youghiogheny River

Fallingwater

Ohiopyle Station

START

OHIOPYLE

381

Ohiopyle
State Park

Youghiogheny River

Ramcat
Hollow

CONFLUENCE

lows time to scan the wooded ridges that tower over the river. All the rugged terrain visible from the trail is part of Laurel Ridge. The section of the Youghiogheny gorge traversed by the bike path is a water gap carved through the ridge.

- Milepost 1 is at the midpoint of the long straightaway. Between mileposts 1 and 2, you can look into the mature forest for more than 100 yards in several places, even in midsummer.

- Milepost 2 or shortly thereafter is where the trail emerges back into the sunlight and reveals a panoramic view of a broad river bend interspersed with rapids. You'll cross a wide, concrete bridge at the apex of the bend over Long Run, your first tributary mountain stream.

- Milepost 3, like several other places along this portion of the trail, is marked by vertical cliffs of native stone where the former railroad cut into the hillside. Many have groundwater slowly seeping from the rock, thus keeping the exposed faces moist throughout the year. In spring these cliff faces are veritable hanging gardens, adorned with wild columbine and early saxifrage, growing from beds of bright green moss.

- Milepost 4 or just beyond presents a grassy side trail on the left, leading across the field to the river's edge, where a pond-size pool of calm, deep water is framed by rapids and wooded banks. You won't be able to ride a bike past the edge of the field, but the scenery is worth a short hike.

- Milepost 5 includes some sections immediately above the river and some out of the river's sight and sound. A state park sign just past the milepost announces that a hiking trail emerging from the woods on the right will parallel the bike trail for the next 1.5 miles.

- Milepost 6 is passed on a shaded section of path. About 0.5 mile later the hiking trail disappears back into the woods to the right. If you leave your bike to follow the hiking trail on foot, you will climb up to a terrace above an unnamed Youghiogheny tributary; a side trail from the terrace will lead you to half a dozen apple trees growing wild on the level patch of ground.

- Milepost 7 is just after some 15- to 20-foot cliffs towering above the path's right side. Wherever patches of soil have accumulated, moss, ferns, and columbine now grow on the damp rock. After passing this vertical wild garden, you'll have views of the Youghiogheny River's rapids and pools of calm water. As you round a bend, the trail passes through a 150-yard-long railroad-carved canyon. The rock walls here rise for 12 feet on your left side and as high as 20 feet on your right. Young tulip trees share this narrows with the bike path, and when in leaf, their overlapping branches create a living tunnel.

■ Milepost 8 is in a long straightaway, which is followed by the bike path's most impressive river scenery: a panoramic view of the white, water-filled bend known as Ramcat Rapids. This rock-and-moving-water obstacle course is a good example of the Class II rapids found on the Youghiogheny between Confluence and Ohiopyle. The steel cables strung across the river directly above these rapids are used to suspend gates in the foaming water for competitive slalom paddling. Just before the bend a wide, grassy area on the path's left edge offers a convenient place to pull off and watch canoeists and kayakers negotiate the tumbling water.

■ Milepost 9 is at the Ramcat Hollow Launch Area, the gravel parking lot of the trail's eastern terminus in the Ohiopyle State Park. Actually, outside the park the trail continues for another 2 miles to the town of Confluence, where the Youghiogheny River, Casselman River, and Laurel Hill Creek join to begin the long journey through the watergap. To get to Confluence, ride out the road from the parking lot. Cross the first paved road to continue straight on the trail for another mile. At the sign TRAIL END, turn left onto the narrow paved road, following the sign CONFLUENCE 1 MILE. Turn left at the stop sign to cross the bridge and immediately turn left into Confluence. Turn around and return the same way you came to get back to Ohiopyle.

26

Ligonier Wildlife Challenge

Ligonier—Darlington—Stahlstown
Jones Mills—Rector—Ligonier

If you love hills, wildlife, hills, beautiful wooded scenery, and more hills, this western Pennsylvania ride is for you. On the route you're likely to see deer, mallard ducks, Canada geese, black bear, wild turkey, pheasants, and other wildlife. Plus there are breathtaking panoramic vistas of the surrounding countryside from the tops of the climbs. For those thrilled by rollercoaster rides, on one downhill stretch you can coast at up to 40 miles per hour!

The shorter 31-mile version is a cruise for those wanting to enjoy the best of the scenery while cutting off the worst of the climbs. But the 49-mile challenge will satisfy even the fittest, strongest cyclist, with a total of about 3,000 feet of hill climbing and grades ranging from 10 to 18 percent.

Yes, 18 percent, as measured by an inclinometer on the top tube of his bicycle, affirms Noel P. Grimm, board member of the Western Pennsylvania Wheelmen (WPW), who submitted this ride. (Eighteen percent would be the grade of a hill where you climbed 180 feet over a horizontal travel of 1,000 feet.) "This is a steep hill!" he exclaims. The steepest hills of 15 to 18 percent grade are seldom more than 0.25 mile long, but the climbs of 10 to 12 percent grade can be more than 1.0 mile long. "The hills on this ride are sharp, choppy ups and downs," Noel Grimm warns. "You need low gears on your bicycle. Also, on the downhills riders need well-adjusted brakes and some expertise on applying the brakes."

This "Ligonier Wildlife" ride is no. 94 in the package of 150 western Pennsylvania rides available from the WPW, a Pittsburgh-based, 1,000-member bicycle club founded in 1969. The route explores the foothills between the Chestnut and Laurel ridges in Westmoreland County between Ligonier and Donegal.

A few notes about road designations in this part of Pennsylvania: The highways prefixed *PA* have a keystone-shaped sign with a one-, two-, or three-digit number. The PA highways are also marked with State Route (SR) numbers as well as the keystone sign. Four-digit SR roads—which are also county roads—are the less traveled access roads preferred by cyclists; they can be marked either by black letters on white signs or even by small numbers on reflective tape on a 5-foot-high pole about every 0.5 mile. Roads marked with a *T* followed by three digits are township roads that have little traffic and are usually very narrow; when the roads are marked—and often they are not—the *T* designation appears on a green city street sign with white letters. Having noted all this, "the local people will not know the T route numbers and they usually don't know the SR route numbers even though they are signed," remarks Grimm, so pay close attention to the cue-sheet mileages and the map.

The Basics

Start: Ligonier, in front of the National Guard Armory on Walnut St. north of Main St. To reach Ligonier take Route 30 east to 0.3 mile before Route 711 in Ligonier, and turn left onto Walnut Street and then left into the parking lot of the Giant Eagle grocery store. There you can provision up, and in the public rest rooms, fill your water bottles. Continue north on Walnut St. for another 0.5 block, cross Main St. at the stop sign, and park on Walnut Street alongside the National Guard Armory.

Length: 31 or 49 miles.

Terrain: Moderately hilly on the 31-mile cruise; very hilly with exceptionally steep climbs on the 49-mile challenge. Outside of Ligonier itself and the crossing of Rte. 30, traffic is exceptionally light (maybe two cars in 10 miles).

Food: Several stores and restaurants in Ligonier. Stock up, because this ride is so rural that there are long stretches between convenience stores and public rest rooms.

Miles & Directions

Note: Follow directions carefully as not every small street is shown on the map.

- ■ 0.0 From your parking spot on Walnut St. north of Main St., head 1 block south to Main St.
- ■ 0.1 Turn right onto Main St., heading west.
- ■ 0.4 Turn right (north) at the gas station onto SR1021 (where deer have been seen on some rides).
- ■ 2.1 Turn left to stay on unmarked SR1021.
- ■ 2.9 Here the ride splits. For the 49-mile challenge turn right onto PA259N.

For the 31-mile cruise turn left (instead of right) onto PA259S, and ride 2.0 miles; resume following the directions below at mile 14.1.
After climbing a few hills, you'll reach a high plateau where Chestnut and Laurel ridges can be seen.

- ■ 6.3 Turn left onto SR1008 at the top of the hill. This is a pleasant, narrow, tree-lined backroad dotted with a few infrequent houses. Follow SR1008 as it bends left.
- ■ 8.7 Continue straight onto T954/T721 where SR1008 heads right. After passing a fancy red barn, you'll encounter a sharp left on SR1021 and a long, fast downhill all the way to Latrobe Reservoir. Depending on what season it is, you should see mallard ducks or Canada geese on the water.
- ■ 11.8 Turn right at the T intersection onto PA259S. *Soon the 31-mile ride rejoins the main ride.*
- ■ 14.1 Turn right onto Rte. 30, riding on the shoulder of this busy road. Fortunately, this heavy-traffic stretch lasts only about 300 feet.
- ■ 14.2 Turn right onto T949 (Orme Rd.). Now you're riding another loop of wooded area with summer and year-round homes.
- ■ 15.6 Turn left onto T719. At mile 17.3 cross Rte. 30, using extreme caution both here and on the downhill that follows.

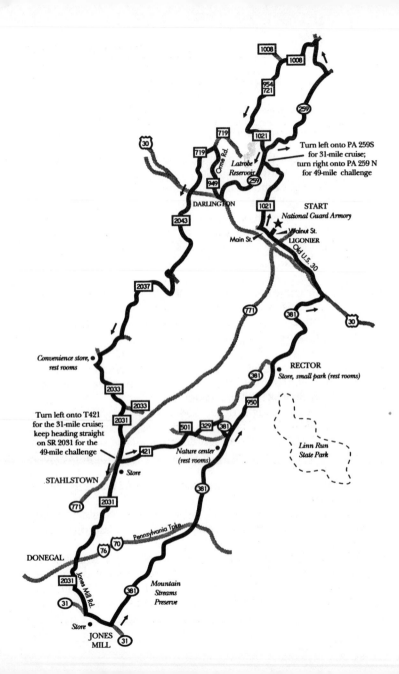

Turn left onto PA 259S
for 31-mile cruise;
turn right onto PA 259 N
for 49-mile challenge

START
National Guard Armory

Walnut St.
LIGONIER
Main St.

Latrobe
Reservoir

DARLINGTON

Convenience store,
rest rooms

RECTOR
Store, small park (rest rooms)

Turn left onto T421
for the 31-mile cruise;
keep heading straight
on SR 2031 for the
49-mile challenge

*Nature center
(rest rooms)*

*Linn Run
State Park*

STAHLSTOWN

Store

Pennsylvania Tpke.

DONEGAL

*Mountain
Streams
Preserve*

Store

JONES
MILL

- 17.6 Turn left onto SR2043 in Darlington, after crossing the bridge. Now you can let 'er rip along a stretch of fast, flat riding.
- 20.2 Turn right onto SR2037, to continue the flat run.
- 23.2 Bear right at the Y intersection to stay on SR2037.
- 24.0 Turn left at the T intersection onto SR2033. The convenience store at this intersection, which has public rest rooms, makes a good rest stop for both rides (14.8 miles into the 31-mile ride), because soon you'll be facing some climbs.
- 26.1 Continue straight onto SR2031 where SR2033 heads left.
- 27.5 Turn right at the stop sign onto PA711. Shortly the 49- and 31-mile rides split again.

For the 31-mile cruise, in 0.3 mile turn left onto unmarked T421. This corresponds to mile 18.6 of the 31-mile cruise. At mile 21.0 of the 31-mile cruise, turn right at the T intersection onto the unmarked T501. At mile 21.3 turn left onto the unmarked T329. At mile 22.1 turn right at the stop sign onto PA381. At mile 22.6 turn left onto T950 at the bottom of the hill. Here is where you rejoin the 49-mile challenge. Resume following the directions below from mile 40.7.

For the 49-mile challenge pass the left turn taken by the 31-mile cruise and pedal 0.2 mile farther.

- 28.0 Bear left onto the continuation of SR2031 (unmarked) at the gas station. Continue straight past the Brass Duck restaurant in Stahlstown. At about mile 29.0 is a great view to your left, sweeping down to the Pennsylvania Tpke. (I–76) several hundred feet below and then up again to the mountains in the distance.
- 31.0 Turn left at the T intersection to stay on SR2031 (Jones Mill Rd.).
- 31.1 Bear right at the Y intersection to stay on SR2031, and cross over the Pennsylvania Tpke. (I–76/I–70). Test your brakes, for now you'll drop down some fast hills.
- 33.0 Turn left at the stop sign onto PA31. Stay single-file on this road because the traffic is fast. A corner store offers food, drink, and an excuse for a rest.
- 33.7 Turn left onto PA381N, and ride through the Mountain

Streams Preserve. This road has little traffic and is a slight uphill all the way to the Pennsylvania Tpke. After crossing over the turnpike, you're in for the best downhill plunge of the entire ride—speeds of up to 40 mph are possible. Braking is required on downhills, and always be alert for uneven road surface and gravel until the road flattens out. Soon after it flattens out, on your left there is a nature center with public rest rooms.

- 40.7 Continue straight onto T950, leaving PA381N. *Here the 31-mile cruise joins the route of the challenge.* This is another tree-lined, relatively flat road.
- 43.4 Turn right onto PA381N and ride into Rector. If you want more snacks and drinks, there is a store on the right at the entrance to Linn Run State Park. Rest rooms are in the small park to the left of the store. Continue past the beautiful scenery of the Rolling Rock horse farms.
- 46.4 Turn left to cross Rte. 30 and make an immediate right onto Old Rte. 30. Soon you'll reenter Ligonier.
- 48.1 Continue straight at the stop sign onto Main St. Now, you'll half-circle the gazebo in the center of town.
- 48.8 Turn right onto Walnut St. and 0.1 mile later you'll reach the starting point, the National Guard Armory on the right.

27

Paean to Petroleum Ramble

Oil Creek State Park—Titusville—Oil Creek State Park

Oil Creek State Park commemorates the booming oil industry that once filled the Oil Creek Valley. The Oil Creek Bike Trail, a 9.7-mile paved trail in Venango County, is built on an abandoned railroad grade. After beginning at the historic site of Petroleum Center, an oil-boom town of the late nineteenth century, the trail winds its way north through the scenic Oil Creek river valley to Drake Well Museum at Titusville, the site of the world's first commercial oil well.

With the discovery of rich oil fields here in northwestern Pennsylvania in 1863 (during the Civil War), this area was suddenly transformed into a lively town of 5,000 people. By 1870 there were theaters, hotels, stores, saloons, a whiskey mill, and an oil refinery. But as the oil boom waned, the town began to die as rapidly as it sprang up, and a fire in 1878 reduced it to ashes.

Today the park's wooded hills look almost as they did before the boom. It is difficult to believe that the valley once supported as many as 20,000 people, that its hillsides were covered with oil derricks as far as the eye could see, and that its air was filled with the raucous noise of pumps and trains and the acrid odors of oil and smoke.

Petroleum Center has a park office with trail maps and literature, as well as displays and programs on the history of the park and the region. The Egbert Farm Day Use Area, across from the park office, has picnic tables, a pavilion, rest rooms, and a playground; also, there is a parking lot for the cars of bike trail users. Opposite the lot are a concession stand and a center where you can rent a bicycle if you did not bring your own. Call (814) 676–5915 before your trip to confirm park office hours and to reserve a rental bike.

This ride is one of two contributed by Paul g. Wiegman, director of natural science and stewardship of the Western Pennsylvania Conservancy (the other is Ride 25).

The Basics

Start: Oil Creek State Park office parking lot at Petroleum Center. To get to the start, take Route 8 north of Pittsburgh to Oil City. At Oil City take the Route 8 bypass. After the bypass continue on Route 8 north across a large bridge over Oil Creek. Continue past oil refineries to another bridge over Oil Creek on the north side of Oil City. Look for an Oil Creek State Park sign and a right turn just beyond. Follow this road and the signs to the park office at Petroleum Center.

Length: 19.4 miles.

Terrain: Mostly flat. No automobile traffic.

Food: A snack bar and rest rooms at the start; services also at the Drake Well Park Museum and in Titusville.

Miles & Directions

Note: Because there are no turns off the trail on this trip, the narrative descriptions below are indications of the scenery you will enjoy at different mileposts.

■ 0.0 The bike trail begins beside the parking lot and is clearly marked. Swing right onto the trail and head into the cool valley. The trail heads upstream on the east side of Oil Creek, and a steep slope laced with hemlocks and tiny waterfalls immediately rises on the right. Watch for a fork in the trail where the bike path bears left and descends gently to a sharp left. At this sharp bend note the beaver pond on the right of the trail, with the

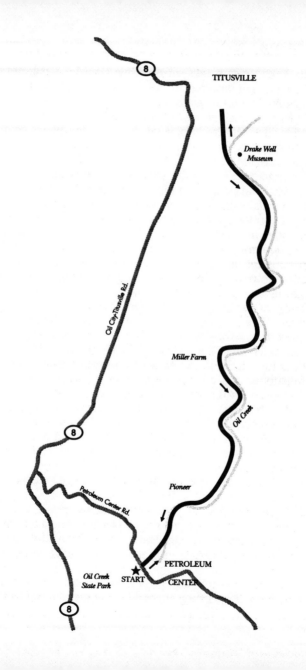

stark, bare tree trunks surrounding it reaching skyward. From here the trail descends to the very edge of Oil Creek and turns sharply right under an iron bridge.

■ Milepost 1.0 is followed by a brief rise that will bring you to a bridge over Oil Creek. Here you have a good vantage point from which to take in the view of the steep-walled valley, a small upstream island, fish and frogs in the clear waters below, and the active tour railroad that runs along the east side of the valley. (You can take a 23-mile round-trip ride on this Oil Creek & Titusville Railroad by making reservations at 814–827–2797.)

As you leave the bridge, you may notice rusting, abandoned oil pipes on the left—reminders, scattered all along the trail, of the booming oil industry that once thrived in the valley. A parking lot on the left marks Pioneer, the site of another oil-boom town of 2,000. The trail continues to follow Oil Creek upstream, now along its west bank.

■ Milepost 2.0 is passed just before you ride under some power lines. Note the handsome shelter where visitors can rest on rainy days. Now you are pedaling on a mile-long straightaway past milepost 3.0 through shady hemlock forest.

■ Near milepost 4.0 the trail passes through Shaffer Farm, which functioned as a major transportation center in the valley. The floodplain on the west side of the creek broadens once again, and white-barked sycamores stand along the opposite shore. In midsummer this section of the bike trail is lined with blackberries ripe for picking; in the fall, with witch hazel in bloom. In 0.5 mile a clearing on the left offers picnic tables and primitive pit toilets. If you're up for a strenuous hike, you can follow the yellow blazes and climb to the top of the ridge for a magnificent view of the Oil Creek Valley.

■ Milepost 5.0 is just after the location of historic Miller Farm, the terminus of the first successful oil pipeline, where oil was stored and transferred to rail cars. Shortly thereafter is a hiking trail upstream alongside Miller Run; the trail will bring you to a lovely waterfall.

For the next few miles, Oil Creek snakes through the picturesque valley, cutting alternately into the east and west banks of the creek. The occasional ripplings in the water create a pleasant background sound in the otherwise quiet valley. Groundwater emerges from the steeper slopes, forming small waterfalls along the trail.

Between mileposts 8.0 and 9.0, rusted remnants of the oil boom become more prominent as the trail nears Drake Well Museum. Drake Well marks the site where oil was struck on August 27, 1859, and both the oil industry and the oil boom in Oil Creek Gorge were born. The trail ends as the paved path bears right out of the forest and into sunshine and civilization.

To return, retrace the entire path back to Petroleum Center.

28

Hanover Horse Farms to Gettysburg Battlefield Century Classic

Hanover—Gettysburg—Rossville—Hanover

Although dubbed a classic, this route through Adams and York counties is actually a group of three rides that can be enjoyed by cyclists of almost any ability. As the terrain is flat to rolling farmland and the traffic mostly light, the 25-mile ramble is suitable even for novices early in the spring; the 50-mile cruise will delight stronger cyclists midseason; and the century classic will exercise the experts. Since the three rides overlap by a minimum of 20 miles, several cyclists of varying abilities can time their separation and reunion to spend some time riding together.

These three rides, devised by Connie and Clair Bentzel, were originally used by their club The Hanover Cyclers for its annual Labor Day Century. All three routes first take you through the Hanover Shoe Horse Farms, the largest standardbred nursery in the world, which has produced champion harness-race trotters and pacers since 1926. You'll pedal past a few of the thirty sprawling farms totaling 3,000 acres in Adams and York counties; the main farm is open for self-guided tours Monday through Saturday from 8:00 A.M. to 3:00 P.M. For information call (717) 637–8931.

The 50- and 100-mile routes then go on to circle Gettysburg, allowing you to visit the national military parks and steep yourself in the memorial to the bloodiest battle in American history. Time your visit for the last weekend in June and the first week in July, and you may take in the city's annual commemoration of the battle as well as the annual Civil War Collectors Show and the Civil War Book Fair. Call the Gettysburg Travel Council at (717) 334–6274 for information.

Both Hanover and Gettysburg have many places to stay overnight. Aside from the usual chain hotels and restaurants, the seven-room Beechmont bed-and-breakfast inn (800–553–7009 or 717–632–3013) in Hanover offers afternoon tea and a full gourmet breakfast with—among other luxuries—the option of being served breakfast in bed. Right on the Gettysburg battlefield is the Doubleday Inn (717–334–9119), which features a candlelight country breakfast.

Those preferring to camp under the stars also have choices. Two miles southeast of Hanover on Route 216 is the Codorus State Park (717–637–2816), with 3,320 acres of woodland and water offering boating, fishing, and hiking—and swimming in one of the nation's largest pools; the campgrounds are open from the second Friday in April to the third Sunday in October. Closer to Gettysburg is the Drummer Boy Campground at the junction of Routes 116 and 15; call (800) 336–3269 or (717) 334–3277 for information.

In this part of Pennsylvania, hardly any roads go straight for more than a few miles; thus, these directions have a fair number of turns. But be patient, for following them will allow you to explore some of Pennsylvania's most beautiful secondary roads. The 25- and 50-mile rides stay within Adams County; the century ride continues into York County.

The Basics

Start: McSherrystown, at the South Street Recreation Park. To get to the start from Rte. 30, head south on Rte. 194 and then turn right onto Rte. 116 into McSherrystown. Turn south off Rte. 116 at the McSherrystown Fire Company, go 1.5 blocks on South Street, and turn left into the park's hidden entrance. Here there are public parking and rest rooms.

Length: 25, 50, or 100 miles. The 100-mile extension is long and skinny, but there are several cutoffs that, at your discretion, could shorten it as well.

Terrain: Flat to rolling farm land. Traffic is generally light to very light.

Food: In McSherrystown there is a Hardee's about 6 blocks from the start at the intersection of Rte. 116 and Elm St. There are also choices around Gettysburg. But elsewhere the territory is so rural that choices are limited; plan to carry snacks and lunch.

Miles & Directions

Note: Follow directions carefully, as not every small street is shown on the map.

- 0.0 Turn left out of the park onto S. 3rd St., which becomes Mt. Pleasant Rd.
- 1.7 Cross over Rte. 194 (Hanover Pike) and head straight onto Narrow Dr.
- 2.4 At the three-way stop, turn right onto unmarked Lovers Dr.
- 3.2 Cross Rte. 194 and head straight on Race Horse Rd. Here the main barns of the Hanover Shoe Horse Farms are on your left; visitors are welcome.
- 5.2 Turn left at the T intersection onto Hostetter Rd.
- 6.6 Bear left at the Y intersection onto Hoover Rd.
- 7.7 Turn right at the T intersection onto the unmarked Sell's Station Rd.
- 7.9 At the stop sign, cross Littlestown Rd. and head straight onto Flatbush Rd.
- 8.6 Where Flatbush Rd. turns right, head straight onto Schoolhouse Rd.
- 9.3 Turn left at the T intersection onto Honda Rd.
- 9.4 Turn right onto White Hall Rd.
- 11.8 Turn left onto Two Taverns Rd. where Locust St. heads right.

For the 25-mile ramble turn right onto Locust St. instead. At mile 11.9 turn left onto Rte. 116 (Hanover Rd.). At mile 12.0 turn right onto N. Pine St., which becomes Granite Station Rd. At mile 14.3 turn right onto Low Dutch Rd. At mile 15.1 turn right onto Salem Church Rd. At mile 16.7 turn left onto Kilpatrick Rd. At mile 17.0 turn right onto Centennial Rd. Ride for 1.8 miles and then follow the directions from mile 91.5 to the end.

- 14.7 Turn left at the T intersection onto Rte. 97 (Baltimore Pike).
- 14.8 Turn right onto Hoffman Home Rd.
- 16.9 Turn right onto Orphanage Rd.
- 18.4 Turn right onto Furney Rd.
- 19.0 Cross Barlow–Two Taverns Rd. and continue straight onto White Church Rd.
- 20.9 Turn left onto Goulden Rd., which becomes Sachs Rd.
- 23.0 Turn right at the T intersection onto Rte. 134 (Taneytown Rd.).
- 23.1 Make the first left onto Wheatfield Rd. You have now entered the grounds of the Gettysburg Battlefield, through which you will be riding for the next 2.2 miles. At mile 24.3 cross Business Rte. 15 (Emmitsburg Rd.).
- 25.3 Turn right onto Black Horse Tavern Rd. On your left is the Eisenhower National Historic Site, where former President Dwight D. Eisenhower lived and farmed; for tickets call (717) 334–1124.
- 27.0 Turn right onto Rte. 116 (Fairfield Rd.).
- 27.1 Turn left onto Bream Hill Rd.
- 27.3 Turn left onto Herr's Ridge Rd. At mile 29.1 jog right to cross Rte. 30 (Chambersburg Rd.). Here on your right is the Eternal Light Peace Memorial.
- 30.1 Turn left onto the unmarked Mummasburg Rd.
- 31.0 Turn right onto Russell Tavern Rd.
- 33.2 Turn right onto Goldenville Rd. At mile 33.5 you'll cross Rte. 34 (Biglerville Rd.).
- 35.5 Turn right at the T intersection onto Rte. 394 (Shrivers Corner Rd.). At mile 36.6 you may wish to refresh yourself at the Distelfink Drive-Inn Restaurant (closed Mondays). At mile 36.7 cross Business Rte. 15 and then Through Rte. 15.

Old York Rd.

Carlisle Rd.

ROSSVILLE

74

Carroll St.

WELLSVILLE

Community St.

74

Main St.

Wellsville Rd.

Ridge Rd.

Ridge Rd.

Kralltown Rd.

Creek Rd.

Ridge Rd.

194

Red Rd.

Mount Rd.

Pordtown Rd.

Lake Meade Rd.

Bragglown Rd.

Latimore Valley Rd.

Oyster Church Rd.

94

Gun Club Rd.

Wierman's Mill Rd.

White Church Rd.

224

Van Cleve Rd.

Cashman Rd.

Tape Worm

15

224

Oxf

burg Rd.

Turn left here for
100-mile classic;
head straight for
50-mile cruise

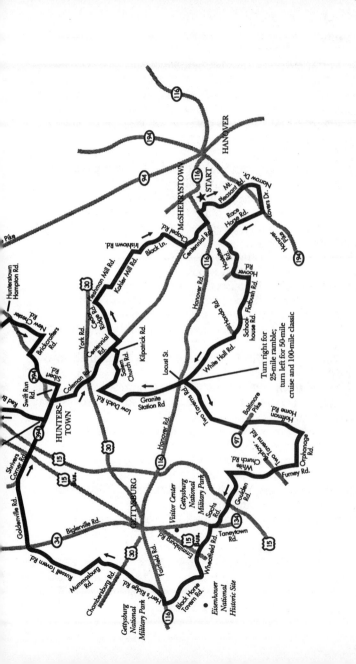

■ 38.4 In Hunterstown, turn left onto Red Bridge Rd.

For the 50-mile cruise do not turn left. Instead, bypass Red Bridge Rd. to keep heading straight on Rte. 394 (now called Hunterstown-Hampton Rd.). At mile 39.0 turn right onto Coleman Rd. Ride for 1.7 miles and then follow the directions from mile 89.7 to the end.

■ 42.3 Turn left onto Oxford Rd. At mile 43.7, after crossing Rte. 234, keep heading straight onto White Church Rd.
■ 45.5 Turn right onto the unmarked Wierman's Mill Rd.
■ 46.0 Turn left onto Gun Club Rd. At mile 48.0, after crossing Rte. 94 (Carlisle Pike), keep heading straight onto Quaker Church Rd.
■ 49.9 Turn left onto Latimore Valley Rd.
■ 52.4 Turn right onto Braggtown Rd.
■ 54.8 At the five-road intersection, bear slightly left onto the unmarked Pondtown Rd. Soon you will enter York County.
■ 55.6 After crossing Rte. 194, keep heading straight on Ridge Rd. At mile 57.7 you'll cross Kralltown Rd.; at mile 59.4 you'll cross Rte. 74.
■ 62.4 Turn right at the T intersection onto the unmarked Old York Rd.
■ 63.8 In the town of Rossville, turn right onto Rte. 74 (Carlisle Rd.). Across the intersection is a small store. About 3 miles away in Pinchot Park are campgrounds.
■ 65.1 In the town of Wellsville turn right onto Carroll St. at the small grocery store.
■ 65.3 Turn left onto Community St.
■ 65.5 Turn left onto Rte. 74 (Main St.).
■ 65.6 Turn right onto York St., which becomes Wellsville Rd.
■ 68.6 Turn right onto Kralltown Rd.
■ 69.1 Mark a sharp left onto Creek Rd., which eventually bends right.
■ 71.5 Turn left onto Rte. 194.
■ 71.9 Turn right onto Red Mount Rd. Now you have reentered Adams County. Red Mount Rd. changes its name four times in the next 10 miles. At mile 72.9, after crossing Braggtown Rd. to

your right and Stoney Point Rd. to your left, keep heading straight onto Lake Meade Rd. At mile 76.7 you'll cross Rte. 94 (Carlisle Pike). At mile 78.4, after crossing Rte. 234, keep heading straight on Van Cleve Rd. In 0.2 mile after crossing Cashman Rd., keep heading directly on Tape Worm Rd., which, like its namesake, writhes through many turns.

- 81.5 Turn right at the T intersection onto Plum Run Rd.
- 81.7 Turn left at the T intersection onto Oxford Rd.
- 82.3 Turn right onto Rte. 394 (Hunterstown-Hampton Rd.).
- 82.6 Turn left onto New Chester Rd.
- 83.8 Turn right onto Brickcrafters Rd.
- 84.5 Turn left onto Rte. 394 (Hunterstown-Hampton Rd.).
- 85.3 Turn left onto Sibert Rd.
- 86.6 Turn right at the T intersection onto Swift Run Rd.
- 88.0 Turn left onto Coleman Rd. *This is where the 50-mile cruise rejoins the century classic.*
- 89.7 Turn right onto Rte. 30 (York Rd.) and immediately turn left onto Centennial Rd. *This is where the 25-mile ramble rejoins the century classic.*
- 91.5 Turn left onto Cedar Ridge Rd.
- 93.2 Turn right onto Fleshman Mill Rd. At mile 93.7 cross Bon Ox Rd.
- 94.2 Turn left to stay on Fleshman Mill Rd. At mile 94.4 head straight onto Kohler Mill Rd. At mile 94.9 cross Poplar Rd. At mile 95.3 keep heading straight onto Irishtown Rd. At mile 96.1 keep heading straight onto Black Ln.; do not follow Irishtown Rd. as it turns right.
- 97.1 Turn right onto Chapel Rd.
- 98.0 Turn left at the T intersection onto Centennial Rd.
- 99.2 Turn left at the T intersection onto Rte. 116 (Hanover Rd.).
- 99.6 Turn right onto Academy St.
- 99.7 Turn left onto South St.
- 99.9 Turn right onto 3rd St.
- 100.0 Turn left into the South Street Recreation Park. *Congratulations!*

29

Mount Gretna–Cornwall Cruise

Annville—Mount Gretna—Cornwall—Annville

The area south of Lebanon around Cornwall and Cornwall Iron Furnace includes some of the most beautiful and historic parts of Pennsylvania Dutch country. On this ride—contributed by the Lebanon Valley Tourist and Visitors Bureau—you'll pass handsome old stone farm buildings still in use and ride along a part of the Furnace Hills ridge, affording you memorable vistas of rural Lebanon County. Although much of the terrain is gently rolling, the segment through Rexmont to the Lebanon Reservoir on Rexmont Road has a few short grades steeper than 10 percent that may prove too arduous for inexperienced cyclists.

The first part of this ride out of Annville is through level cornfields and dairy farms. Then you'll shift into lower gears as you ascend Mount Pleasant. The climb affords glimpses of the Lebanon Valley below through the cool forests of the low mountain. You'll then pedal through Colebrook and more beautiful forest to Mount Gretna, where you can gaze at the view of Conewago Lake on your left. As a special treat you'll pass on your right the renowned Jigger Shop Ice Cream Parlor, which is open during the summer.

The effort at the climb now pays off with an easy descent to historic Cornwall, a restored miner's village reminiscent of southwest England. The village was built around iron mining and manufacturing. The open-pit mine called Cornwall Banks, the greatest iron-ore deposit east of Lake Superior, was once the greatest source of iron in the eastern United States; now it is filled in with blue water

---

that beautifully reflects the golds and reds of fall foliage. The village's heart was the Cornwall Iron Furnace, which fired and bellowed day and night from 1742 to 1883. During peacetime it produced pig iron, household goods, and stoves; during the revolutionary war it supplied George Washington's army with cannon, shot, and shells.

Today the furnace is the only completely intact nineteenth-century charcoal–iron-making complex left in the country. Pay the nominal admission fee to walk in and gaze at the massive stone furnace and its steam-powered air-blast machinery (open Tuesday through Saturday 9:00 A.M. to 5:00 P.M. and Sunday noon to 5:00 P.M. Call 717–272–9711). Slake your thirst at the Minersvillage Store while you marvel at the statue of a miner that was sculpted with a chainsaw!

The final stretch of the ride brings you out of the hills and back into Pennsylvania's rich farmland. Return to Annville, where each December the Friends of Old Annville conduct candlelight tours through the historic town.

Note on automobiles: Traffic can be moderately heavy around Cornwall Iron Furnace during the summer when the facility is open to the public. On a Monday when it is closed, however, the tourists seem to desert the spot; you will miss seeing the furnace and exhibits, but as compensation the roads are delightfully quiet and car-free.

The Basics

Start: The Annville-Cleona High School on Rte. 934, just south of Annville; park in the visitor spaces. To get to the start, take exit 29 off I–81 and drive 7 miles south on Rte. 934; after passing through the heart of Annville, turn left into the high school. Parking is also available at Cornwall Center, should you wish to start from there instead.

Length: 28 miles.

Terrain: Gently rolling, with some steep climbs. Traffic is light along most of the route, although there are brief sections of riding along the wide shoulders of busier roads. Be especially cautious about cars while entering Cornwall Center and the village of Rexmont on summer days when Cornwall Iron Furnace is open.

Food: Widely available at Annville if you ride about 0.75 mile north of the start; available in Cornwall Center and Rexmont and, between April and October, at Mount Gretna.

Miles & Directions

- 0.0 Exit Annville-Cleona High School following the one-way signs, and turn right onto the painted shoulder of Rte. 934N.
- 0.1 Turn left onto Reigerts Ln. You'll pass residences on your right, but the tone of the entire ride is set by the cornfields on your left.
- 0.9 Turn left at the T intersection onto the unmarked Mt. Pleasant Rd., a delightful, narrow rural lane that curves past dairy farms.
- 3.8 Turn right at the T intersection onto the unmarked Rte. 322W. The traffic is moderately heavy, but the shoulder is wide (although the pavement is rough). Watch for cars for the next 0.4 mile.
- 4.2 Make the first left to continue on Mt. Pleasant Rd. at the big blue sign for Thousand Trails. Soon you'll begin climbing, and then you'll be coasting through forest.
- 6.7 Turn right at the T intersection onto the unmarked Rte. 241.
- 7.0 Follow the main road as it bears left and joins Rte. 117S.
- 7.8 Turn left to continue on Rte. 117S (Mt. Gretna Rd.). At mile 10.1 look left for a view of Conewago Lake. At mile 10.4 is the Jigger Shop Ice Cream Parlor on your right; at mile 10.7 you can stop for refreshments at the Mt. Gretna store or pizza parlor on your left. Here the shoulder is wide but the pavement is rough.
- 13.1 After passing under the overpass for Rte. 322, keep heading straight onto the unmarked Ironmaster Rd. (where the sign says END RTE. 117).

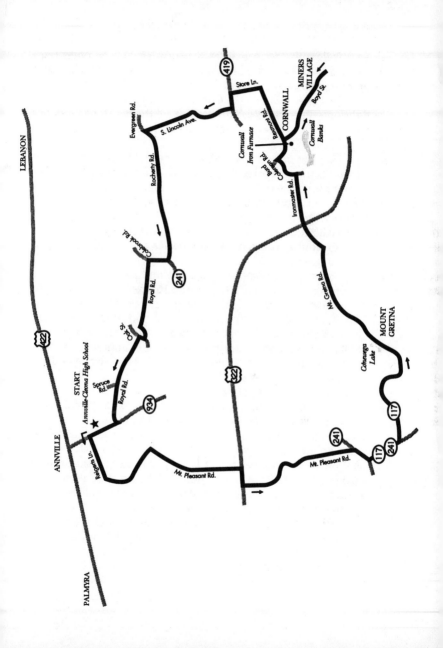

- 14.0 Follow the main road as it bends left and becomes Burd Coleman Rd. Now you're riding through a small development of multifamily stone houses.
- 14.4 Just after you pass the Cornwall Garage on your right, turn right onto Rexmont Rd. At mile 15.0 are the red stone buildings of the Cornwall Iron Furnace museum, where you can begin to explore the exhibit.
- 15.1 Past the museum bear right at the yield sign and the stop sign onto the unmarked Boyd St. Pass the Cornwall Children's Center on your left. In less than 0.25 mile, gaze to the right to the lake of Cornwall Banks. At mile 15.4 you'll enter the miner's village with its stone buildings. At mile 15.7 you'll reach the Minersvillage Store and its chainsaw-carved statue. When you're done exploring, *turn around and leave the miner's village the same way you entered.*
- 16.3 Turn right at the T intersection and make an immediate right to stay on Rexmont Rd. At mile 16.7 keep heading straight at the yield sign, enjoying the view of the valley to your left.
- 17.5 Turn left at the brick firehouse and white clapboard church onto Store Ln. Now you'll begin a gentle downhill.
- 18.0 At the T intersection turn left onto the unmarked Rte. 419. *Caution* for the next 0.25 mile—the traffic is moderate and the shoulder is below road level!
- 18.3 Make the first right onto S. Lincoln Ave.
- 18.7 Bear right at the T intersection to stay on S. Lincoln Ave. Be careful crossing the railroad tracks in 0.5 mile.
- 20.1 Turn left at the stop sign onto the moderately busy Evergreen Rd., which immediately becomes Rocherty Rd. The shoulder is wide but the pavement is rough. Keep heading straight through the traffic lights at miles 20.8 and 21.1 to stay on Rocherty Rd. After the second light the traffic becomes lighter and the shoulder narrower but smoother.
- 22.7 Turn right at the T intersection onto Rte. 241 (here called Colebrook Rd.), which is moderately busy but has a wide shoulder.
- 23.1 Turn left onto Royal Rd.

- **24.6** Turn right at the stop sign onto Oak St., following the sign TO ROYAL RD.
- **25.7** Turn left onto the continuation of Royal Rd. Pass the golf course on your right. At mile 26.7 keep heading straight through the stop sign to stay on Royal Rd. (where Spruce Rd. heads right).
- **27.6** Turn right at the T intersection onto Rte. 934N, another road that is fairly busy but has a wide shoulder.
- **28.1** Turn right into the parking lot of the Annville-Cleona High School.

30

Pennsylvania Dutch Sampler Cruise

Lampeter—Iva—Intercourse
Weavertown—Strasburg—Lampeter

On this ride it is likely that you will want to spend as much time off the bike as on, for you will be pedaling through some of the most beautiful Amish farmland in Lancaster County, as well as near or through two of Pennsylvania's several hundred still-standing covered bridges.

The terrain varies from gently rolling in the northern half of the ride to longer and steeper hills south of Rte. 741. Because farm country is so open and there is little shade, riding could be hot on very warm summer days. Road surfaces are good, but there are occasional ruts left by the wheels of Amish buggies, pockmarks from horses' hooves, and "road apples" deposited by the horses. Although the secondary roads are narrow—usually less than 20 feet wide—the traffic is light.

Film buffs may appreciate the fact that near the beginning of the ride, the route passes the farm where much of the 1985 movie *Witness* (about an Amish family drawn into a murder case) was made; next the route goes through the town of Intercourse, where the fight scene was filmed. But anyone will enjoy the fact that this single bicycle trip will take the rider through most of what is famous about the Pennsylvania Dutch country, notes its contributor, William N. Hoffman of the Lancaster Bicycle Club.

Give yourself plenty of time to stop and explore, for in the area you will have opportunities for taking tours of the working Amish Farm and House (717–394–6185), wandering through the Amish Village (717–687–8511), and watching the animated re-creation of a class at the Weavertown One-Room Schoolhouse (717–768–3976). For more information about what to see in the area, call the Intercourse Tourist Information Center at (717) 768–3882 or the People's Place interpretive center at (717) 768–7171 (both of which you will pass on this route).

You can also eat your way through this tour, tasting the best of Pennsylvania Dutch smoked meats or shoofly pie at the Bird-in-Hand Farmers Market (717–393–9674) or other restaurants and shops along the way. Should you wish to stay overnight, there are three campgrounds right in the thick of things: the Beacon Camping Lodge in Intercourse (717–768–8775) right on the route, Flory's Cottages and Campground in Ronks (717–687–6670), and Mill Bridge Village and Campground in Strasburg (717–687–8183). Moreover, there are numerous bed-and-breakfast inns in the area, as well as a few "farm vacation homes"—working farms licensed by the state to have overnight guests, who may help with the farm chores.

The Basics

Start: Lampeter, at the Lampeter-Strasburg High School. To get to the start, take Rte. 222S from Lancaster; turn left onto Rte. 741 (Village Rd.) into Lampeter; the high school is at the corner of Book Rd. and Rte. 741 (Village Rd.), 0.5 mile east of the traffic light in Lampeter. Park in the school parking lot on weekends. (This school is a starting point for several of the rides of the Lancaster Bicycle Club.)

Length: 37 miles.

Terrain: Rolling to hilly. Traffic is light except in the village of Intercourse and while crossing Rtes. 30, 340, and 741.

Food: A few farm stands with seasonal vegetables and baked goods; Amish restaurants in Intercourse and Strasburg. Take water, but save your appetite for the goodies en route.

Miles & Directions

Note: Follow directions carefully, as not every small street is shown on the map.

- **0.0** Turn right out of the school parking lot onto Book Rd.
- **0.2** Turn right at the T intersection onto Village Rd., and then immediately turn left onto Bridge Rd.
- **1.1** Turn right at the T intersection onto the unmarked Penn Grant Rd. (Before turning at this T intersection, look left to see the covered bridge through which you will ride at the end of the route.)
- **1.3** Turn left onto Pequea Ln.
- **2.4** Turn left at the T intersection onto the unmarked Lime Valley Rd. (If you were to turn right instead, in 0.2 mile you would see the second covered bridge near this route.)
- **2.8** Turn right onto Walnut Run Rd.
- **3.6** Turn left onto Deiter Rd.
- **5.2** Turn right onto the unmarked Bunker Hill Rd.
- **5.9** Turn right to stay on Bunker Hill Rd. At mile 6.5 on your right—although not visible from the road—are the farmhouse and barn filmed in the movie *Witness.*
- **6.7** Turn left onto Sandstone Rd.
- **7.5** Turn left at the T intersection onto Old Rd.
- **7.8** Turn left onto Winter Hill Rd.
- **8.9** Turn left onto Stively Rd.
- **9.1** Turn right to continue on Winter Hill Rd.
- **9.7** Head straight onto Weaver Rd. (which joins from the left).
- **10.9** After crossing May Post Office Rd., head straight onto Lantz Rd.
- **11.1** Turn left at the T intersection onto Strubel Rd.
- **11.3** Turn right onto the unmarked Girvin Rd.
- **12.3** Turn left onto the unmarked Summit Hill Rd.
- **12.5** Turn left at the T intersection onto Iva Rd.
- **12.9** Turn right at the T intersection onto Paradise Ln.
- **13.3** Head straight across the busy Rte. 896 (Georgetown Rd.) to stay on Paradise Ln. *Caution!* This intersection has poor visibil-

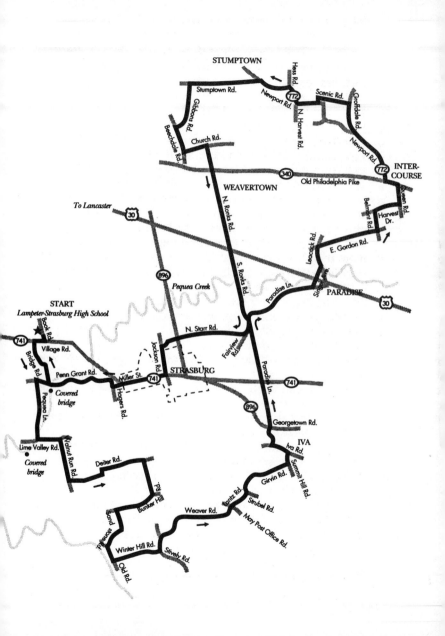

ity. (If you were to turn left at the next intersection—Rte. 741—you could visit the Railroad Museum of Pennsylvania.)

- 15.4 Bear right at the Y intersection to stay on Paradise Ln.
- 16.9 Turn left onto Singer Ave. Cross busy Rte. 30.
- 17.2 Turn left onto Leacock Rd.
- 17.8 Turn right onto Vigilant St.
- 17.9 Turn left at the T intersection onto E. Gordon Rd.
- 19.0 Turn left at the T intersection onto Belmont Rd.
- 19.4 Turn right at the T intersection onto Harvest Dr.
- 19.9 Turn left at the T intersection onto Queen Rd.
- 20.3 Turn left at the T intersection onto Rte. 772 (Newport Rd.) and then make an immediate left onto Rte. 340 (Old Philadelphia Pike). Here are the Intercourse Tourist Information Center and the People's Place. If you're hungry now that you're a bit more than halfway through the ride, in 500 feet you can turn right for a stop at the Kitchen Kettle Shops. But forgo dessert for a little later in the route.
- 20.7 Turn right onto Rte. 772 (Newport Rd.). Soon you'll pass the Beacon Camping Lodge on your right.
- 21.7 Turn right onto Groffdale Rd.
- 22.3 Turn left onto Scenic Rd.
- 23.0 Turn right at the T intersection onto Rte. 772 (Newport Rd.).
- 23.4 Turn right at N. Harvest Dr. to stay on Rte. 772 (Newport Rd.).
- 23.8 Turn left at Hess Rd. to stay on Rte. 772 (Newport Rd.).
- 24.4 Turn left onto Stumptown Rd.
- 25.8 Turn left onto Gibbons Rd. At mile 26.2 you can now pick up dessert at the Amish Bake Shop on your right.
- 26.7 Turn left at the T intersection onto Beechdale Rd.
- 27.2 Turn left onto Church Rd.
- 27.7 Turn right onto N. Ronks Rd. Cross Rte. 340 (Old Philadelphia Pike). At that intersection you are in Weavertown; the one-room schoolhouse is to your left. After crossing Rte. 30, keep heading straight onto S. Ronks Rd.
- 31.1 Turn right onto Fairview Rd.
- 31.3 Bear right to stay on Fairview Rd.

- 31.4 Turn right onto N. Starr Rd.
- 33.1 Turn left onto Jackson Rd.
- 33.7 Turn right onto W. Main St. and immediately bear left at the Y intersection onto Rte. 741 (Miller St.) through downtown Strasburg. At mile 34.6 keep heading straight where Rte. 741 heads right.
- 34.8 Turn right at the T intersection onto Hagers Rd.
- 35.0 Turn left at the cemetery onto Penn Grant Rd.
- 36.2 Turn right onto Bridge Rd. and pass through the covered bridge over Pequea Creek.
- 37.1 Turn right at the T intersection onto Village Rd. and then left onto Book Rd. Turn left into the parking lot of the Lampeter-Strasburg High School.

31

Daniel Boone Homestead Challenge

Berks County, although barely an hour from Philadelphia, is overwhelmingly rural. Undoubtedly, that is due to the influence of the German immigrants who settled the area in the late 1600s and became known as the Pennsylvania Dutch. On many of these country roads, the traffic is light, and it is not uncommon to see Mennonites driving horse-drawn carriages, as they have for more than a century. In late June and early July, tiger lilies are in bloom, adding a bright splash of orange to the landscape.

You will pedal through rolling farmland dotted with covered bridges and grazing sheep, interspersed with stone barns and houses dating back two centuries. In fact, one of this ride's charms is the way a road may suddenly narrow and then wind and squeeze between the buildings of a farm. The lovely valleys are separated by wooded hills, some of which will challenge the most seasoned cyclist. And throughout the ride keep your ears open for the musical splashing of water in stony creek beds.

Time your visit for Independence Day, and near the start you can listen to some of the nation's best folk and country-and-western singers at the annual Kutztown Folk Festival. And any Saturday in Kutztown, take a moment to stroll through Reninger's Antique Market to survey the offerings of the area's largest collection of antiques dealers.

The full 54.5-mile challenge starts from the campus of the university at Kutztown (with the *u* pronounced as a short "oo," as in *cook* or *shook*). Kutztown University was the site of the 1993 League of American Wheelmen rally, hosted by the Lehigh Wheelmen Association, Inc. This ride, devised for the rally, is based on a cue sheet designed and contributed by Mark Scholefield of Birdsboro. You may still see the arrows painted on the road for the rally; if so, you'll be following the orange ones marked *67*.

The ride can be shortened to a 34.5-mile cruise by starting south of Kutztown in Oley, a town listed on the National Register of Historic Places for having the largest concentration of stone architecture in the country.

Take your camera, as both rides have a special treat: They take you through two 150-year-old covered bridges whose main structures are supported by curved wooden beams—a method known as the Burr Arch Construction, named after Theodore Burr, a renowned nineteenth-century designer of covered bridges.

The Daniel Boone Homestead, settled in 1730, is the birthplace and boyhood home of Daniel Boone, one of America's best-known pioneers. For a modest admission fee, you can learn about the saga of the region's settlers; you can also refill your water bottles at the public rest rooms in the visitor center. The homestead is open Tuesday through Saturday from 9:00 A.M to 5:00 P.M. and Sunday from noon to 5:00 P.M.; it is closed Mondays and all but summer holidays. For more information call (215) 582–4900.

The Basics

Start: Kutztown, at Kutztown University. To get to the start from I–78, take exit 12 onto Rte. 737S directly into the heart of Kutztown. Turn right onto Main St. and drive straight to the entrance of the university. Turn right onto College Blvd. and immediately left into the Student Union parking lot.

The alternate start is at King's Market at the intersection of Friedensberg Rd. and Memorial Hwy. in Oley. Please park at the far end of the lot, which is covered by gravel. To get to this starting place, continue south from Kutztown by following the directions below for the first 14.5 miles, which follow the most direct route.

Length: 34.5 or 54.4 miles.

Terrain: Rolling to moderately hilly. Traffic is generally moderately light to very light, except in Kutztown, in Oley, and at the crossings of major highways.

Food: Plenty of options in Kutztown and Oley; a few convenience stores and restaurants elsewhere along the route. But there is a 20-mile stretch with no food services at all; carry snacks, water, and tools.

Miles & Directions

Note: Follow directions carefully, as not every small street is shown on the map.

The directions below start from the Student Union parking lot at Kutztown University. If you are starting instead from King's Market at Oley, turn left out of King's onto Friedensberg Rd.; at mile 0.2 turn right at the T intersection onto Main St.; at mile 0.6 turn left onto DeTurk Rd., and then continue the directions below at mile 14.5.

- ■ 0.0 Turn right out of the Kutztown Student Union parking lot onto College Blvd.
- ■ 0.1 Head straight through the traffic light onto Normal Ave., passing the university's main entrance. Normal Ave. is a gentle downhill that will take you through four stop signs and past the Kutztown Elementary School.
- ■ 1.2 After crossing over the railroad tracks, keep heading straight onto Kohler Rd. Now just follow this road's double yellow line through all its ninety-degree turns until you encounter the first stop sign.
- ■ 4.8 Turn right at the stop sign onto Old Bowers Rd.
- ■ 5.2 Turn left at the T intersection onto Bowers Rd. at the Bowers Hotel. At mile 5.4 continue straight at the stop sign to stay on Bowers Rd.
- ■ 6.6 Turn left at the stop sign at the end onto the unmarked Lyons Rd.
- ■ 7.0 Turn right onto Forgedale Rd., following the sign to Price-

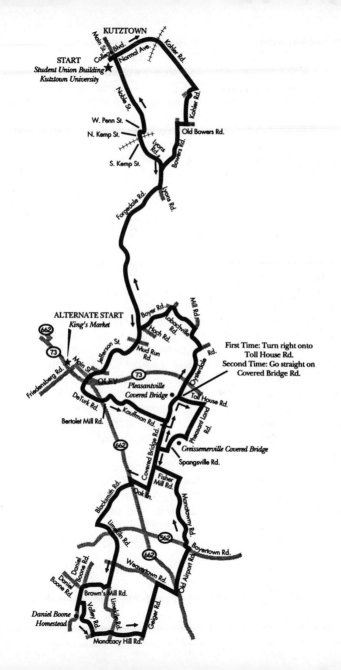

town. At mile 8.9 head straight at the stop sign to stay on Forgedale Rd.; Boyer's Market is a convenience store at this intersection. At mile 10.9 continue straight at the stop sign to stay on Forgedale Rd.; at mile 11.3 bear left to stay on Forgedale Rd., which eventually becomes Hoch Rd.

■ 11.8 Turn right onto Jefferson St.

■ 12.6 Turn right at the T intersection onto Mud Run Rd., and then make an immediate left to continue on Jefferson St. Soon you will enter Oley.

■ 14.5 Turn left at the T intersection onto Main St. in Oley, and then make an immediate right onto DeTurk Rd. *The 34.5-mile cruise joins the main 54.4-mile ride at this point.* At mile 14.6 continue straight at the stop sign to stay on DeTurk Rd. (At this intersection with Rte. 662, there are public rest rooms, a convenience store, water, and a restaurant—your last chance to get food directly on this route for the next 20 miles. Stock up!)

■ 15.1 Turn right at the T intersection onto busy Rte. 662, and then make an immediate left onto Bertolet Mill Rd.

■ 15.8 Turn right at the T intersection onto Kauffman Rd.

■ 17.2 Turn left at the T intersection onto Covered Bridge Rd. Get your camera ready, for the road delivers on the promise of its name. At mile 18.0 walk your bike through Pleasantville Covered Bridge, rebuilt in 1856. (Although now blocked to automobile traffic, it is open to pedestrians and bicycles; *Walk* your bike through the bridge, as the wooden surface is treacherous.)

■ 18.0 Immediately after the bridge turn right onto Toll House Rd.

■ 18.8 Turn right at the stop sign onto the unmarked Pheasant Land Rd. (where Tollhouse Rd. continues straight).

■ 20.7 Turn right onto Spangsville Rd. Cock your camera again, for coming up at mile 21.0 is Greissemersville Covered Bridge, a striking red-painted bridge with a double Burr arch and an entrance graced by a large painted hex sign.

■ 21.2 Bear left to stay on the curvy Spangsville Rd. (where Church Rd. heads right).

■ 21.9 Turn left at the T intersection onto the unmarked Covered Bridge Rd.

■ 23.0 Turn right after the stone farmhouse onto Oak Ln.; watch carefully for this turn, as it is hidden by trees.

- 23.6 Turn left at the T intersection onto the busy Rte. 662, and then immediately turn right onto Blacksmith Rd.

- 25.3 Turn left at the T intersection onto the unmarked Limekiln Rd. At mile 25.8 continue straight at the next two stop signs to stay on Limekiln Rd.

- 27.4 Turn right onto Brown's Mill Rd.

- 28.2 Turn left at the T intersection onto Daniel Boone Rd. At mile 28.3 keep heading *straight* on the main Daniel Boone Rd. where a smaller Daniel Boone Rd. heads right (yes, there is indeed a signpost showing the intersection of Daniel Boone Rd. and Daniel Boone Rd.). At mile 29.1 on the right is the entrance to the Daniel Boone Homestead. After your visit turn left out of the homestead to retrace 0.5 mile back along Daniel Boone Rd.

- 29.7 Turn right onto Valley Rd.

- 30.9 Turn left at the T intersection onto Monocacy Hill Rd.

- 31.4 Turn left onto Limekiln Rd. and make an immediate right to stay on Monocacy Hill Rd. At mile 31.8 begin climbing into the forest of Monocacy Hill.

- 32.4 Turn left at the T intersection onto Geiger Rd. Now you're at the crest and will begin descending.

- 33.9 Turn right at the T intersection onto Weavertown Rd.

- 34.6 Turn left onto Old Airport Rd. In 0.1 mile continue straight at the traffic light to stay on Old Airport Rd. At this intersection is a convenience store, the first food stop in 20 miles.

- 36.0 Turn left at the T intersection onto Rte. 562W (Boyertown Rd.), and then make the first right onto the unmarked Manatawny Rd.

- 36.6 Bear left at the Y intersection to stay on Manatawny Rd., keeping the river on your left.

- 38.2 Turn left onto Fisher Mill Rd. After crossing a bridge you will soon be pedaling through flat farm fields.

- 38.9 Turn right at the T intersection onto Covered Bridge Rd. and once again walk your bicycle through Pleasantville Covered Bridge (mile 41.1).

- 41.5 Head straight at the traffic light across Rte. 73 onto Oysterdale Rd.

- 42.3 Bear right at the Y intersection to stay on Oysterdale Rd.
- 42.6 Make the first left onto the unmarked Lobachville Rd. and begin climbing. At mile 43.4 follow the main road as it bends left to stay on Lobachville Rd. (where Mill Rd. continues straight). At mile 43.7 continue straight through the stop sign to stay on Lobachville Rd.
- 44.3 Turn left onto Boyer Rd. At mile 45.0 continue straight through the stop sign (Bortz Rd.) to stay on Boyer Rd.
- 45.1 Turn right at the T intersection onto Hoch Rd., which in 0.25 mile becomes Forgedale Rd.

To end the 34.5-mile cruise, turn left onto Hoch Rd. instead. In 0.3 mile make the first right onto Jefferson St. In another 0.6 mile make a right onto Mud Run Rd. and then an immediate left to continue on Jefferson St. In 1.9 mile turn right at the T intersection onto Oley's Main St. In 0.4 mile turn left at the stop sign onto Friedensberg Rd. In 0.2 mile turn right into the parking lot of King's Market.

- 49.7 Turn left at the T intersection onto Lyons Rd.
- 51.0 Go straight at the stop sign (following the sign KUTZTOWN 3) onto the unmarked S. Kemp St., which becomes N. Kemp St. after you cross the railroad tracks. Follow the road as it bends right and becomes W. Penn St.
- 51.4 Turn left at the stop sign (following the sign KUTZTOWN 3) onto the unmarked Noble St.
- 53.9 Turn left at the stop sign onto Normal Ave.
- 54.3 Continue straight through the traffic light onto College Blvd., passing the main entrance to Kutztown University.
- 54.4 Turn left into the Student Union parking lot.

32

Hopewell Furnace Classic

Kutztown—Oley—Birdsboro—French Creek State Park
Hopewell Furnace National Historic Site
Stowe—Earlville—Kutztown

Lightly traveled, tree-lined country roads winding between corn-fields, horse corrals, and barns painted with hex signs are the main attraction of this lovely meander through the rolling farmland and forested hills in Berks County. Several of the roads are positively rollercoaster rides, swooping downhill past farms selling corn or apples and cider (depending on the time of year).

If you are an American history buff, you should particularly enjoy this ride, for a bit more than halfway through the route you can stop at Hopewell Furnace National Historic Site (215–582–8773), an iron-making village that cast cannon and shot for the revolutionary war and then reached its peak making everything from kettles to machinery during the Industrial Revolution. You can wander around the reconstructed buildings and gaze at the restored anthracite furnace that blew day and night from 1771 to 1883. Stop at the visitor center not only to browse through its excellent selection of books on early iron making but also to refill your water bottle at the public rest rooms and—as a bonus in autumn—to get a permit to pick your own apples at orchards near the site.

For those desiring fewer miles in a day, the 81-mile classic can be broken neatly in half into two cruises by camping overnight in one of the 310 sites at French Creek State Park. The route takes you through the campground, which is midway through the route (and 3 miles before Hopewell Furnace). French Creek also offers swimming in its three lakes and 32 miles of hiking trails; for information and reservations call (215) 582–1514.

Alternatively, this classic can be shortened to a 59-mile challenge by starting south of Kutztown in Oley, a town noted for having the largest concentration of stone architecture in the country. By the way, the first 16 and last 18 miles of the classic overlap those of Ride 31; both rides were designed by Mark Scholefield of Birdsboro for the 1993 League of American Wheelmen (LAW) rally, which was hosted by the Lehigh Wheelmen Association, Inc., on the campus of Kutztown University.

One special note: Directions are given for two alternative routes out of Birdsboro to French Creek State Park. The main route takes you over a hill by Cocalico (pronounced "co-CAL-i-co") Road. But Mark Scholefield's original cue sheet for the 1993 LAW rally included an option along a 2-mile stretch of abandoned road outside of Birdsboro that was partly washed out by flooding in the early 1980s and has been blocked off to cars ever since. According to local residents, the reason the road has not been repaired is primarily that people in the area don't want it to be: They too much enjoy jogging, walking, and cycling along its quiet, forested, pine-scented length. Despite the gates locking out cars, it is still a public road open to pedestrians and nonmotorized vehicles. If you choose to pedal this traffic-free stretch of abandoned road (thus subtracting a mile from the mileage of either route), *ride with extreme caution at your own risk:* Stick close to the road's center double line, as in several sections the edges of the road, along with the guardrail, have slumped into the river below.

The Basics

Start: Kutztown, at Kutztown University. To get to the start from I–78, take exit 12 onto Rte. 737S directly into the heart of Kutztown. Turn right onto Main St. and drive straight to the entrance of the university. Turn right onto College Blvd. and immediately left into the Student Union parking lot.

The alternate start is at King's Market at the intersection of

Friedensburg Rd. and Memorial Hwy. in Oley. Please park at the far end of the lot, which is covered by gravel. To get to this starting place, continue south from Kutztown by following the directions below for the first 14.5 miles, which is the most direct route.

Length: 59 or 83 miles; subtract 1 mile from either if you take the alternative route on the section of abandoned road at the edge of Birdsboro.

Terrain: Rolling to moderately hilly. Traffic is generally moderately light to very light, except it is heavier in Kutztown, Oley, and Stowe (a suburb of Pottstown) and at the crossings of major highways.

Food: Plenty of options in Kutztown, Oley, and Stowe; elsewhere there are convenience stores about every 10 to 15 miles along the route.

Miles & Directions

Note: Follow directions carefully, as not every small street is shown on the map.

The directions below start from the Student Union parking lot at Kutztown University. If you are starting instead from King's Market at Oley for the 59-mile ride, turn right out of King's onto Friedensberg Rd., and you're already on the main route. Continue the directions below at mile 16.7 (the left turn onto West School Rd., 1.6 miles from King's).

- **0.0** Turn right out of the Kutztown Student Union parking lot onto College Blvd.
- **0.1** Head straight through the traffic light onto Normal Ave., passing the university's main entrance. Normal Ave. is a gentle downhill that will take you through four stop signs and past the Kutztown Elementary School.
- **1.2** After crossing over the railroad tracks, keep heading straight onto Kohler Rd. Now just follow this road's double yellow line through all its ninety-degree turns until you encounter the first stop sign.

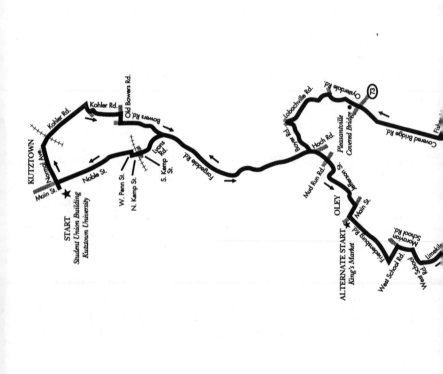

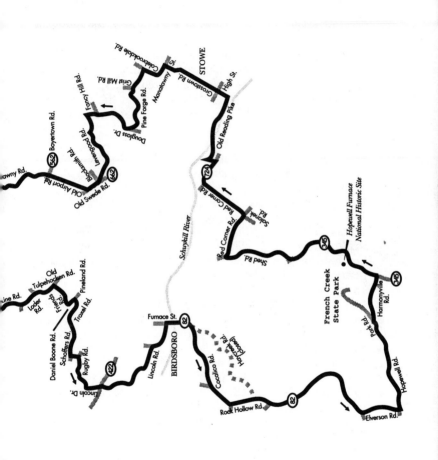

- 4.8 Turn right at the stop sign onto Old Bowers Rd.
- 5.2 Turn left at the T intersection onto Bowers Rd. at the Bowers Hotel. At mile 5.4 continue straight at the stop sign to stay on Bowers Rd.
- 6.6 Turn left at the stop sign at the end onto the unmarked Lyons Rd.
- 7.0 Turn right onto Forgedale Rd., following the sign to Pricetown. At mile 8.9 head straight at the stop sign to stay on Forgedale Rd.; Boyer's Market is a convenience store at this intersection. At mile 10.9 continue straight at the stop sign to stay on Forgedale Rd.; at mile 11.3 bear left to stay on Forgedale Rd.
- 11.8 Turn right onto Jefferson St.
- 12.6 Turn right at the T intersection onto Mud Run Rd., and then make an immediate left to continue on Jefferson St. Soon you will enter Oley.
- 14.5 Turn right at the stop sign onto Main St. in Oley.
- 14.9 Turn left at the stop sign onto Friedensburg Rd. At mile 15.1, you will pass King's Market on your right. *The 59-mile challenge joins the 83-mile classic at this point.* In Oley you will find rest rooms, food stores, water, and restaurants; the next opportunity is in 15 miles.
- 16.7 Turn left onto West School Rd.
- 17.2 Turn right at the T intersection onto Moravian School Rd.
- 17.7 Follow the main road right (where Quarry Rd. goes straight) onto the continuation of West School Rd.
- 18.2 Turn left onto Limekiln Rd.
- 19.3 Turn left at the T intersection onto the Oley Tpke.
- 19.4 Turn right onto the continuation of Limekiln Rd.
- 19.8 Turn right onto Oley Line Rd. In 0.75 mile you'll pass a stone marker on the grounds of the Hidden Valley Farm noting that this is the original site of the log cabin of George Boone III, Daniel Boone's father.
- 20.7 Turn left at the T intersection onto Loder Rd. In less than 0.5 mile, you'll pass a deli on your right.
- 21.6 Head straight at the stop sign (crossing Rte. 562) onto Old Tulpehocken Rd.

- 21.8 Turn right onto Friends Rd., exercising care on the rough pavement. Soon you'll pass under high-tension power lines.
- 22.4 Turn left at the T intersection onto Daniel Boone Rd.
- 22.5 Turn right onto Pineland Rd.
- 22.8 Turn right onto Troxel Rd.
- 23.4 Turn left at the T intersection onto Schoffers Rd.
- 24.5 Bear left at the Y intersection onto Rugby Rd. (where Schoffers Rd. continues straight).
- 24.7 Bear right to stay on Rugby Rd. (where Stonetown Rd. goes straight).
- 25.4 Turn left onto Lincoln Dr. into the modern housing development. Immediately turn left at the T intersection onto Diane Ln. Now you'll circle halfway around the development and then out the other side. At the end of Diane Ln., turn right onto Fairway Dr., and then turn left at the continuation of Lincoln Dr.
- 25.9 Head straight through the traffic light (crossing Rte. 422) onto Lincoln Rd. Keep following the double yellow line of Lincoln Rd. through all its ninety-degree turns. Now you're riding through industrial suburbia, with somewhat more traffic.
- 29.0 Turn right at the stop sign onto Rte. 82S, taking the bridge over the railroad tracks. Watch for potholes!
- 29.1 Continue straight through the traffic light to stay on the former Rte. 82, now called Furnace St. After passing through downtown Birdsboro, the road becomes Haycreek Rd.
- 29.6 Bear right at the Y intersection onto Cocalico Rd. *(If instead you want to ride the stretch of abandoned road—the alternative shown as a dashed line on the map—bear left at the T intersection instead to stay on Haycreek Rd. At mile 30.4 you can stop for a snack at the Birdsboro Rustic Picnic Area on your right. Just beyond the picnic area, walk your bike around the gate to continue on the closed road. **Ride carefully, as some sections of this abandoned road are treacherous.** At mile 31.8 walk your bike around the second gate to resume riding on opened road. At mile 32.9 turn left to stay on Rte. 82 where Rock Hollow Rd. heads right; here you resume riding on the main route. At various turns keep following all the signs for Rte. 82. Pick up the directions below at mile 38.9—the left turn onto Elverson Rd.)*

- 30.0 Bear right at the Y intersection (stop sign) to stay on Cocalico Rd.
- 30.4 Bear left at the Y intersection to stay on Cocalico Rd.
- 32.7 Turn left onto Rock Hollow Rd.
- 33.9 Head straight at the stop sign onto Rte. 82S.
- 34.0 Turn right at the T intersection to stay on Rte. 82S.
- 38.9 Turn left at the stop sign onto Elverson Rd. to stay on Rte. 82S. (*If you took the stretch of abandoned road, resume following the directions at this turn.*)
- 39.0 Bear left at the Y intersection onto Hopewell Rd.
- 41.4 Head straight onto Park Rd. (where Pineswamp Rd. heads right). At mile 42.2 you'll pass a sign for French Creek State Park. At mile 42.6 keep heading straight past the sign for Hopewell Furnace National Historic Site. At mile 42.8 you'll enter French Creek State Park. The park headquarters will be on your right. Take some time to see the park, which has water and rest rooms in addition to picnic grounds, swimming beaches, and campsites. When departing, backtrack 0.3 mile to the sign for Hopewell Furnace National Historic Site.
- 43.1 Turn left at the sign for Hopewell Furnace National Historic Site onto unmarked Harmonyville Rd.; watch for potholes!
- 44.2 Turn left at the T intersection onto Rte. 345N, leaving French Creek State Park. A quarter-mile up this road is French Creek General Store, which is open in the summer. At mile 45.7 is the Hopewell Furnace National Historic Site on your left; the visitor center is about 0.25 mile up the road. When you leave the site by this entrance, turn left to continue the ride on Rte. 345N.
- 46.5 Turn right at the top of the hill onto Shed Rd. Now you'll begin a long, gentle descent.
- 48.4 Turn right at the T intersection onto Red Corner Rd. Continue descending.
- 49.7 Turn left to stay on Red Corner Rd. (where Salanek Rd. heads right). In 0.75 mile you'll pass the Blackwood Golf Course clubhouse and driving range. At the clubhouse is a restaurant, along with water and rest rooms. Continue the long, gentle downhill.

- 51.1 Turn right at the T intersection onto Rte. 724. Soon you'll be paralleling the Schuylkill River.
- 51.7 Turn left, following the sign to Douglassville, to cross the bridge over the Schuylkill River.
- 52.5 Just after the bridge turn right onto the unmarked Old Reading Pike.
- 54.4 Turn left onto S. Grosstown Rd. *Walk* your bike across the bridge over the railroad tracks (it is closed to cars but passable to bicycles and pedestrians).
- 54.8 Continue straight through the traffic light (across High St.) onto Grosstown Rd.
- 56.3 Turn left at the T intersection onto Manatawny St.
- 56.8 Turn right onto Colebrookdale Rd.
- 57.3 Turn left onto Pine Forge Rd. Be careful on the downhill— there's a stop sign at the bottom of the hill.
- 57.9 Turn left at the T intersection to stay on Pine Forge Rd. (Grist Mill Rd. goes right). Cross the bridge over the beautiful river.
- 59.1 Turn right at the T intersection onto the unmarked Douglass Dr. Now you're riding through open fields and apple orchards.
- 60.3 Turn left onto Fancy Hill Rd.
- 60.6 Turn left onto Levengood Rd., past dairy farms.
- 61.1 Turn left to stay on Levengood Rd. (where Worman Rd. goes straight). Now you'll descend steeply into the forest, cross a bridge over a river, and climb back out.
- 62.7 Turn left at the T intersection onto Blacksmith Rd.
- 62.8 Turn right at the T intersection onto Rte. 662 (Old Swede Rd.).
- 63.1 Turn right at the traffic light (in Earlville) onto Old Airport Rd., a wonderful rollercoaster ride.
- 64.3 Turn left at the T intersection onto Rte. 562W (Boyertown Rd.), and then make the first right onto the unmarked Manatawny Rd.
- 65.0 Bear left at the Y intersection to stay on Manatawny Rd., keeping the river on your left.
- 66.6 Turn left onto Fisher Mill Rd. After crossing a bridge you

will soon be pedaling through flat farm fields.

- 67.3 Turn right at the T intersection onto Covered Bridge Rd. At mile 69.6 the road delivers on the promise of its name as you approach Pleasantville Covered Bridge (blocked to cars but accessible to bicycles and pedestrians). *Walk your bicycle through the bridge.*
- 69.9 Head straight at the traffic light across Rte. 73 onto Oysterdale Rd.
- 70.7 Bear right at the Y intersection to stay on Oysterdale Rd.
- 71.0 Make the first left onto the unmarked Lobachville Rd. and begin climbing. Follow the main road as it bends left to stay on Lobachville Rd. (where Mill Rd. continues straight). Continue straight through the stop sign to stay on Lobachville Rd.
- 72.6 Turn left onto Boyer Rd. Continue straight through the stop sign to stay on Boyer Rd.
- 73.4 Turn right at the T intersection onto Hoch Rd., which in 0.25 mile becomes Forgedale Rd.

To end the 59-mile challenge, turn left onto Hoch Rd. instead. In 0.3 mile make the first right onto Jefferson St. In another 0.6 mile make a right onto Mud Run Rd. and then an immediate left to continue on Jefferson St. In 1.9 mile turn right at the T intersection onto Oley's Main St. In 0.4 mile turn left at the stop sign onto Friedensburg Rd. In 0.2 mile turn right into the parking lot of King's Market.

- 78.0 Turn left at the T intersection onto Lyons Rd.
- 79.3 Go straight at the stop sign (following the sign KUTZTOWN 3) onto the unmarked S. Kemp St., which becomes N. Kemp St. after you cross the railroad tracks. Follow the road as it bends right and becomes W. Penn St.
- 79.7 Turn left at the stop sign (following the sign KUTZTOWN 3) onto the unmarked Noble St.
- 82.2 Turn left at the stop sign onto Normal Ave.
- 82.6 Continue straight through the traffic light onto College Blvd., passing the main entrance to Kutztown University.
- 82.7 Turn left into the Student Union parking lot.

33

Blue Bell All-Class Challenge

Blue Bell—Finland—East Greenville
Green Lane—Blue Bell

Although dubbed a challenge, this ride through Montgomery County was devised by Richard, Nancy, and Richard Jr. Liebert of Ambler, Pennsylvania, to be an all-class ride for the Pennsylvania Bicycle Club's John Pixton Memorial Poker Ride. As an all-class ride it has four options—17, 27, 50, and 60 miles; as the shorter rides are also less hilly than the longer ones, the 17-mile route is an easy ramble and the 27-mile route is a good cruise. The 50-mile ride is a somewhat easier challenge than the 60-mile version but still a challenge nonetheless. Ideally, because the route is long and skinny, all four options take you varying distances along the same path, with the cutoffs being so simple that you can decide whether to shorten any section almost on the spur of the moment.

The ride starts in Blue Bell, an outer suburb of Philadelphia, and takes you out into farmland and game preserves. According to Rich Liebert, the riding is ideal: "Ninety percent of the roads are virtually free of traffic," with good surfaces, taking cyclists through rural country. Moreover, the route is marked with a yellow spade from a playing card, painted on the road with traffic paint that survives the elements throughout the year. "Also, the locals ride the 17- and 27-mile rides all the time," he notes.

If you're inclined, take along a portable fishing pole on the longest route, because the destination—Green Lane Reservoir—is stocked with big northern pike and crappies (you'll need a Pennsylvania fishing license and a county permit if you are not a resident of Montgomery County). The two longer rides also pass close to the Country Creek Vineyard and Winery in Telford (215–723–6516), which may be open for tastings; even a slight lengthening of the 27-mile option will take you there. All four rides pass the Peter Wentz Homestead (a restored early Pennsylvania farm) and take you past the eastern tip of Evansburg State Park in Collegeville (215–489–3729), which has picnic grounds, hiking trails, and public rest rooms and allows trout fishing in Skippack Creek, running its length (again, you need the proper licenses).

Should you wish to ride the route in company, the John Pixton Memorial Poker Ride has been run annually the third Sunday in May since 1990, attracting about 200 cyclists. It is called a poker ride because at each of the five check points set up for the event, each cyclist draws a playing card; at the end of the ride, the cyclist with the best five-card-stud poker hand wins up to $65. For a modest registration fee, you'll also get a patch, all the food you can eat, and sag-wagon support. For the current year's registration packet and flyer, send a self-addressed, stamped envelope to Rich Liebert, 609 Montgomery Road, Ambler, PA 19002.

The Basics

Start: Blue Bell, at the Montgomery County Community College, at the corner of Rte. 202 (DeKalb Pike) and Morris Rd. Park in the lot for the Physical Education Center.

Length: 17, 27, 50, or 60 miles.

Terrain: The 17-mile ramble is easy and virtually flat; the 27-mile cruise has one difficult hill; the 50-mile challenge has three difficult hills; and the 60-mile ride is very challenging, with more than four difficult hills. Traffic is light on all four versions.

Food: There is no food, water, or rest rooms at the start. There are only two restaurants (both informal) on the entire ride: On the 60-mile ride you can eat at the Upper Perkiomen Golf Club; on the 50- and 60-mile challenges during the summer, there are rest rooms and a good snack bar in Montgomery County Park; on the 27-, 50-, and 60-mile rides, you'll also pass The Tea Room at the five-way corner in Lederach, a restaurant with "great food and coffee," Rich Liebert notes. *Bring food and water.*

Miles & Directions

Note: Follow directions carefully, as not every small street is shown on the map.

- ■ 0.0 Turn left out of the Physical Education Center parking lot onto Cathcart Rd. In 0.3 mile take a dogleg left and then right to stay on Cathcart Rd.
- ■ 0.7 Turn left onto Township Line Rd.
- ■ 2.4 Turn left onto N. Wales Rd.
- ■ 2.5 Make a sharp right onto Morris Rd.
- ■ 4.0 Turn left onto Schultz Rd., passing the Peter Wentz Homestead.
- ■ 5.3 Continue straight onto Shearer Rd.
- ■ 5.5 Ride straight through the driveway and parking lot of the Central Schwenkfelder Church.
- ■ 5.7 Turn left onto unmarked Fisher Rd. Follow it as it doglegs right and then left.
- ■ 7.5 Turn right at the T intersection onto Bustard Rd.
- ■ 7.8 Turn left at the T intersection onto Kriebel Rd.
- ■ 8.3 Turn left to stay on unmarked Kriebel Rd.

For the 17-mile ramble: At mile 8.2 turn right onto Kulp Rd.; at mile 9.0 turn right onto Old Morris Rd. You've now rejoined the 60-mile ride. At mile 9.4 continue following the directions below at mile 52.7 (beginning with the right turn onto Springer Rd.).

- ■ 9.1 Turn left onto Old Forty Foot Rd.
- ■ 9.2 Make the first right onto Bridge Rd., which becomes Quarry Rd. after you cross Store Rd.
- ■ 10.8 Turn left onto Morris Rd.
- ■ 10.9 Turn right onto Landis Rd. There are rest rooms and water at Heckler Plains Farmstead.

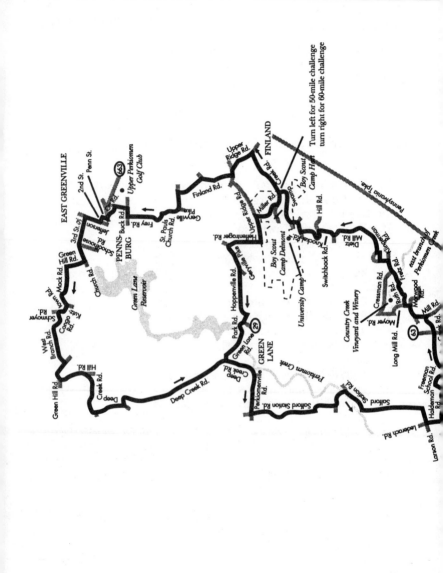

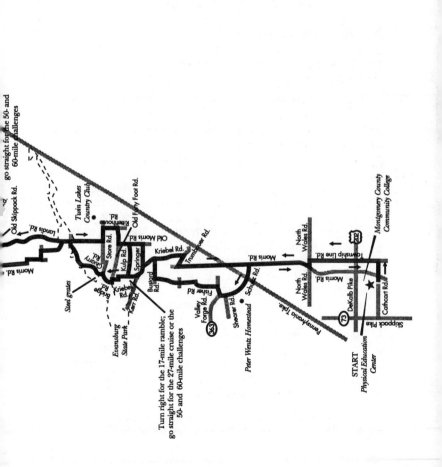

- 12.7 Turn right at the T intersection onto Old Skippack Rd.
- 13.0 Turn left at the T intersection onto Groffs Mill Rd.
- 13.2 Turn right at the T intersection onto Salfordville Rd.

For the 27-mile cruise: At mile 13.2 turn left onto Haldeman Rd.; at mile 14.1 turn left at the T intersection onto Camp Wawa Rd. You've now re-joined the 60-mile ride. At mile 15.1 continue following the directions below at mile 49.5 (beginning with the right turn at the T intersection onto Salfordville Rd.). By the way, to visit the Country Creek Vineyard and Winery, continue following the directions below through the options given at mile 16.5; then backtrack again to this cutoff. Adding the winery will lengthen the 27-mile option to about 34 miles.

- 13.7 Turn right onto Freeman School Rd.
- 14.2 Turn left at the T intersection onto Indian Creek Rd.
- 15.7 Turn left at the T intersection onto Mill Rd.
- 16.0 Follow Mill Rd. as it bends right and joins Morwood Rd.
- 16.3 Turn left onto Long Mill Rd.
- 16.5 Turn right onto Ruth Rd. (To visit the Country Creek Vineyard and Winery, which is across the east branch of Perkiomen Creek, stay on Long Mill Rd. instead as it bends left; make the first right on Moyer Rd. to cross the bridge over the creek, and turn right onto Cressman Rd. to reach the winery. Then retrace your path and turn left onto Ruth Rd. to resume the main route.)
- 17.1 Turn left onto Fretz Rd.
- 17.8 Turn left onto Klingerman Rd.
- 18.8 Bear left at the Y intersection onto Dietz Mill Rd. Follow it as it doglegs right and left.
- 20.2 Bear left onto the paved Switchback Rd., which becomes Hill Rd.
- 20.5 Turn right at the top of the hill onto the paved Knockel Rd.
- 21.3 Turn right at the T intersection onto the unmarked Swamp Creek Rd. Now you're entering several campgrounds.
- 22.4 Turn right to stay on the unmarked Swamp Creek Rd. (where Miller Rd. heads left).

For the 50-mile challenge: Turn left instead onto Miller Rd. to climb the hardest hill on the course; at mile 23.4 turn left at the T intersection onto

Upper Ridge Rd.; at mile 24.0 turn right onto Heffentrager Rd.; at mile 24.9 turn left at the T intersection onto Geryville Pike; at mile 25.4 turn right onto Hoppenville Rd; at mile 26.9 turn right at the T intersection onto Rte. 29 in the town of Green Lane; at mile 27.0 turn left onto Park Rd., watching carefully for traffic at this busy intersection; at mile 27.2 turn left onto Green Lane Rd. through the park south of the Green Lane Reservoir; at mile 28.3 turn left at the T intersection onto Deep Creek Rd. You've now rejoined the 60-mile ride. At mile 29.3 resume the directions below at mile 40.5, beginning with the right turn onto Perkiomenville Rd.

- 23.5 Turn left at the T intersection onto unmarked Upper Ridge Rd.
- 24.4 Turn right onto Finland Rd.
- 26.2 Turn right at the T intersection onto Geryville Pike.
- 26.4 Turn right and then immediately left onto St. Pauls Church Rd.
- 27.0 Turn right onto Frey Rd.
- 27.6 Turn right at the T intersection onto Buck Rd.
- 27.9 Turn left onto Ott Rd., riding through the grounds of the Upper Perkiomen Golf Club. If you're hungry, a diner is here at the golf course.
- 28.6 Turn left on Rte. 663, watching carefully for traffic as you ride into downtown Pennsburg. Now there are several quick turns; follow carefully.
- 28.7 Turn right onto Penn St.
- 29.1 Turn left onto 2nd St.
- 29.2 Turn right onto Jefferson St.
- 29.4 Turn left onto East Greenville's 3rd St.
- 30.1 Bear left onto Church Rd.
- 30.4 Turn right onto Green Hill Rd., which bends left at the top of a hill and becomes Mack Rd.
- 31.6 Turn left at the T intersection onto Kutztown Rd.
- 31.8 Make the first right onto Congo Rd., which bends left (where Schmoyer Rd. heads straight). Eventually Congo Rd. becomes W. Branch Rd. and finally Green Hill Rd.
- 34.0 Turn left onto Hill Rd.
- 34.8 Turn right onto Deep Creek Rd., a very narrow road.
- 36.6 Turn left to stay on the unmarked Deep Creek Rd., follow-

ing the sign for Montgomery County Park. *At mile 39.8 the 50-mile cutoff joins the main 60-mile ride where Green Lane Rd. comes in from the left.* At the Montgomery County Park in the summer, there are rest rooms, water, a good snack bar, and swimming.

- 40.5 Turn right onto Perkiomenville Rd.
- 41.5 Turn left onto Salford Station Rd.
- 44.3 Turn right to stay on Salford Station Rd.
- 46.4 Turn right onto Larson Rd.
- 46.8 Turn left onto Lederach Rd.
- 47.5 Ride straight onto Camp Wawa Rd. *At mile 48.5 the 27-mile cutoff joins the main 60-mile ride where Haldeman Rd. comes in from the left.*
- 49.5 Turn right at the T intersection onto Salfordville Rd., which after the next intersection becomes Morris Rd. Carefully watch signs to follow Morris Rd. through its various turns.
- 51.0 Turn left at the T intersection onto Store Rd.
- 51.3 Turn right onto Rittenhouse Rd.
- 51.6 Turn right onto Old Forty Foot Rd.
- 52.0 Turn left onto Old Morris Rd. *At mile 52.3 the 17-mile cutoff joins the main 60-mile ride where Kulp Rd. comes in from the right.*
- 52.7 Turn right onto Springer Rd.
- 53.3 Turn left onto unmarked Kriebel Rd.
- 54.5 Turn right onto Trumbauer Rd.
- 54.8 Turn left at the T intersection onto Morris Rd. In a couple of miles, you'll start retracing your outbound route.
- 58.0 Turn left onto N. Wales Rd.
- 59.1 Turn right onto Township Line Rd.
- 59.8 Turn right onto Cathcart Rd.
- 60.2 Dogleg left and then right to stay on Cathcart Rd.
- 60.5 Turn right into the parking lot of Montgomery County Community College.

34

Ringing Rocks Ramble

*Kintnersville—Uhlerstown—Ringing Rocks
County Park—Kintnersville*

This ride between Kintnersville and Uhlerstown is among the most spectacular you'll find in Bucks County, with the Delaware River and Canal stretching out along the left side of the road and steep palisades rising above your right shoulder. Its beauty and its ease make it an ideal early-season ride, as well as a wonderful introduction to the charms of bicycle touring.

The canal, part of a system of state-built public works started in 1827 to connect Philadelphia, Pittsburgh, and Lake Erie, carried barges of freight for more than a century. The Delaware Canal section of the Pennsylvania Canal ran from the Lehigh River in Easton north of Kintnersville to Bristol in the south. Nine years after it was closed in 1931, it was turned into a state park. Now it is open to cyclists, picnickers, and others to enjoy.

At Uhlerstown pause to gaze at the historic collection of houses and canal buildings before passing through the Uhlerstown covered bridge. Built of oak in 1821 and spanning a remarkable 101 feet, this structure is the only covered bridge crossing the Delaware Canal, and it has windows on both sides, affording a view of the canal and locks. Shortly thereafter you'll ascend a steep wooded hill—the only steep climb of the trip, but it is mercifully short. If you must walk your bike, take advantage of your leisurely pace to enjoy the coolness of the forest.

At the top you'll pedal through rolling farmland, cycling past Ringing Rocks County Park. Stop for a few moments to hike out a few hundred feet on one of the trails to this small valley of boulders, deposited there during the Ice Age. The boulders rest on one another in such a way that sound is not damped, and if struck by a hammer or a thrown fist-size rock, they emit bell-like ringing tones. After leaving Ringing Rocks, you'll coast back down to Kintnersville.

This ride, one of the favorites of Steven Getzow, member of the board of directors of the Bucks County Tourist Commission in Doylestown, should be taken only in the direction described in this cue sheet; the grades and crossings make it much less safe when taken in the opposite direction. Also, this ride can be taken only in the spring, summer, and fall, as the steep section of Uhlerstown Hill Road is closed from December 1 through April 1.

The segment between Kintnersville and Uhlerstown can be covered either on Route 32 or on the Delaware Canal towpath. Route 32 is smooth but without shoulders, and on lovely weekends it has fairly heavy traffic at 35 to 40 miles per hour; the towpath is somewhat bumpy so that speeds above about 6 miles per hour may not be comfortable, but it hugs the water's edge and is free of auto traffic. A cross (hybrid) bike or a mountain bike might handle best on the towpath's hard-packed dirt, although any thin-tire bike will also do fine. The towpath may be muddy, though, right after a heavy rain.

The only places to buy food and snacks are at the start, in Kintnersville. The Great American Grill at the intersection of Routes 611 and 32 makes huge deli sandwiches of all descriptions, some quite fancy. Take your goodies to go, as the canal towpath is dotted with picnic tables and an occasional pit-toilet rest room. There are also pit toilets at Ringing Rocks but no water, so take with you all you'll want to drink.

If you wish to stay overnight to allow yourself more time to explore the full length of the canal's towpath, two inns in Uhlerstown are within a mile south of the turn at mile 8.1: EverMay-on-the-Delaware country inn (215–294–9100) for dining and lodging and the Isaac Stover Bed & Breakfast (215–294–8044).

The Basics

Start: Kintnersville, at the parking lot of the Post Office on Rte. 611, just 500 feet off Rte. 32. To get to the start from Easton, take Rte. 611S to Kintnersville.

Length: 17.5 miles.

Terrain: Generally flat to gently rolling, except for one steep climb. Traffic is very light on the second half of the route, although it can be moderately heavy on the first half; to avoid most cars for the first 8 miles, ride on the canal towpath.

Food: Kintnersville only; stock up on both snacks and drinks at the beginning.

Miles & Directions

- 0.0 Turn left out of the post office parking lot onto Rte. 611N (Easton Rd.).

- 0.1 Bear right at the Y intersection onto Rte. 32S (River Rd.). If you want to take the Delaware Canal towpath, 0.5 mile down Rte. 32S, use the footbridge on your left to cross the canal, and turn right onto the towpath to parallel Rte. 32S. The wide Delaware River will be on your left.

- 8.1 Turn right onto Uhlerstown Hill Rd., just after the Uhlerstown-Frenchtown Bridge over the Delaware River. At mile 8.4 you'll pass through a covered bridge that was built in 1832. On the other side of the bridge, follow the road as it takes a sharp right. It rises very steeply and the pavement deteriorates. But at mile 8.8 it will level out again and then head downhill.

- 9.2 Turn right onto Upper Tinicum Church Rd.; this is the right turn immediately *before* the T intersection (which is Perry Auger Rd.). At the Bridgeton Township line (mile 10.7), the road changes its name to Chestnut Ridge Rd.

- 12.3 Turn left at the T intersection onto Bridgeton Hill Rd.

- 12.8 Turn right onto Ringing Rocks Rd. At mile 13.0 is the entrance to Ringing Rocks County Park on your right.

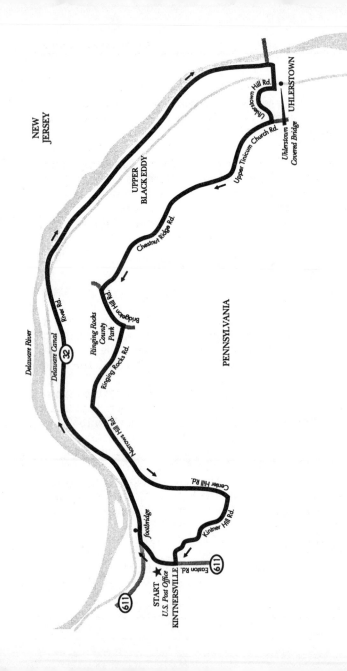

- 13.9 Turn left at the T intersection onto Narrows Hill Rd., which climbs gently but steadily; it changes its name to Center Hill Rd. when you cross into Nockamixon Township.
- 16.1 Turn right onto Kintner Hill Rd., which is a fairly steep descent with winding switchbacks.
- 17.2 Turn right at the T intersection onto the unmarked Rte. 611N (Easton Rd.). Watch for traffic as you enter Kintnersville.
- 17.5 Turn left into the post office parking lot.

Washington, D.C.

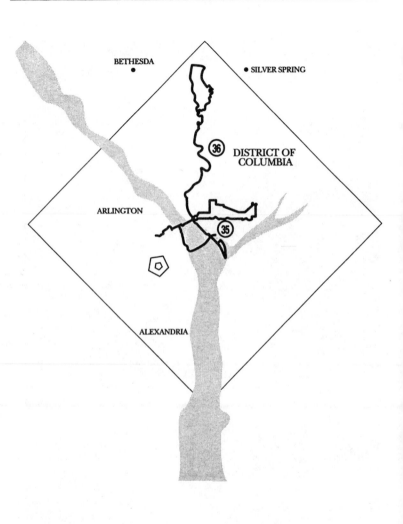

Washington, D.C.

35

Washington Monuments Ramble

Washington, D.C.—Arlington, Va.—Washington, D.C.

In 1988 *Bicycling* magazine named the District of Columbia one of the top ten cycling cities in the United States. No wonder, as it has more than 670 miles of paved paths exclusively for bicycles and pedestrians and another 480 miles of bicycle routes marked on roads and streets shared with automobiles.

As you will see on this urban route, many of Washington, D.C.'s most famous monuments, memorials, and museums are accessible on two wheels, giving you the option of stopping where and when you wish without wondering where to park the car. You'll pedal right past the Lincoln Memorial, the Arlington Cemetery, the Washington Monument, nine Smithsonian museums (all of which are free), the Supreme Court, the U.S. Capitol, Union Station, the FBI Building, the White House, and the Vietnam Veterans Memorial.

Although this virtually flat 22-mile ramble can be ridden in only an hour or two, there is so much to stop and see that you may well decide to take several days. This ride, which combines two routes in Michael Leccese's best-seller *Short Bike Rides in and around Washington, D.C.* (The Globe Pequot Press, second edition, 1993), is within the ability of even novice or out-of-shape cyclists.

The most beautiful time of year for cycling in the District is the spring, especially in mid-April when thousands of blooming cherry and dogwood trees on both sides of the Potomac River are adorned in their lacy pink finery. Late autumn, with its crisper air and fiery leaves, is also a lovely time. Even on a mild winter's day this short outing can be done before early darkness falls. Avoid summer, however, when the steaming humidity combines with automobile exhaust to make outdoor exercise in the city less than fun or healthful.

The Basics

Start: Washington, D.C., at the Harry T. Thompson Boat Center just off Virginia Ave. and the Rock Creek Potomac Pkwy. NW. (Bicycles can be rented at the boat center.) To get to the start from the north, take Rock Creek Potomac Pkwy. south to Thompson's parking lot and turn right. From the Mall, take Virginia Ave. west across Rock Creek Potomac Pkwy. to Thompson's parking lot.

Length: 22 miles. It may be combined as noted below with the "Rock Creek Potomac Park Cruise" (Ride 36) for a cruise of 38.8 miles.

Terrain: Flat except for Arlington Cemetery and Capitol Hill. Traffic ranges from nonexistent on the paved bicycle paths to very heavy on the main streets.

Food: Water and rest rooms at the start. Food is available at various spots on the Mall and at Arlington Cemetery.

Miles & Directions

- 0.0 Turn right (southeast) out of the Harry T. Thompson Boat Center onto the bike path heading toward the Watergate apartments. The Potomac River will be on your right, and the Kennedy Center on your left. At mile 1.3 dismount and walk through two short bridge underpasses. Continue straight through the traffic circle at the John Ericsson Monument at Independence Ave. and Ohio Dr. Southwest.
- 1.4 Proceed northeast on Ohio Dr., a one-way road with many potholes.
- 2.3 After crossing over a graceful bridge with gargoyle fountains, turn right at the circular flower bed to stay on Ohio Dr.,

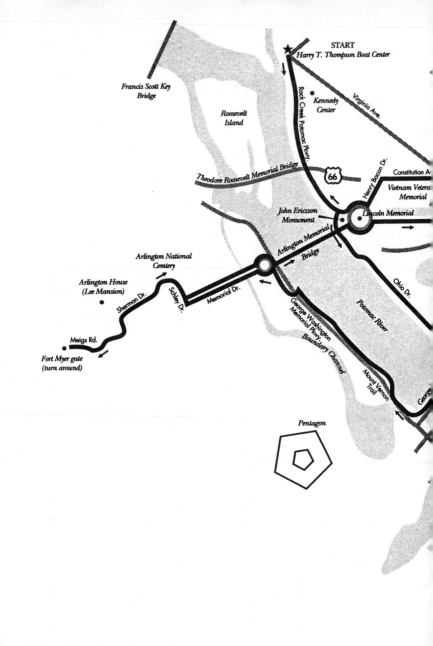

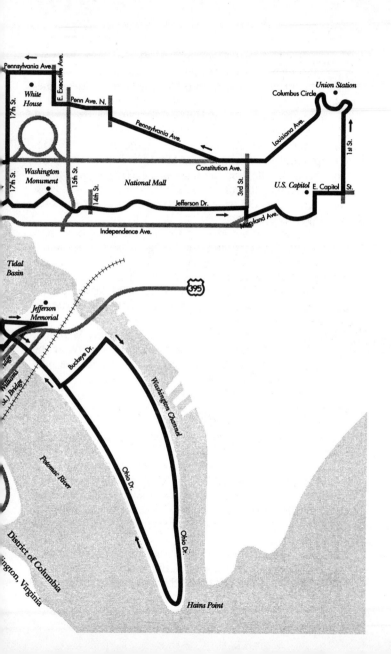

following signs to East Potomac Park (Hains Point). Cross under four bridges for cars, Amtrak, and Metrorail.

- 2.9 Turn left at the stop sign onto Buckeye Dr. to follow a one-way loop around East Potomac Park. Follow the road as it makes a sharp right around Hains Point and passes Seward Johnson's 1980 statue *The Awakening*. Now you're headed back north, parallel to the Potomac River. At the end of the one-way loop, continue straight onto Ohio Dr. Pass again under the four bridges, following the signs to the Jefferson Memorial.

- 7.4 At the parking lot for the Jefferson Memorial, look for a curb cut leading to the wide, smooth bike path over the 14th St. Bridge. Cross the bridge.

- 8.0 At the base of the bridge on the Virginia side, bear right onto a bike path that parallels the George Washington Memorial Pkwy. You're now on the Mt. Vernon Trail, with the Potomac River on your right and the Boundary Channel on your left. Pass Lady Bird Johnson Park, with its 2,700 dogwoods and 1 million daffodils. Continue on the bike path toward the Arlington Memorial Bridge.

- 9.2 Bear left to avoid passing under the Arlington Memorial Bridge. Cross the George Washington Memorial Pkwy. at the cross walks. Cross the traffic circle and turn left onto the sidewalk paralleling Memorial Drive.

- 10.2 Turn right onto Schley Dr. to enter Arlington National Cemetery.

- 10.3 Bear left onto Sherman Dr.

- 10.5 Bear right onto Meigs Rd., which leads to Arlington House (Lee Mansion).

- 10.9 Turn around at the gate to Ft. Myer. Retrace your route back to Arlington Memorial Bridge. Cross the bridge back to Washington, D.C., by riding on the sidewalk. Walk your bike across the traffic circle to the grounds of the Lincoln Memorial. Ride up a short road (where the sign reads TAXIS ONLY) to the Lincoln Memorial.

- 13.5 Facing east, head down a slight slope past a souvenir stand on your right and ride on the bike path parallel to the 0.5-mile-long Reflecting Pool. Continue past the fountains and jog to the left on the sidewalk to the 17th St. pedestrian crossing (traffic light).

- 14.2 Take the bike path heading directly uphill to the Washington Monument. Ride on the bike/foot paths across 15th and 14th Streets to Jefferson Dr.

- 15.0 Follow one-way Jefferson Dr. along the National Mall, past nine Smithsonian museums (including the Smithsonian Castle, the National Air and Space Museum, and the National Gallery of Art), an ice-skating rink, and a Dept. of Agriculture building.

- 15.9 Turn right onto 3rd St. and then immediately left onto Maryland Ave. On the right is the U.S. Botanical Gardens. Ride past the statue of James Garfield on the grounds of the U.S. Capitol.

- 16.1 Turn right onto footpaths that bear left around the south side of the U.S. Capitol to the east front, passing the Library of Congress and the Supreme Court. Pass through stone gates.

- 16.4 Turn right onto E. Capitol St.

- 16.5 Turn left onto 1st St. Ride about 0.75 mile to Columbus Circle in front of Union Station.

- 17.0 Turn right onto Columbus Circle and left into the service road in front of the train station. After exiting the station area on the service road, turn left. At mile 17.3, take the second right onto Louisiana Ave.

- 17.7 Bear right at the end of Louisiana Ave. onto Constitution Ave. Two blocks later bear right onto Pennsylvania Ave., riding along the same route the presidential inaugural parade has always taken since the inauguration of Thomas Jefferson. Pass the Canadian Chancery, the National Archives, the FBI Building, and the Old (1897) Post Office.

- 18.8 Turn right onto 13th St. and immediately left onto Pennsylvania Ave. Pass the National Theatre and the Willard Hotel. Cross 15th St. at the signal to continue straight onto Alexander Hamilton Pl.

- 19.2 Turn right onto E. Executive Ave. Exit through iron gates; turn left onto the sidewalk to arrive at 1600 Pennsylvania Ave.—the White House. Walk your bike to 17th St. and cross the street.

■ 19.5 Turn left onto 17th St. and ride three long blocks (passing the Corcoran Gallery and the Organization of American States Building).

■ 20.1 Cross Constitution Ave. and turn right onto a parallel bike path, passing Constitution Gardens and the Vietnam Veterans Memorial.

■ 20.6 Turn left onto Henry Bacon Dr. to the Lincoln Memorial. Return to the Ericsson statue. Turn right onto the bike path to retrace the route back to the Thompson Boat Center.

To combine this route with the "Rock Creek Park Cruise" (Ride 36) for a total length of 38.8 miles, continue north past the boat center and pick up the directions at mile 0.0 of the Rock Creek Park ride.

36

Rock Creek Park Cruise

Thompson Boat Center—Pierce Mill and Art Barn
Rock Creek Park—Pierce Mill and Art Barn
Thompson Boat Center

The Rock Creek Park bicycle path is one of the best-known classic routes of Washington, D.C., cyclists. Right within the center of the nation's urban capital, the bike path is an escape to the country with deep wooded glades, cooling even in the hot summer's humidity. During the week the bike path is a regular commuter run for city cyclists riding to work from the north; on weekends it is a favorite of recreational strollers and hikers as well.

This ride, a combination of two routes in Michael Leccese's marvelously written best-seller *Short Bike Rides in and around Washington, D.C.* (The Globe Pequot Press, Second Edition, 1993), takes you north into the hilly reaches of Rock Creek Park—a superb aerobic workout for stronger riders. The ride can be turned into a longer cruise of 38.8 miles by joining it with the "Washington Monuments Ramble" (Ride 35). Ride carefully on nice weather weekends, as the recreational traffic can be heavy and the path is both bumpy and narrow in spots—sometimes only eight feet wide. But riding more slowly gives you more time to take in its refreshing, rustic beauty.

The most beautiful time of year for cycling in the District is the spring, especially in mid-April when the cherries and dogwoods are abloom. Autumn and even mild winter days are also good times to be cycling in D.C. Summer, however, is less than ideal, as steaming humidity combines with automobile exhaust to make outdoor exercise in the city physically stressful—and not much fun.

The Basics

Start: Washington, D.C., at the Harry T. Thompson Boat Center just off Virginia Ave. and the Rock Creek Potomac Pkwy. NW. (Bicycles can be rented at the boat center.) To get to the start from the north, take Rock Creek Potomac Pkwy. south to Thompson's parking lot and turn right. From the Mall take Virginia Ave. west across Rock Creek Potomac Pkwy. to Thompson's parking lot.

Length: 16.8 miles. It may be combined as noted above with the "Washington Monuments Ramble" (Ride 35) for a cruise of 38.8 miles.

Terrain: Rolling south of Pierce Mill and Art Barn; very hilly north of Pierce Mill and Art Barn. Automobile traffic is nonexistent on the paved bicycle paths to heavy on the main streets. Note that you're likely to share the bike path with many joggers and strollers on weekends.

Food: Water and rest rooms at the start and at Pierce Mill and Art Barn. None elsewhere on the route, so bring snacks or a picnic lunch.

Miles & Directions

- **0.0** From the boat center cross the short one-lane bridge to the parking lot. At the curb cut, turn left (north) onto the Rock Creek Park bike path, keeping the Watergate apartment complex and the Kennedy Center on your right. For the next three miles, the path runs parallel to the Rock Creek Potomac Pkwy, crossing Rock Creek five times via bridges. (At mile 1.5 you may turn left onto the Massachusetts Ave. bike path and proceed 0.5 mile to reach the U.S. Naval Observatory.) After passing the exercise course that parallels the route, dismount and cross Rock Creek Potomac Pkwy. at the crosswalk and continue north.
- **2.2** Bear right at the fork in the path and ride under the arches of the Duke Ellington Memorial Bridge.

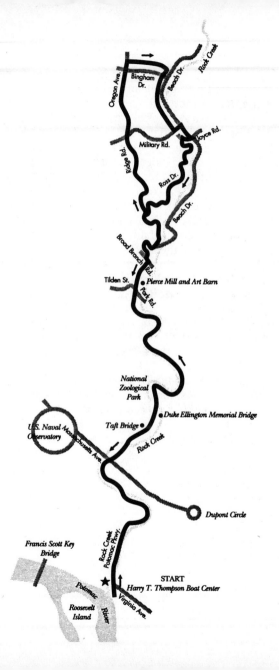

- 3.3 Just before the tunnel, turn left and ride through a gate onto a smooth path paralleling Rock Creek. At the service road crossing, take a short detour to your left over a stone bridge into the National Zoological Park. At mile 4.0 pass Pierce Mill and Art Barn and waterfalls, a nice spot for a snack.
- 4.3 Turn left onto the two-lane Broad Branch Rd. and make an immediate right onto Ridge Rd. Climb a steep hill for 0.5 mile.
- 4.0 Bear left at the sign for the Nature Center to stay on Ridge Rd.
- 5.6 At the Military Rd. traffic light, keep heading straight onto Oregon Ave. or take the bike path parallel to it.
- 6.3 Turn right onto Bingham Dr. or take the parallel bike path.
- 6.6 Turn right onto the Beach Dr. bike path.
- 7.5 At the four-way stop, turn right onto Joyce Rd. and make an immediate left onto Ross Dr.
- 8.3 Bear left onto Ridge Rd. near the Nature Center.
- 8.9 Turn left onto the two-lane Broad Branch Rd. and make an immediate right into the bike path, retracing your route south. At mile 13.1 pass the Pierce Mill and Art Barn parking area. At mile 16.8 arrive back at the Thompson Boat Center.

To combine this route with the "Washington Monuments Ramble" for a total length of 38.8 miles, continue south past the boat center and pick up the directions at mile 0.0 of the monuments ride.

West Virginia

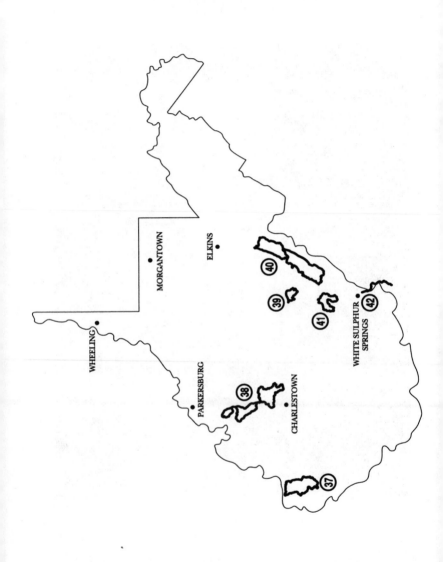

West Virginia

37

Milton Getaway Challenge

Milton—Dudley Gap—Ona—Balls Gap—Milton

If you're hankering for some real hill climbing and the cure for too much civilization, this loop will exercise your granny gear and quest for solitude, along with providing lovely views of West Virginia's rows of forested ridges. The westernmost ride in this book, this route through Cabell County is a true challenge, despite its moderate length of 41 miles. A favorite of the Mountain State Wheelers Bicycle Club, it is the contribution of Jim Saulters of St. Albans, West Virginia.

At the start in Milton, you could take a public tour of Blenko Glass, famous for its hand-blown commemorative glassware. And 17.6 miles into the ride, you can make a 0.5-mile detour to Ona Air Park, a small country airport that offers rides in private planes. But outside of Milton and the town of Ona halfway through the ride, the route follows backroads in the Mountain State so isolated and so lightly traveled that you will not run across so much as a picnic ground. There are no bed-and-breakfast inns, although Ona does offer the Foxfire Camp Grounds (304–743–5622), allowing you to turn this challenge into a two-day cruise. Despite the solitude, all the roads are paved.

The Basics

Start: Milton, at the Little League fields on County Fair Rd. To get to the ride's start, take the Milton exit (exit 28) off I-64; drive 0.3 mile south; turn right (west) at the traffic light onto Rte. 60; and drive 0.4 mile into downtown Milton. At the next traffic light, turn left (south) onto County Fair Rd. Drive 0.2 mile and park along the road near the Little League playing fields. Please do *not* park in the visitor lot for Blenko Glass.

Length: 41 miles.

Terrain: Hilly, no doubt about it. Traffic is normally light, except for around Milton and Ona.

Food: Convenience stores and fast-food restaurants in Milton and halfway through the ride at Ona; no other services along the route. Carry snacks, water, and tools.

Miles & Directions

Note: Follow directions carefully, as not every small street is shown on the map.

- 0.0 Head north (it could be either left or right, depending on the side of the road on which you parked) along County Fair Rd. back into Milton. At mile 0.2 you can stock up on snacks at the Chevron convenience store on your right. At the traffic light continue straight north.
- 0.4 Turn right at the stop sign onto Mason St.
- 0.45 Turn left onto Rte. 15 (Glenwood St.). Pass under I–64.
- 4.1 Turn right onto Rte. 9 (Dudley Gap Rd.). In 0.75 mile, you'll begin a long climb up to Dudley Gap. "Hope you brought your granny!" notes Jim Saulters.
- 6.1 Turn left onto Rte. 11 (Barkers Ridge Rd.), which rolls and weaves in a wonderful rollercoaster ride, offering lovely views of the forested ridges. At mile 10.5 you'll pass some television towers on your right.
- 12.0 Continue straight onto Rte. 1 (Union Ridge Rd.), which intersects from your right.
- 12.3 Bear left (south) to stay on Rte. 1; stay on the ridge, *not* taking the obvious downhill to the right (which is Big Seven Rd.). In 0.25 mile you'll begin a long, pleasurable downhill.
- 16.8 Bear to the right to stay on Rte. 1, where Rte. 21 (Prichard

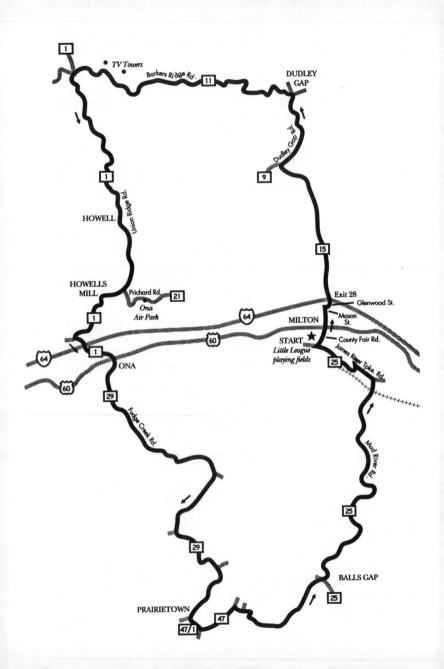

Rd.) comes in from the left. If, however, you'd like a nice 0.5-mile detour and maybe take a ride in a private plane, turn left onto Rte. 21 to visit the Ona Air Park. Then return to this spot to continue the ride. At mile 17.6 cross the Mud River at Howells Mill.

- 20.3 Here you can refuel at the Exxon convenience store where Rte. 1 ends at Rte. 60. Then continue straight across the intersection onto Rte. 29 (Fudges Creek Rd.). Around mile 26 you'll climb up to the top of a ridge; on the downhill use caution on the steep switchbacks.

- 28.8 Turn left onto the unmarked Rte. 47/1 at the unmarked community of Prairietown. In 0.3 mile bear left onto Rte. 47. In 1.2 miles you'll grind up a *steep* hill, followed by a slightly less steep descent.

- 32.4 Turn left onto Rte. 25 (Mud River Rd.) and ride over the top of Balls Gap, marked by a church on your right. Watch your speed on the left-hand sweeper on the other side!

- 35.2 Before crossing the Mud River, turn left at Zoar Baptist Church onto Rte. 25/12 (W. Mud River Rd.).

- 39.5 After passing under a railroad trestle, turn left onto Rte. 25 (James River Tpke. Rd.). At mile 40.7 pass the warehouse for Supervalu Food Distributors.

- 40.9 Bear right at Blenko Glass onto County Fair Rd.

- 41.0 Arrive back at your car.

38

Sternwheel Regatta Century Classic

Elkview—Sissonville—Liberty—Given
Fairplain—Sissonville—Elkview

This 100-mile ride north of Charleston takes you on a challenging tour through Kanawha, Putnam, and Jackson counties in western central West Virginia. You will climb forested ridges to behold panoramic vistas, soar down slopes into a river valley, and cycle through cultivated farmland. You may choose to picnic at the top of Allen Fork Road where it intersects with Route 34 about 35 miles into the ride and then take a tour of Fisher Ridge Winery a few miles later.

The ride's unusual name originated from the Sternwheel Regatta, a festival that started in Charleston on Labor Day in 1970 and whose highlight is a boat race among sternwheel riverboats. Over the years the Sternwheel Regatta has grown to a celebration ten days long that attracts more than 100,000 spectators for the events and concerts, all of which are free. In 1979 the Mountain State Wheelers Bicycle Club was asked to organize a bike ride for the festival; now the challenging ride attracts some 400 cyclists each year. "You can mention that if riders do the Regatta bike ride the last weekend in August during the festival, they will enjoy full support, which includes sag wagons, food, water, security and emergency services, and a dinner the night before the ride," notes Dennis A. Strawn of Elkview, West Virginia, who contributed the map and cue sheet.

Although the Sternwheel Regatta classic was originally conceived as a one-day century ride, you can modify it in several ways. Because the 105-mile ride is three successive loops, it can be shortened to a 43-mile challenge or an 85-mile classic by returning after only the first or second loop. Alternatively, the ride can be turned into a two-day weekend by staying overnight at the Wildwood Campground (304–372–2436) at Staats Mill, 6 miles from Fairplain, about 70 miles into the ride.

Like most locales isolated enough to be ideal for road riding in West Virginia, here, too, places to get food are few and far between. There are a few convenience stores, but load up on snacks, water, and tools—unless, of course, you join the riders with sag support at the actual Sternwheel Regatta!

The Basics

Start: Elkview, at Crossings Mall, just off the Elkview exit from I-79.
Length: 43, 85, or 105 miles.
Terrain: Very hilly. Traffic is light on weekend mornings, but during the week it can get heavy with commuter traffic in the mornings and evenings.
Food: Occasional restaurants and convenience stores, but places can be up to 15 miles apart; carry snacks, water, and tools.

Miles & Directions

- 0.0 Turn right out of the parking lot at Crossings Mall onto Rte. 45 (Little Sandy Creek Rd.).
- 6.3 Turn right onto Rte. 119.
- 8.5 Turn right onto Rte. 41/114 (Coopers Creek Rd.). Here there are a Hardee's and Smith's Grocery Store.
- 9.4 Turn right to stay on Rte. 41 (Coopers Creek Rd.) and stay on the obvious main road as it changes number from Rte. 41 to Rte. 28 to Rte. 26 to Rte. 26/1. At mile 13.8 start climbing. At mile 14.2 you'll reach the crest and start a steep downhill.

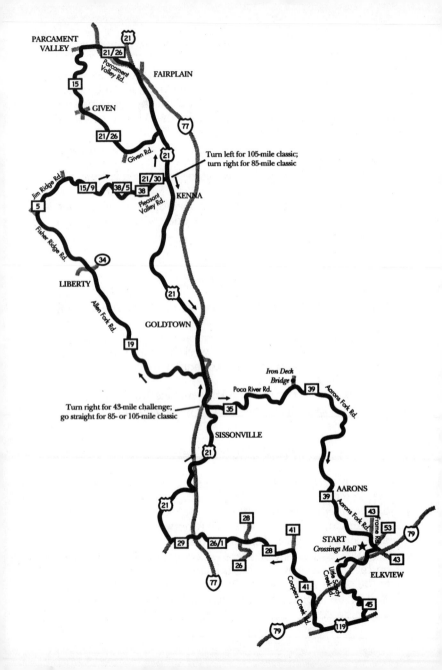

PARCAMENT VALLEY

FAIRPLAIN

GIVEN

Parcament Valley Rd.

Jim Ridge Rd.

Given Rd.

Turn left for 105-mile classic;
turn right for 85-mile classic

KENNA

Pleasant Valley Rd.

Fisher Ridge Rd.

LIBERTY

Allen Fork Rd.

GOLDTOWN

Iron Deck Bridge

Poca River Rd.

Aarons Fork Rd.

Turn right for 43-mile challenge;
go straight for 85- or 105-mile classic

SISSONVILLE

AARONS

START
Crossings Mall

Frame Rd.

Aarons Fork Rd.

Coopers Creek Rd.

Little Sandy Creek Rd.

ELKVIEW

At mile 16.0 start another climb, followed 0.2 mile later by a very steep downhill. Control your speed on the sharp turns.

- 16.8 Bear right at the sharp turn to stay on Rte. 26/1. Watch your speed—the safe maximum is 15 mph. At mile 17.7 ride under I–77 and keep heading straight onto Rte. 29.
- 18.9 Turn right onto Rte. 21N. At mile 20.1 are a grocery store and restaurant; continue straight at the traffic light. At mile 25.1 you'll enter the limits of Sissonville. At mile 26.8 continue straight on Rte. 21 at the intersection of Poca River Rd. (Markles convenience store is here.)

For the 43-mile challenge: At mile 26.8 turn right onto Poca River Rd. (instead of continuing straight) and pick up the directions below at mile 88.5.

- 28.3 Turn left onto Rte. 21/19 (Allen Fork Rd.), which passes under I–77. At mile 35.0 start a steep but short climb.
- 35.8 Turn left onto Rte. 34S.
- 36.0 Make the first right onto Fisher Ridge Rd., passing the Fisher Ridge Winery. At mile 42.5 be careful! This is the start of a very steep downgrade, which has a stop sign at the bottom.
- 43.0 Turn right onto Rte. 5 (Jim Ridge Rd.). At mile 43.3 begin climbing.
- 45.8 Bear right at the Y intersection to stay on Rte. 5. In 500 feet you can refuel at the Jim Ridge convenience store on your right, where the owner is friendly toward visiting cyclists. At mile 51.8 continue straight at the intersection of Rock Castle Rd. After Rock Castle the road you are on will change route numbers several times (from Rte. 2 to Rte. 15/9 to Rte. 38/5 to Rte. 38 to Rte. 21/30), but continue to follow the evident main road.
- 56.9 Turn left at the T intersection onto Rte. 21N.

For the 85-mile classic: Turn right onto Rte. 21S instead, and pick up the directions at mile 76.0.

- 59.3 Turn left onto Rte. 21/26 (Given Rd.), which changes to Rte.

38. At mile 63.8 you'll pass through the community of Given, which has no services. Continue north of Given onto Rte. 15.

■ 67.3   Bear right at the Y intersection onto Parcament Valley Rd. to Fairplain.

■ 68.1   After crossing over I–77, bear right to stay on Parcament Valley Rd. (Rte. 21/26).

■ 70.4   Turn right at the T intersection onto Rte. 21S and proceed under the interstate. You'll just stay on Rte. 21S for the next 18 miles. At mile 73.6 pass the intersection of Given Rd. At mile 76.0 pass the intersection of Pleasant Valley Rd. *This is where the 85-mile ride joins the 105-mile route.* At mile 76.9 continue straight as Rte. 34 joins from the left. At mile 77.8 begin climbing Divide Hill. At mile 78.3, at the crest of the hill, continue straight on Rte. 21S where Rte. 34 turns right. Coast down Divide Hill. At mile 84.0 pass under I–77 at Goldtown (a small community with no services). At mile 87.0 pass the intersection of Allens Fork Rd.

■ 88.5   Turn left onto Rte. 35 (Poca River Rd.). *This is where the 43-mile ride joins the 105-mile route.* Once again you can refuel at Markles convenience store. At mile 92.0 use caution crossing Iron Deck Bridge over Hicumbottom Creek; when wet this bridge is *very slippery,* and you must walk your bike. Bear right onto Rte. 39 (Aarons Fork Rd.).

■ 104.4   Continue straight onto Frame Rd. (Rte. 43).

■ 104.5   Turn right onto Little Sandy Creek Rd., and then make an immediate right into Crossings Mall.
Congratulations!

39

Williams River Trail Cruise

Little Laurel Overlook—Woodrow
Tea Creek Campground—Little Laurel Overlook

West Virginia is famed for its mountain biking, not its road riding, so it's only right to include an easy introduction to that very distinct sport. This ride along a well-marked former railroad grade paralleling the Williams River in Pocahontas County is accessible even to novices. But if you're one of those road riders who love to coordinate the color of their water bottle cages with their Descente jackets and their Hind shorts, be forewarned: Mountain biking is a filthy sport. On the Williams River Trail, several springs run off the mountain and can make the trail wet and slippery; you must also ford Little Laurel Creek about halfway through the ride. Mud can be liberally splashed all over your clothes and equipment, finding its way into your bottom bracket and even into your pockets and onto your glasses. Save the fashion statement for a dry day on the highway.

For safety's sake do this ride only on the 2-inch knobbies of a true mountain bike; otherwise you risk injury slipping on the moist trail or down the first gravel descent. If you've brought only a road bike, never fear: You can readily rent a true West Virginia mountain steed from the Elk River Touring Center in Slatyfork (304–572–3771), just 12 miles from the ride's start. In fact, the touring center includes ten rooms and two cabins at a bed-and-breakfast lodge, a hot tub where overnight guests can soak the aches out of their quadriceps, and a very nice restaurant (The Restaurant at Elk River, also 572–3771)—one of the few in the state that caters to the high-carbo, low-fat nutritional needs of active cyclists. Other overnight options can be found in Marlinton, about 10 miles south (see Ride 40).

This ride, based on one in the book *Mountain Bike Rides in Pocahontas County, West Virginia* (Roadrunner Press, 1992), written by the owners of the Elk River Touring Center, veteran mountain-bike tour guides Gil and Mary Willis, gives you several options. Although this ride is written to start from the Little Laurel Overlook on the Highland Scenic Highway 150, you could also start from the Tea Creek Campground or from the Handley Public Hunting and Fishing Area.

The cue sheet below directs you only on the paved and gravel roads and not on the trail. Taking the actual Williams River Trail would cut off either U.S. Forest Service (USFS) Road 115 or USFS86. The least hilly option (only about 300 feet of altitude gained) for riding the trail would be to start at either campsite and take USFS86; the option taking full advantage of the views from the scenic highway—but requiring much more climbing—would be to take USFS115 after starting at the Little Laurel Overlook of the scenic highway.

The Highland Scenic Highway 150, a fantastic two-lane road running for 23 miles along the tops of ridges, would itself make a wonderful road trip (although there are no services along its length outside of the primitive campgrounds). Reminiscent of the gorgeous Blue Ridge Parkway in Virginia, the scenic highway commands spectacular views of line after line of the forested ridges that are so beautifully characteristic of West Virginia. Moreover, its pavement is so superb and the automobile traffic so light that "we Rollerblade all over it," remarks Gil Willis, and in the winter locals cross-country ski on it because it remains unplowed.

There is *nowhere* to buy food or drink on this ride, so you must stock up at Slatyfork. The Little Laurel Overlook has a sheltered picnic table and a chemical toilet (as well as a great view). At both Handley and Tea Creek there are primitive campsites with pit toilets and drinking water (at Tea Creek you heave the long handle of an old-fashioned hand pump to draw up the frosty well water). Bring any tools you anticipate needing.

Oh, yes, one other note: Hunting season in West Virginia starts the last week in November. Mountain biking during hunting season is *not* recommended.

The Basics

Start: The Little Laurel Overlook on Highland Scenic Hwy 150. From the Elk River Touring Center in Slatyfork, drive (or pedal) 8 miles south on U.S. Rte. 219/State Rte. 55; turn right onto Hwy. 150; in 3.9 miles turn left into the overlook's parking lot.

Length: 16 miles if only the paved and gravel roads are taken (as the ride is written); 14 or 15 miles if the Williams Creek Trail is taken.

Terrain: One long descent at the beginning; one stiff climb at the end. Traffic is light.

Food: *None*—stock up in Slatyfork; water is available at the Tea Creek and Handley campgrounds.

Miles & Directions

- **0.0** Turn right out of the Little Laurel Overlook onto Highland Scenic Hwy. 150N toward Rte. 219/Rte. 55.
- **1.8** Turn right onto the gravel Friel Run Rd. and make an immediate left onto the gravel unmarked USFS115. Descend slowly on the gravel, taking care when passing over the cattle grates in 0.5 mile and 1 mile.
- **3.5** Turn right at the T intersection (stop sign) onto the semi-paved Rte. 17/3, passing some of the trailer homes and farm buildings of the community of Woodrow.
- **4.9** Bear right at the church, and immediately turn right at the next T intersection (stop sign) onto the nicely paved two-lane unmarked Rte. 17/1, following the sign WILLIAMS RIVER 5 MI. Soon you're riding through a farm valley.
- **6.4** Bear left onto Rte. 17/4.

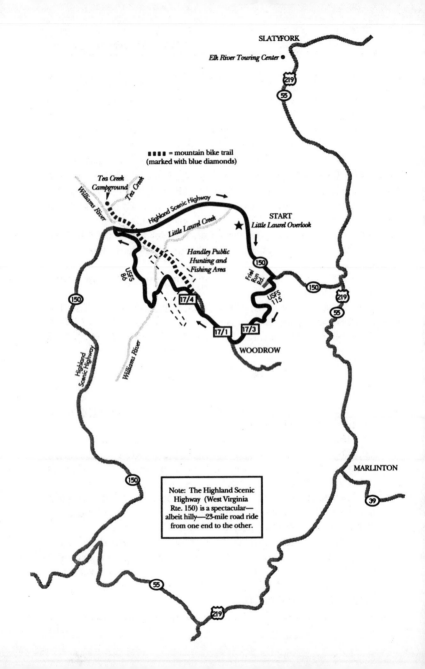

SLATYFORK

Elk River Touring Center ●

219
55

■■■■ = mountain bike trail
(marked with blue diamonds)

*Tea Creek
Campground*

Tea Creek

Williams River

Highland Scenic Highway →

Little Laurel Creek

START
Little Laurel Overlook

★

150

*Handley Public
Hunting and
Fishing Area*

*Trail
Run
Rd.*

USFS
86

USFS
115

150

150

219

17/4

55

17/1   17/3

WOODROW

Williams River

*Highland
Scenic
Highway*

150

MARLINTON

39

Note: The Highland Scenic
Highway (West Virginia
Rte. 150) is a spectacular—
albeit hilly—23-mile road ride
from one end to the other.

150

55

219

To ride the Williams River Trail, keep heading straight here (instead of bearing left) to enter the Handley Public Hunting and Fishing Area (the sign reads HANDLEY WILDLIFE MANAGEMENT AREA*). In 1.0 mile bear left at the Y intersection, following the sign to* MANAGER'S RESIDENCE *(the right-hand fork goes to the campground); 0.1 mile later pass through a gate marked with a blue diamond onto an old two-track dirt road. This is one end of the Williams River Trail, which is marked with blue diamonds all along its 3.75-mile length to the Tea Creek Campground. At Tea Creek Campground you'll emerge at a circular parking area, in the center of which is the hand water pump. Exit the campground by heading left onto the bridge over the Williams River. Turn left at the T intersection and ride another mile on gravel USFS86. Immediately after passing under the overpass for Scenic Hwy. 150, turn right onto the paved onramp and follow the directions from mile 12.3 below.*

- 8.8 Cross the bridge over the Williams River.
- 9.2 Bear right at the Y intersection onto the unmarked gravel USFS86, following the sign TO SCENIC HIGHWAY 150, and begin climbing. In about 3 miles you'll approach the concrete bridge over the Williams River that is part of Scenic Hwy. 150.
- 12.3 Turn left onto the paved onramp leading up to the overpass of Scenic Hwy. 150.
- 12.5 Turn right at the T intersection onto Scenic Hwy. 150. Begin a 3.5-mile-long, arduous, steady climb.
- 16.1 Turn right into the Little Laurel Overlook.

40

Observatory and Railroad Classic

Marlinton—Green Bank—Bartow—Cass—Marlinton

This entire classic is within the Monongahela National Forest, which spreads 848,000 acres over nine counties. The first half of the ride is a 35-mile-long, relatively gentle uphill all the way from Marlinton to Bartow. You'll pass through the Seneca State Forest (304-799-6213), where there is picnicking and primitive camping. The entire ride is within Pocahontas County.

If you don't feel like pedaling the whole 90-mile classic, you can still hit the two main attractions in a shorter challenge of 58 miles, whose route is based on the suggestion of Rachel Alpert, program director of the Greenbrier River Leadership Center in Bartow (which, among other activities, offers a variety of mountain-bike tours—call 304-456-5191), and Karen G. Carper, owner of the Bikeworks bicycle shop in Elkins.

The first attraction, some 27 miles into the ride, is the National Radio Astronomy Observatory (NRAO) in Green Bank (304-456-2011). The observatory is open to the public at no charge. You may walk around and gaze at the giant dish-shaped telescopes, which stand in the open air and are used to listen to radio emissions from the heavens twenty-four hours a day. Free tours are given in the summer.

If it is late afternoon when you leave NRAO, you can easily turn the 90-mile classic into a two-day ride by spending the night in Bartow 9 miles north (36 miles into the 90). The nicest place in Bartow is The Hermitage (304-456-4808), a motel and restaurant on the bank of the east fork of the Greenbrier River. The rear door of every room opens onto a long porch, which overlooks a large green and the river—perfect for enjoying a sunset drink and listening to the peepers as the stars come out.

Five miles after leaving Bartow, the second half of the ride becomes almost like mountain biking on pavement: winding, rolling, with rollercoaster-sharp turns and steep climbs, on the appropriately named Back Mountain Road. Sixty-seven miles into the classic, stop for the second main attraction: a ride on a turn-of-the-century, 90-ton steam-powered Shay logging locomotive at the Cass Scenic Railroad State Park (304–456–4300). On selected Saturday evenings throughout the summer, you can make reservations on a "dinner train," which includes a barbecue and live bluegrass entertainment. Cass also has The Shay Inn (a bed-and-breakfast) and fully equipped six- or eight-person cottages, complete with linens and kitchen utensils. For reservations, call either (304) 456–4652 or 572–3771.

The last half of the classic, from Bartow through Cass and back to Marlinton, has almost no services. Stock up well at the ride's start in Marlinton, at Green Bank, or at Bartow if you're taking the 58-mile challenge. Route 66 passes The Amish Bakery—an unmarked white farmhouse open Wednesday through Saturday from 12:00 noon to 5:00 A.M. Don't rely on Cass except during the summer: Even in late May right before Memorial Day, daytime services at Cass—including the country store, snack bar, and rest rooms—are closed except for an outdoor soft drink machine. As there are no bike shops anywhere, be sure to take all the tools you may need.

Marlinton has several places to stay overnight, among them the Marlinton Motor Inn (304–799–4711) and the Jerico B&B (304–799–6241). A night at Marlinton would allow you also to explore the Greenbrier River Hike, Bike, and Ski Trail. The restored railroad depot that is now the Marlinton Visitors Center is an access to the Greenbrier River Trail, the level former bed of the Greenbrier Division of the C&O Railway built at the turn of the century to serve the booming timber industry of the time. Now the public trail passes through numerous small towns and traverses thirty-five bridges and two tunnels, much of the route adjacent to the beautiful Greenbrier River. You can ride along the hard-packed gravel bed as far north as Cass (24 miles) or as far south as North Caldwell (53 miles). For a detailed map and guide to the trail, write to the Greenbrier River Trail Association, Inc., Slatyfork, WV 26291.

The Basics

Start: Marlinton, at the parking lot of the Marlinton Visitor Center (an old converted railroad station) on Rte. 39 0.2 mile east of Rte. 219/15.

Length: 58 or 90 miles.

Terrain: Rolling to hilly. Traffic ranges from moderate to light on the main roads outbound and is practically nonexistent on the return.

Food: Convenience stores and restaurants in Marlinton, Green Bank, and Bartow; food available at Cass between Memorial Day and Labor Day; that is *it!* Moreover, on the 90-mile ride other than in the summer, there could be a stretch of *37 miles without food or water* (from Durbin to Marlinton). Take all necessary tools.

Miles & Directions

- 0.0 Turn left out of the Marlinton Visitor Center parking lot onto Rte. 39E (Main St.). Ride through the quaint, brick downtown district of Marlinton. Load up here on snacks and water; your next opportunity is in 21 miles. After leaving the outskirts of town, you'll begin climbing.
- 5.5 Turn left onto Rte. 28N, continuing your gradual climb through farm land. At mile 15.8 you'll pass the entrance to the Seneca State Forest.
- 21.0 Turn left at the stop sign to stay on Rte. 28N, where Rte. 92N joins your route. At this intersection are an Exxon gas station and a small convenience store—the first in 21 miles.
- 24.4 At this intersection with Rte. 66W, continue straight to stay on Rte. 28N/92N.

west fork

1

DURBIN

92 250 BARTOW

east fork
of the
Greenbrier River

28 250

11 20

The Hermitage

1

Back Mountain Rd.

Greenbrier River

28
92

National Radio
Astronomy Observatory

The Amish
Bakery

The Country Store

GREEN
BANK

66

66/1

CASS

28

92

Turn left here for 58-mile challenge;
go straight for 90-mile classic

66

Cass Scenic
Railroad State
Park

92

STONY
BOTTOM

1

Convenience store

9

Back Mountain Rd.

28

CLOVER
LICK

1

9

Fairview Rd.

1

15

1/c

Seneca
State Forest

55
219

28

Airport Rd.

Greenbrier River

START
Marlinton
Visitor Center

★ MARLINTON

55
219

39

28

■ 27.6 Turn left to enter the grounds of the National Radio Astronomy Observatory. To continue the 90-mile route, leave the observatory grounds by turning left to continue north on Rtes. 28N/92N.

For the 58-mile challenge, leave the observatory grounds by turning right instead and retracing 3.2 miles south along Rte. 28S/92S. Then turn right onto Rte. 66W, coast 4.6 miles down to Cass, and pick up the directions at mile 67.3.

By the way, only 0.6 mile down Rte. 66 from Rtes. 28N/92N is The Amish Bakery; a small sign will direct you to turn right and continue for 0.5 mile. The bakery is actually a white farmhouse with no sign but with a small gravel area for cars to park; walk in the front door and you'll know you've arrived.

■ 36.2 Bear left to stay on Rte. 92N/250 as Rte. 28N heads right. You are entering Bartow. Not 500 feet later, just after crossing over the east fork of the Greenbrier River, The Hermitage motel is on your left. At mile 38.9 you'll pass a grocery market in the town of Durbin. At mile 40.0 you'll pass a gas station on your left, which has a small convenience store. This is your *last chance* before Cass—or possibly Marlinton—to stock up on food and drink.

■ 41.4 Turn left onto Rte. 1 (Back Mountain Rd.).

■ 42.7 Make a *sharp* right to stay on Rte. 1 (Back Mountain Rd.), where Rte. 251/11 (Grant Vandevender Rd.) goes straight. This is real backwoods West Virginia, where tumbledown farms with rusting trucks and buses in the muddy yards overlook boulder-strewn fields and forested hills of stunning beauty. Just keep going for nearly 15 miles.

■ 67.2 Turn left at the T intersection onto the unmarked Rte. 66E. This is Cass. In a few hundred feet, just across the railroad track, you'll be at the Cass Country Store and Soda Fountain and Restaurant, the terminus for the scenic railroad. Across the parking lot there are picnic tables with barbecue grills on the bank of the Greenbrier River.

■ 67.3 To resume the ride turn right out of the Cass Scenic Railroad State Park parking lot onto the unmarked Rte. 66W. You'll pedal through the restored village of Cass, past the rental cabins and gift shops, rejoining Rte. 1. Cass is also the northernmost access to the Greenbrier River Trail, which is an alternate return to Marlinton (24.6 miles to the south by the trail).

- **69.0** Turn left onto the continuation of Rte. 1 (Back Mountain Rd.), heading south. At mile 72.1 you'll descend into Stony Bottom, where amid all this wildness you'll suddenly encounter Moore's Lodge Motel (304–456–4721) on your right next to the river; there are no other services. Then you'll begin a very steep climb. At mile 75.0 Rte. 9 (Linwood Rd.) joins Rte. 1 (Back Mountain Rd.) from the right. A mile later you'll enter the small community of Clover Lick—another access to the Greenbrier River Trail for an alternate return to Marlinton (15 miles south by the trail through its most wild and remote section).
- **76.1** Turn right at the T intersection to stay on the unmarked Rte. 1/9, following the sign reading MARLINTON 14 MI.
- **82.9** Bear right at the Y intersection to stay on Rte. 1 (Back Mountain Rd.) where Rte. 1/6 (Fairview Rd.) heads left.
- **83.6** Turn left at the triangle onto Rte. 15 (Airport Rd.), a two-lane road of excellent pavement that now seems like a veritable freeway. This is a lovely downhill glide past farms.
- **88.8** Turn left at the T intersection onto the unmarked and very busy Rte. 55/219. Watch for cars! If you're hungry, you now have a choice between Kentucky Fried Chicken and Dairy Queen.
- **89.8** Turn left onto Rte. 39E into Marlinton.
- **90.0** Turn left into the parking lot of the Marlinton Visitor Center.

41

Hillsboro Farmland Cruise

Hillsboro—Lobelia—Droop Mountain—Hillsboro

For a true appreciation of West Virginia farmland and countryside, this 25-mile tour in Pocahontas County can't be beat. You'll start in the town of Hillsboro, birthplace of Pearl S. Buck (1892–1973)—the only American woman to be awarded both the Pulitzer Prize in literature (in 1932 for *The Good Earth*) and the Nobel Prize in literature (1938). In fact, just 0.75 mile north of this ride's start on Route 219, the white clapboard home where she was born is now a museum, open to the public Monday through Saturday (for hours call 304-653-4430).

The ride, suggested in part by Cara L. Hefner, director of the Pocahontas County Tourism Commission, first meanders through farms where you may see sheep and cattle grazing. But this is no tame and pastoral farmland like the somnolent rolling fields of Pennsylvania. No, this is red-knuckled farmland clinging to the steep sides of hollows, surly in its strong beauty lying naked among the tree-covered rocky hills.

And those rocky hills you will climb. The roads become very twisty, very narrow, and very steep—up to 9 percent grade as you approach and leave Droop Mountain, site of the most extensive Civil War battle in West Virginia. The site is now a state park with a small museum, picnic areas, and a stacked-log lookout tower commanding a spectacular view.

But there's a great payoff for all that climbing: the gorgeous land and its sheer isolation. There is nothing to disturb your contemplation of nature other than the rhythmic sound of your own deep breathing in grinding up switchbacks; in the whole route it is doubtful you'll encounter as many as half a dozen cars (except for the brief stretch on Route 219).

The first half of the ride (up Droop Mountain) is a net climb, with the second half being a net descent, from a high of 3,060 feet above sea level to a low of 2,200 feet. But as in Nepal, there are considerable ups and downs in between; the probable total of a couple of thousand feet gained and lost is the reason this short ride is definitely not a ramble. But it is one of the simplest routes in this book, taking only four roads: Lobelia Road its full length, left onto Route 219 for 2.6 miles, right onto Locust Creek Road for 3 miles, and left onto Denmar Road until its end back in Hillsboro.

These roads are so little traveled that there are *no* services outside of Hillsboro. Stock up there on food and water before you leave, and be sure to take your tools. There are, however, a couple of inns in the area to stay a night: the Yew Mountain Lodge (304–653–4821) and The Current Bed & Breakfast (304–653–4722) halfway through the ride. (The Current, by the way, is adjacent to the Greenbrier River Trail, a generally level former railroad bed now devoted to hiking and biking along the river.) Bicycle campers can pitch a tent and enjoy a hot shower at the 10,000-acre Watoga State Park a few miles northeast of Hillsboro (304–799–4087).

The Basics

Start: Hillsboro, on Rte. 219 at the corner of Rte. 29 (Lobelia Rd.). Park along Rte. 219 across from the Rosewood Cafe.
Length: 25 miles.
Terrain: Very hilly. Virtually no traffic on the side roads, although traffic may be moderately heavy on the unavoidable 2.6-mile stretch on Rte. 219. *Watch for gravel.*
Food: No services outside of Hillsboro. Take more snacks, water, and tools than you think you might need.

Miles & Directions

■ 0.0 From Rte. 219 through the center of Hillsboro, head west (the only direction you can go) on Rte. 29 (Lobelia Rd.). First

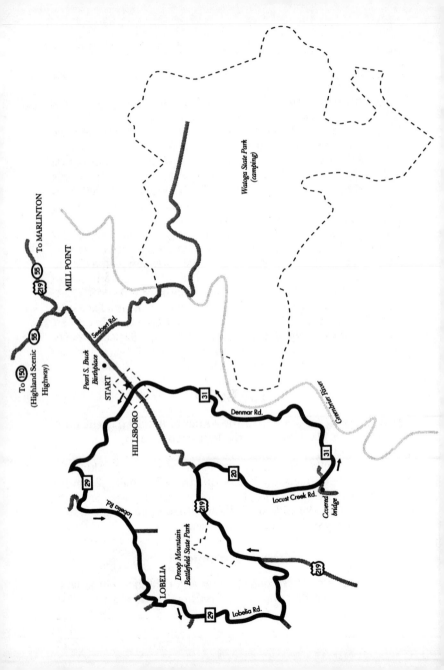

you'll ride through open farmland with cows and sheep, and soon you'll be climbing through forest. At mile 4.9 you'll pass Rte. 22 (Russell Scott Rd.) on your left; at mile 6.6 you'll pass Rte. 29/21 (Bruffy's Creek Rd.) on your right. At mile 7.2 follow Rte. 29 (Lobelia Rd.) as it makes a ninety-degree left turn through the town of Lobelia (a few sagging buildings with no services), following the sign TO 219. At mile 8.4 keep heading straight through the intersection of two gravel and dirt roads (George Hill Rd. and Briery Knob Rd.), following the sign TO 219.

- 10.9 Bear left at the unsigned Y intersection to stay on Rte. 29 (Lobelia Rd.). A mile later begin a *steep* climb up the back of Droop Mountain, taking time to enjoy the expansive vista at your left over the valley to forested West Virginia ridges.

- 13.1 Turn left at the T intersection onto Rte. 219. Watch for cars! At this point you are nearly at the summit of the mountain, which has an altitude of 3,060 feet. At mile 13.7 you'll pass one entrance to Droop Mountain State Park on your left. At mile 14.1, after passing a second park entrance, you'll begin a *steep* descent of a 9 percent grade down tight switchbacks for the next 0.75 mile. *Caution! Watch for gravel and cars!*

- 15.7 Turn right onto Rte. 20 (Locust Creek Rd.).

- 18.8 Turn left at the T intersection onto the unmarked Rte. 31 (Denmar Rd.). But before you make the turn, you might want to detour 100 feet to your right to walk through the century-old covered bridge, no longer in service for automobile traffic but preserved for posterity as a landmark.

- 20.1 Bear left at the small white church to stay on Rte. 31 (Denmar Rd.). At mile 20.7 you'll pass the stark white building of the Denmar State Hospital for the chronically ill, which overlooks the beautiful Greenbrier River. You've now descended to the lowest point on the ride, 2,200 feet. The rest is a relatively gentle ascent.

- 21.4 Turn right at the T intersection to stay on the unmarked Rte. 31 (Denmar Rd.). Now you're pedaling through farmland.

- 25.1 Arrive back at Rte. 219 at your starting point, across the highway from Rte. 29 (Lobelia Rd.). (To visit the Pearl S. Buck Birthplace, turn right onto Rte. 219 and ride another 0.75 mile.)

42

Springs to Springs Cruise

White Sulphur Springs—Sweet Chalybeate Springs
White Sulphur Springs

Grab your swimsuit and towel! This beautiful ride through rolling West Virginia hills, farmland, meadows, and creeks has as its destination a dip in the seventy-two-degree pools of Sweet Chalybeate Springs in the neighboring state of Virginia.

In the nineteenth century the refreshing mineral waters of Sweet Chalybeate (pronounced "ka-LEE-bee-ah") were famed for their healing powers, and bottled water from the area is locally available. The two beautiful swimming pools filled by the cool, continuously flowing natural springs are perfect for sluicing off a cyclist's sweat after a hot summer's day of pedaling. They are open to the public for a modest fee during the summer whenever the owner, Myron Pierson—a hippie-era former attorney from Atlanta who wears a Boy Scout cap and drives a 1968 black Chevy—takes a mind. *Note:* As this tucked-away refuge is *not* a standard tourist attraction, it has no attendant or lifeguard, and you swim at your own risk. There is no phone number to call; you'll know the springs are open only by arriving and seeing the gate open. (And should the gate be closed, you can instead swim in nearby Dunlap Creek.)

The ride to Sweet Chalybeate is a favorite of Dr. Alinda L. Perrine, owner of Free Spirit Adventures and Bike Sales in Lewisburg (800–877–4749), where you can rent a bicycle or sign up for group mountain-bike tours. The route starts in White Sulphur Springs in West Virginia's Greenbrier County, home of the world-famous 6,500-acre resort The Greenbrier (800–624–6070 or 304–536–1110), which—among other attractions—has bicycle trails for its guests.

Although this is a relatively easy ride, because of the climb up Alleghany Mountain it is rated as a cruise instead of a ramble. In spite of the climb, the ride out is a net downhill, but then, naturally, the ride back, which retraces the route out, is a net climb. As in many rides in West Virginia, traffic is exceptionally light. Aside from a spring—where you can fill your water bottles on the climb up Alleghany Mountain—and The Eagle's Nest—a rustic, romantic restaurant in the town of Alleghany in Alleghany County, Virginia—there are no other services; pack snacks and tools.

The Basics

Start: White Sulphur Springs, West Virginia, at the Ward Motor Corp., 89 Main St. (Rte. 60), at the corner of Main St. and Mountain Ave. Park along the street.
Length: 28 miles round-trip; retrace the same route out and back.
Terrain: Rolling hills. Outside of White Sulphur Springs, traffic is light.
Food: The Eagle's Nest, an excellent restaurant in Alleghany, Virginia, is open evenings.

Miles & Directions

- 0.0 From Ward Motor Corp. on Rte. 60 (Main St.), turn left onto Mountain Ave., to head south (the only way you can go). Now you're riding on a fairly flat section through a residential area.
- 0.5 Head straight onto Rte. 601 (Tuckahoe Rd.).
- 2.9 Bear left at the Y intersection to stay on the unmarked Rte. 601 (Tuckahoe Rd.); do not cross the one-lane bridge after the intersection. Begin climbing into the woods to the top of Alleghany Mountain. At the summit you will leave Greenbrier County, West Virginia, and enter Alleghany County, Virginia.
- 4.7 Turn right at the base of the mountain onto Rte. 311S (Kanawha Trail). Just after riding through a one-lane tunnel

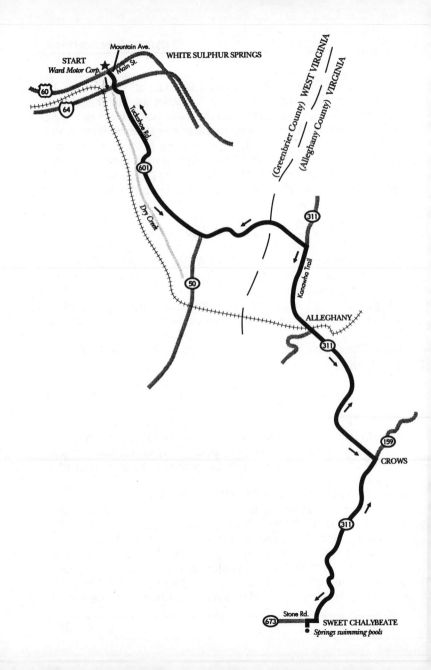

into the community of Alleghany, The Eagle's Nest restaurant will be on your right beside a lovely waterfall.

- 8.6 Bear right in the community of Crows to stay on Rte. 311S where Rte. 159 comes in from the left. Now you can get the old cardiovascular system pumped up with pedaling over rolling hills and flat farmland. You will cross Dunlap Creek three times before entering the community of Sweet Chalybeate.
- 14.4 Take the second right onto Rte. 673 (Stone Rd.), and then turn left into Sweet Chalybeate Springs Swimming Pools. After your swim turn right out of the parking lot onto Rte. 673. Turn left onto Rte. 311.
- 20.4 Turn left at the T intersection in Crows to stay on Rte. 311N (Kanawha Trail).
- 24.4 Turn left onto Rte. 601 (Tuckahoe Rd.) and begin climbing Alleghany Mountain.
- 26.4 Bear right to stay on Rte. 601 (Tuckahoe Rd.).
- 27.9 Bear left onto Mountain Ave.
- 28.4 Turn right onto Rte. 60W back to Ward Motor Corp.

Appendix

Below are some selected references, the major ones pertinent to bicycle touring in the Mid-Atlantic states. The list is not exhaustive. If any organization, set of maps, or other reference that should have been included has been omitted or if an address has changed, please send the necessary information to the author for inclusion in the next edition of this book: Trudy E. Bell, 18 Cherry Place, Maplewood, NJ 07040 (fax: 201–378–2304).

National Cycling Organizations

Adventure Cycling Association
P.O. Box 8308
Missoula, MT 59807
(406) 721–1776

The Adventure Cycling Association is a national, nonprofit organization for recreational cyclists, founded in 1974 as Bikecentennial; since then it has established the 19,000-mile National Bicycle Route Network, for which it publishes maps and marks cross-state and cross-country roads as bicycle routes. It publishes the magazine *BikeReport* nine times a year for members, including the annual reference *Cyclists' Yellow Pages;* sells panniers, tents, guidebooks, and other touring merchandise; and conducts guided bicycle tours, including ones up to three months long across the country.

League of American Wheelmen (LAW)
190 W. Ostend Dr., Suite 120
Baltimore, MD 21230-3755
(410) 539-3399

LAW is a national, nonprofit bicycle-advocacy organization, serving the interests of touring, utilitarian, and club cyclists. It has a full-time government relations advocate, who represents LAW's concerns with legislation and other activities to gain for cyclists greater legal rights and safer access to roads. It publishes the magazine *Bicycle USA* eight times a year for members, including the annual *TourFinder* and *Almanac* reference issues.

State Cycling Organizations

Some telephone numbers are not included, following club policy.

Delaware
Delmarva Bicycle Club
c/o Frances M. Smith
1404 Forrest Ave., #C
Dover, DE 19901-3315
(302) 734-4994

Diamond State Bicycle Club
c/o Tom Hartley
P.O. Box 1729
Dover, DE 19903-1729
(302) 378-4000

White Clay Bicycle Club
c/o Nancy Estilow
1124 12th Ave.
Murray Manor II
Wilmington, DE 19808

Maryland
Annapolis Bicycle Club
P.O. Box 224
Annapolis, MD 21404-0224
(410) 267-2996

Baltimore Bicycling Club
P.O. Box 5906
Baltimore, MD 21208
(410) 792-8308
or
9515 Deereco Rd., Suite 601
Timonium, MD 21093-2146

Cumberland Valley Cycling
Club
P.O. Box 711
Hagerstown, MD 21740-0711
(301) 797-7039

Frederick Pedalers Bike Club
P.O. Box 1293
Frederick, MD 21702-0293
(301) 845-8307

Freestate Derailleurs Bicycle
Club
c/o Frank J. Pondolfina
4424 MacWorth Pl.
Baltimore, MD 21236-2615
(410) 256-6968

Oxon Hill Bicycle & Trail Club
c/o John Kimmons
P.O. Box 81
Oxon Hill, MD 20750-0081
(301) 899-6894

P.A.C.E. (Patuxent Area Cycling)
P.O. Box 1318
Solomons, MD 20688-1318
(410) 535-2938

Salisbury Bicycle Club
c/o Edward K. Payne
708 Walnut St.
Pocomoke City, MD 21851-1525
(410) 957-3089

Salisbury State University
Cycling Club
c/o Joseph K. Gilbert
Office of the Vice President of
Administration
Salisbury State University
Salisbury, MD 21801-6837
(410) 543–6012

New Jersey
Bicycle Touring Club of North
Jersey
P.O. Box 306
Cliffside Park, NJ 07010-0306
(201) 284–0404

Central Jersey Bicycle Club
P.O. Box 2202
Edison, NJ 08818-2202
(908) 654–9228

East Coast Bicycle Club of
Orange County
c/o Pat Cividanes
44 Edith Ct.
Toms River, NJ 08753-2611
(908) 255–5397

Jersey Shore Touring Society
P.O. Box 8581
Red Bank, NJ 07701-8581
(908) 747–8206

Morris Area Freewheelers
P.O. Box 331
Lake Hiawatha, NJ 07034-0331

North Jersey Bicycle Club
c/o John P. Quinn
100 Ridgewald Ave.
Waldwick, NJ 07463-2109

Outdoor Club of South Jersey
583 Ridgewood Ter.
Mt. Laurel, NJ 08054
(609) 235–2457
or
P.O. Box 455
Cherry Hill, NJ 08003-0455
(609) 871–1932

Princeton Freewheelers
P.O. Box 1204
Princeton, NJ 08542-1204

Shore Cycle Club
P.O. Box 492
Northfield, NJ 08225
(609) 628–2358

South Jersey Wheelmen
c/o Arthur Schalick
P.O. Box 2705
Vineland, NJ 08360-1076
(609) 327–1336

Western Jersey Wheelmen
c/o Robert Boysen
41 Philhower Rd.
Lebanon, NJ 08833
(908) 832–7361

New York
Big Wheels Bicycle Club
379 Joe MacCarthy Dr.
Amherst, NY 14228-2610
(716) 691–9461

Bike WNY
P.O. Box 1101
Buffalo, NY 14205-1101
(716) 885–4633

Canton Bicycle Club
P.O. Box 364
Canton, NY 13617-0364

Catskill Wheelmen, Inc.
c/o Robert Klein
21 Katrina Falls Rd.
Rock Hill, NY 12775
(914) 796–3336

C.L.I.M.B.
c/o Pat Astegher
P.O. Box 203
Woodbury, NY 11797

Country Cycle Club, Inc.
c/o Kathy Holmes
1296 Midland Ave., #2A
Yonkers, NY 10704
(212) 755–7656

Cruise Brothers Bike Club Inc.
85 Carmans Rd.
Massapequa, NY 11758
(516) 541–1707

Five Borough Bicycle Club
American Youth Hostels
891 Amsterdam Ave.
New York, NY 10025
(212) 932–2300

Long Island Bicycle Club
c/o Mark Bornfield
415 Argyle Rd., #4J
Brooklyn, NY 11218
(516) 484–2645

Mid-Hudson Bicycle Club
P.O. Box 1727
Poughkeepsie, NY 12601

Mohawk-Hudson Wheelmen
P.O. Box 5230
Albany, NY 12205-0575

New York Bicycling Coalition
P.O. Box 7335
Albany, NY 12224-0335
(518) 373–1831

New York Cycle Club
c/o Richard Rosenthal
P.O. Box 199, Cooper Station
New York, NY 10022
(212) 242–3900

Niagara Frontier Bicycle Club
P.O. Box 211
Buffalo, NY 14226-0211
(716) 836–8359

Onondaga Cycling Club, Inc.
P.O. Box 6307, Teall Station
Syracuse, NY 13217-6307

Orange County Bicycle Club
c/o Alice A. Laughlin
P.O. Box 20
Campbell Hall, NY 10916
(914) 294–5212

Paumonok Bicycle Clubs
P.O. Box 7159
Hicksville, NY 11802
(516) 842–4699

Rochester Bicycling Club
P.O. Box 10100
Rochester, NY 14610
(716) 671–6732

Sound Cyclists Bicycle Club
c/o Jeffrey Ross
Soundvie Loop Rd. 4
South Salem, NY 10590
(914) 533–2711

Southern Tier Bicycle Club
c/o Augie P. Mueller
4009 Drexel Dr.
Vestal, NY 13850-4016
(607) 722–6005

Staten Island Bicycling Club
P.O. Box 141016
Staten Island, NY 10314-0004
(718) 273–0805

Suffolk Bike Riders Association
P.O. Box 404
Saint James, NY 11780

Transportation Alternatives
92 St. Marks Pl.
New York, NY 10009-5840
(212) 475–4600

Pennsylvania
Berks County Bicycle Club
c/o Tom Moyer
4624 Pheasant Run N.
Reading, PA 19606-3542
(215) 370–1239

Bicycle Club of Philadelphia
P.O. Box 30235
Philadelphia, PA 19103
(215) 592–8703 or 440–9983

Bicycle Coalition of the
   Delaware Valley
P.O. Box 8194
Philadelphia, PA 19101-8194
(215) BICYCLE

Brandywine Bicycle Club
P.O. Box 3162
West Chester, PA 19381
(215) 783–0536

Bucks County Biking
P.O. Box 534
New Hope, PA 18938-0534
(215) 862–0733

Central Bucks Bicycle Club
P.O. Box 295
Buckingham, PA 18912-0295
(215) 348–5639

Hanover Cyclers
c/o Jack Housman
129 Baltimore St.
Hanover, PA 17331-3111
(717) 632–7516

Harrisburg Bicycle Club
c/o Bill Wierman
1011 Bridge St.
New Cumberland, PA 17070-1631
(717) 761–4822

Lancaster Bicycle Club
P.O. Box 535
Lancaster, PA 17603-0535
(717) 560–3636 or 387–1149

Lebanon Valley Bicycle Club
408 Wilshire Dr.
Cleona, PA 17042
(717) 272–8071

Lehigh Wheelmen Association, Inc.
P.O. Box 356
Bethlehem, PA 18016-0356
(215) 435–8662

Suburban Cyclists Unlimited
P.O. Box 401
Horsham, PA 19044-0401

Susquehanna Valley Bike Club
P.O. Box 63
Berwick, PA 18603-0063
(717) 784–6856

Western Pennsylvania Wheelmen Bicycle Club
P.O. Box 6952
Pittsburgh, PA 15212-0952
(412) 782–1341

Wyoming Valley Bicycle Club
c/o Carol King
P.O. Box 253
Dallas, PA 18612-0253
(717) 675–2328

Washington, D.C.
Potomac Pedalers Touring Club, Inc.
6729 Curran St.
McLean, VA 22101
(202) 363–TOUR

Spokespeople
P.O. Box 33554
Washington, DC 20033-0554

Washington Area Bicyclist Association (WABA)
1819 H St. NW, Suite 640
Washington, DC 20006
(202) 872–9830

The Wayfarers
P.O. Box 73408
Washington, DC 20056-3408
(202) 265–1418 or 872-9830

West Virginia
Blennerhassett Bicycle Club
P.O. Box 2262
Parkersburg, WV 26102-2262
(304) 485–1611

Harrison County Bicycle Club
c/o Paul Moses
982 W. Pike St.
Clarksburg, WV 26301-2554

Mountain State Wheelers Bicycle Club
P.O. Box 8161
South Charleston, WV 25303-0161
(304) 345–4136

State Bicycling Maps and Guides

The DeLorme Mapping Company has published an *Atlas & Gazetteer* for New York and Pennsylvania and is working on similar editions for other Mid-Atlantic states. The large-format book of topographic maps also shows dirt and paved roads and suggested bicycle routes, and it lists wildlife areas and other local attractions. These maps are accurate and are superb in rural areas; their scale is too small, however, to be helpful in towns and cities. For a list and prices, contact DeLorme Mapping Co., P.O. Box 298, Freeport, ME 04032; (800) 227–1656.

The tabloid-size newspaper *Spokes*, published nine times a year, covers bicycle touring, racing, off-road, recreation, triathalon, and commuting news in the southern Mid-Atlantic states. It is available for free at many area bicycle stores, fitness centers, and sporting establishments in Maryland, Virginia, Washington, D.C., and parts of Delaware, Pennsylvania, and West Virginia. For more information contact the editor and publisher, Neil W. Sandler, at *Spokes*, 5334 Sovereign Pl., Frederick, MD 21710; (301) 846–0326.

DELAWARE
Delaware State and County Road Maps and Maps for Bicycle Users
Contract Administration,
  Delaware Department of
  Transportation
P.O. Box 778
Dover, DE 19903
(302) 739–4318
Send for free map index.

Delaware Valley Commuters Bicycle Map
Greater Philadelphia Bicycle
  Coalition
P.O. Box 8194
Philadelphia, PA 19101
(215) 387–9242
$5.75 ppd. Map (1982) of pre-
ferred commuting roads in
Delaware, New Jersey, and
Pennsylvania counties sur-
rounding Philadelphia.

MARYLAND
Maryland State and County Road Maps
Map Distribution Section
State Highway Administration
2323 W. Joppa Rd.
Brooklandville, MD 21022
(301) 321–3518

The Maryland Department of
Transportation has a toll-free
number for information about
bicycle-compatible transportation facilities and other bicycling information. Call
800–252–8776 Monday–Friday
between 8:30 A.M. and 4:30 P.M.

Baltimore Area Bike Map
Baltimore Regional Council of
  Governments
2225 N. Charles St.
Baltimore, MD 21218
(301) 554–5614
$2.50. Waterproof and tear-
proof. Routes for commuting
and touring in Baltimore and
surrounding counties (1984).

Maryland Bicycle Touring Map
Bicycle Affairs Coordinator
Maryland State Highway
  Administration
707 N. Calvert St.
P.O. Box 717
Baltimore, MD 21203
(800) 252–8776
Free. Cross-Maryland routes,
plus close-up maps of twelve
scenic routes.

Bicycle Tours of Frederick County, Maryland
Tourism Council of Frederick
  County, Inc.
19 E. Church St.
Frederick, MD 21701
(301) 663–8687

$4.00 plus tax at the visitor center; $5.25 ppd. Packet of cue sheets and maps for nine bicycle tours in Frederick County.

Carroll County Classic Country Bicycle Tours

Carroll County Tourist Information Center
210 E. Main St.
Westminster, MD 21157
(301) 848–1388
$1.00. Packet of cue sheets and maps for ten bicycle tours in Carroll County.

Chesapeake & Ohio Canal Map

C&O Canal National Historic Park
P.O. Box 4
Sharpsburg, MD 21782
Free. Map of 184.5-mile-long bicycling and hiking trail on the canal towpath from Cumberland to Georgetown.

NEW JERSEY

New Jersey county maps can be obtained at many local stationery stores and newsstands; the major local publishers are Geographia, Hagstrom, and Patton.

New Jersey County Maps

New Jersey Department of Transportation
Attn. Cashier
1035 Parkway Ave., CN600
Trenton, NJ 08625
(609) 530–2000
$2.00 per map, plus postage (75 cents folded, $1.50 rolled in a tube).

New Jersey Bicycling Information Packet

Pedestrian/Bicycle Advocate
New Jersey Department of Transportation
1035 Parkway Ave., CN600
Trenton, NJ 08625
(609) 530-2000
Free packet, including cue sheets, maps of popular bicycle tours, and a detailed information booklet listing clubs and tour organizations.

Bicycling Suitability Map of Western Jersey

Dan Rappaport
Holly House, #5M
Princeton, NJ 08540
$7.50.

Union County Bicycle Map

Union County Division of Planning and Development
County Administration Building

Elizabeth, NJ 07207
Free (1982). Map of Union
County, with roads colored
for suitability for cycling.

NEW YORK

Maps of New York counties
near New York City can be obtained at many local stationery
stores and newsstands; the
major local publishers are Geographia, Hagstrom, and Patton.

New York State and County Road Maps

Map Information Unit
New York State Department of
Transportation
State Campus, Building 4,
Room 105
Albany, NY 12232
(518) 457–3555
Send SASE for complete list and
prices.

Brooklyn Bike Map

Transportation Alternatives
92 St. Marks Pl.
New York, NY 10009-5840
(212) 475–4600
Map of the borough of Brooklyn, with roads colored for suitability for cycling.

Nassau County Bikeway Map

Nassau County Planning De-
partment
Transportation Division
222 Willis Ave.
Mineola, NY 11501
$1.00 (free at many bike shops).
Map of Nassau County on Long
Island, with roads colored for
suitability for cycling.

Oneida County Bike Map

Oneida County Convention
and Visitors Bureau
P.O. Box AA
Oriskany, NY 13424
(315) 724–7221; (800) 426–3132
(outside New York State)
Free. Detailed tours and routes
for all levels.

PENNSYLVANIA

Pennsylvania State and County Road Maps

Pennsylvania Department of
Transportation (PennDOT)
Sales Store
P.O. Box 2028
Harrisburg, PA 17105-2028
(717) 787–6746 or (800)
VISIT–PA
County maps, $2.00 each
folded, $75.00 per set, one map
per county.

Pennsylvania County Maps
County Maps
821 Puetz Place
Lyndon Station, WI 53844
(608) 666–3331
$11.90 ppd. Book of county
maps with information on history and on natural and recreational areas.

Pennsylvania Bicycling Guide
Pennsylvania Department of
Transportation (PennDOT)
Sales Store
P.O. Box 2028
Harrisburg, PA 17105-2028
(717) 787–6746 or (800)
VISIT–PA
The Pennsylvania Bicycling Guide
(2nd ed., 1986) is an index
map, plus four quadrant maps
of the state, color-coding the
roads best suitable for cross-
state cycling routes; also listed
are bicycle clubs, emergency
phone numbers, sources of
other cycling information, and
historic or scenic areas. Index
map is free; quadrant maps are
$1.25 each.

**Bicycle Touring Guide for
Central Pennsylvania**
Bicycle Division
Pennsylvania State Outing Club
IM Building, Room 8
University Park, PA 16802

$1.00. Network map (1982) of
suggested loop tours in the
State College area.

Lebanon County Bike Trails
Lebanon Valley Tourist and Visitors Bureau
P.O. Box 626
Lebanon, PA 17042
(717) 272–8555
Free with SASE. Map and description of bicycle tours in the
county.

WASHINGTON, D.C.
Washington, D.C., Street Map
Maps
D.C. Committee to Promote
Washington
415 12th St. NW, Suite 312
Washington, DC 20004
(202) 724–4091

**ADC's Washington Area Bike
Map**
ADC, "The Map People"
6440 General Green Way
Alexandria, VA 22312
(800) 232–6277
$6.95. April 1990 map, com-
piled by the Metropolitan
Washington Council of Governments, marks roads suitable
for bicycling, along with 64
miles of paved bicycle paths.

Getting around Washington By Bicycle

Office of Documents, Room 19
District Building
14th St. and Pennsylvania Ave. NW
Washington, DC 20004
(202) 727-5090
$3.00 ppd.; make check payable to "D.C. Treasurer." Eight detailed maps (1982), with recommended routes color-coded by traffic volume. Printed on waterproof paper; guidebook lists bicycle paths, bridge crossings, and so on.

WEST VIRGINIA

West Virginia State, County, and Urban Road Maps

West Virginia Department of Highways
Planning Division, Map Section, Room 851
1900 Washington St. E
Charleston, WV 25305
(304) 348–2868
Call for information and price list. These official county maps are as accurate as U.S. Geological Survey topographic maps, minus the contour lines; the mileages of all segments of numbered roads are given to the nearest 0.1 mile. Names of roads are omitted, however, as are all named but unnumbered city streets.

West Virginia County Maps and Recreational Guide

County Maps
821 Puetz Pl.
Lyndon Station, WI 53844
(608) 666–3331
$14.85 ppd. Fifty-five county maps, with table of state parks and natural and wild areas.

Guide to the Greenbrier River Trail

Greenbrier River Trail Association, Inc.
Slatyfork, WV 26291
$2.00 ppd. Map (1989) of 75-mile-long unpaved railroad right of way along the Greenbrier River, along with information about access points and places to stay overnight.

An Adventure Guide to West Virginia Rail Trails

by Frank Proud and Lynn Hartman
West Virginia Rails-to-Trails Council
P.O. Box 85
Nitro, WV 25143
(304) 722–6558
A booklet expected to be 60–80 pages long, scheduled for publi-

cation mid-1994 at an estimated
cost of $7.00. Call for details.

West Virginia Cycling Maps
Bill Foster
515 S. Linden
Clarksburg, WV 26301
Write for list of maps and prices.

Bicycle Touring Companies

This is only a partial list of locally based commercial touring companies that concentrate their efforts in the Mid-Atlantic states. Many reputable touring companies headquartered outside the area also offer lovely Mid-Atlantic tours. For more information consult Bikecentennial's *The Cyclists' Yellow Pages* or the League of American Wheelmen's *Bicycle USA TourFinder*.

In addition, charities such as the American Cancer Society, the American Lung Association, the March of Dimes, the National Multiple Sclerosis Society, and the United Way sponsor one-day and weekend fund-raising tours, whereby participants take pledges per mile traveled. Contact your local office of the charity for information about fund-raising rides in your area.

American Youth Hostels
P.O. Box 37613
Washington, DC 20013-7613
(202) 783–6161

Appalachian Valley Bicycle
Touring
P.O. Box 27079
Baltimore, MD 21230
(410) 837–8068

Biking Inn to Inn Delaware
The New Devon Inn
P.O. Box 516
Lewes, DE 19958
(302) 645–6466 or (800)
824–8754

Breakaway Vacations
164 E. 90th St., #2Y
New York, NY 10128
(212) 722–4221

Brooks Country Cycling and Hiking (formerly Country Cycling Tours)
140 W. 83rd St.
New York, NY 10024
(212) 874–5151 or (800) 284–8954 (outside New York, New Jersey, and Connecticut)

Classic Adventures
P.O. Box 153
Hamlin, NY 14464
(716) 964–8488 or (800) 777–8090

Elk River Touring Center
Hwy. 219
Slatyfork, WV 26291
(304) 572–3771
Mountain-bike tours. Also offers the book *Mountain Bike Rides in Pocahontas County, West Virginia* by Gil and Mary Willis (1992).

Finger Lakes Cycling Adventures
P.O. Box 457
Fairport, NY 14450
(716) 377–9817

Five Borough Bicycle Club
American Youth Hostels
891 Amsterdam Ave.
New York, NY 10025
(212) 932–2300 Ext. 355

Free Spirit Adventures
104 Foster St.
Lewisburg, WV 24901

(304) 645–2093 or
(800) 877–4749
Mountain-bike tours.

Freewheel Experience
RD1, Box 397
Mohawk, NY 13407

Greenbrier River Leadership Center
P.O. Box 160
Bartow, WV 24920-0160
(304) 456–5191 or (304) 636–0556
Mountain-bike tours.

Lancaster Bicycle Touring, Inc.
3 Colt Ridge Ln.
Strasburg, PA 17579
(717) 396–0456

Northstar Bicycle Tours
113 Crawley Ave.
Pennington, NJ 08534
(609) 737–8346

Pocono Inn-to-Inn Bicycle Tours
Rte. 903, HC2. Box 2245
Jim Thorpe, PA 18229
(717) 325–3656

Ridge Rider Mountain Bikes, Inc.
103 Keller Ave.
Fayetteville, WV 25840
(304) 574–BIKE (2453)
Mountain-bike tours.

Snowshoe Mountain Biking
  Center
P.O. Box 10
Snowshoe, WV 26209
(304) 572–1000
Mountain-bike tours.

True Wheel Tours
3K Woolerton St.
Delhi, NY 13753
(607) 746–2737

Acknowledgments

This book would not have been possible without the generous help of scores of people.

First, my deepest thanks go to the contributors of the individual routes, each of whom is credited in the ride's description. In some cases the contributor is also the person who painstakingly created the ride you may now enjoy. Many of these people spent hours traveling over the route specifically to answer questions I raised while writing this book; they also sent me helpful brochures and maps.

My deep gratitude goes as well to the contributors of the photographs that appear at the beginning of the state sections: for Delaware, Barbara Lloyd of the New Devon Inn in Lewes; for Maryland, the Carroll County Tourism Office; for Pennsylvania, Mark Scholefield of Birdsboro; for Washington, D.C., the Washington, D.C., Convention & Visitors Association; and for West Virginia, Pamela "Sam" Withrow of Camera One in White Sulphur Springs.

Next, I wish to thank those people who donated rides that, for myriad reasons, unfortunately could not be published in this book. I also wish to thank the many people who did not submit rides but were most helpful in steering me to people who did or who sent me useful maps and other supplemental material. These wonderful people include Paul Breeding, volunteer on the 1993 Cycling Committee of the American Lung Association of Maryland, Inc., in Timonium, Maryland; Bruce Clinton of Wilmington, Delaware; the Clinton County Tourist Promotion Agency in Lock Haven, Pennsylvania; L. C. Cole of Coles Bicycle Inc. in Carlisle, Pennsylvania; Greg Cook and Stephanie R. Hughart of the West Virginia Division of Tourism and Parks in Charleston; Angelo Cristinzio of Cycling Enthusiasts in Philadelphia, Pennsylvania; Karl Esch in Randallstown, Maryland; Florence Fink of Shillingham, Pennsylvania, and ride cochairperson of the Berks County Bicycle Club; Gordon V. Gay, chief of interpretation at the Chesapeake & Ohio Canal National Historic Park in Sharpsburg, Maryland; the High Peaks Cyclery in Lake Placid, New York; Nancy Hantman of White Plains,

N.Y.; Joe Hoechne of the Pittsburgh Council of the American Youth Hostels; Liz Holloway, Delaware's state bicycle coordinator in Dover; Michael J. Krajsa, executive director of the Bucks County Tourist Commission in Doylestown, Pennsylvania; C. J. Joyce of the Bicycle Federation of America in Washington, D.C.; Lini Lavin of the New York State Office of Parks, Recreation, and Historic Preservation in Albany, New York; the Lawrence County Tourist Promotion Agency in New Castle, Pennsylvania; Richard C. Lockwood, transportation planning engineer and state bicycle coordinator for the Commonwealth of Virginia in Richmond, Virginia; Mary Jane McGuire, Bicycle Safety Coordinator for New York State in Albany; Robert Nordvall of Gettysburg, Pennsylvania, eastern regional director of the League of American Wheelmen; Brian A. O'Shea of Country Ski and Sports in Wellsboro, Pennsylvania; Edward K. Payne of the Salisbury Bicycle Club in Pocomoke City, Maryland; Bob Piper, Washington, D.C., rides coordinator for the Potomac Pedalers Touring Club; Shari Lawrence Pfleeger of Washington, D.C.; the Pocono hostel at La Anna in Cresco, Pennsylvania; Dan Rappaport of Princeton, New Jersey; Jeffrey Ross of the Sound Cyclists Bicycle Club in South Salem, New York; C. E. Schafer of Rumson, New Jersey, and the Jersey Shore Touring Society; Howard D. Smith of the Wheel Easy bicycle store in Dover, Delaware; Jerry E. Stadd, bicycle affairs coordinator of the Maryland Department of Transportation in Baltimore; Tony Stalls and his Washington, D.C.–area cycling computer bulletin board, The Freewheel (703) 243–8059; Ed Ward of the Seaside Cyclists in Wilmington, Delaware; Kenneth M. Washburn, innkeeper of the Lantern Inn in Betterton, Maryland; Jo Ann Weiss of *Pedal Patter*, the newspaper of the Potomac Pedalers Touring Club, Inc., McLean, Virginia; and Don F. Whitney of the Central Bucks Chamber of Commerce in Doylestown, Pennsylvania. I also wish to thank all the bed-and-breakfast innkeepers who contacted me and sent me descriptive brochures of their inns.

Behind the scenes were my parents, R. Kenneth and Arabella J. Bell, who lovingly cared for their granddaughter Roxana on several occasions when I headed to Westchester County in New York, the Monongahela National Forest in West Virginia, and southern

Pennsylvania to verify routes and devise cue sheets from maps. This book is dedicated to them for all their love, guidance, encouragement, and support throughout my life.

I also wish to thank my husband, Craig B. Waff, for all his driving in verifying several Pennsylvania routes, for his work on the maps as the manuscript headed into final production, and for his steady and daily support and love.

About the Author

Trudy E. Bell is an avid touring cyclist and a certified bicycle mechanic (East Coast Bicycle Academy, Harrisonburg, Virginia, 1989). She has taught an introductory course in bicycle touring at the South Orange–Maplewood Adult School in New Jersey and at the Learning Annex in New York City.

Either with groups or solo, she and her 1984 Univega SportTour have cycled all over the Mid-Atlantic states and in Colorado, Utah, and California, including down the length of Baja California. In addition, she commuted by bicycle on the streets of New York City for five years (worth about 6,000 miles).

A former editor of *Scientific American* and *Omni* magazines, she is now senior editor for the engineering magazine *IEEE Spectrum* in New York City. She has a master's degree in the history of science (American astronomy) from New York University. Articles of hers on bicycling have been published in *The New York Times, Bicycle USA, Essence, Science Probe,* and *The Bicyclist's Sourcebook* (edited by Michael Leccese and Arlene Plevin, Woodbine House, 1991).

She lives with her husband, historian of science Dr. Craig B. Waff, and daughter, Roxana, in Maplewood, New Jersey.